What People Are Saying About

Michael Hauge's
WRITING SCREENPLAYS THAT SELL

"By far the best screenwriting book I've ever read. Michael Hauge's wise and humane approach to story and character development is the only one that consistently works for me. I make sure to consult this book whenever I begin a project—and again when I run into trouble."
—Bob Fisher, co-writer: *Wedding Crashers*; screenwriter/executive producer: *Mixed Signals*

"Don't come to Hollywood without reading this book, because everyone else has." —Terry Rossio, co-writer: *Shrek*; *Pirates of the Caribbean 1, 2, 3 & 4*

"Michael Hauge's principles and methods are so well argued that the mysteries of effective screenwriting can be understood—even by directors."
—Phillip Noyce, director: *Patriot Games*; *Clear and Present Danger*; *Salt*

"What Michael Hauge does seems quite simple but is in fact quite rare. He takes your ideas and makes them better."
—Christopher Murphey, screenwriter: *The Karate Kid*; *Body of Proof*

"In a field choked with alleged 'script doctors,' Michael Hauge remains the surest, most sensible alternative. When I pick up the phone for help, he's the call I make."
—Shane Black, screenwriter: *Lethal Weapon 1 & 2*; *The Last Boy Scout*; *The Long Kiss Goodnight*; screenwriter/director: *Kiss Kiss Bang Bang*

"If you're serious about becoming a screenwriter, start by reading this book." —Robert Mark Kamen, screenwriter: *The Karate Kid*; *Transporter 1, 2 & 3*; *Taken*

WRITING
SCREENPLAYS
THAT SELL

THE COMPLETE GUIDE

TO TURNING STORY CONCEPTS INTO
MOVIE AND TELEVISION DEALS

NEW TWENTIETH ANNIVERSARY EDITION

WRITING
SCREENPLAYS
THAT SELL

MICHAEL HAUGE

methuen | drama

Methuen Drama

1 3 5 7 9 10 8 6 4 2

Methuen Drama is an imprint of Bloomsbury Publishing Plc

Methuen Drama
Bloomsbury Publishing Plc
36 Soho Square
London W1D 3QY
www.methuendrama.com

Originally published: New York: McGraw-Hill, © 1988
First HarperPerennial edition published in 1991
First HarperResource paperback edition published in 2002
First Collins edition published in 2007
First Collins Reference edition published in 2011

This edition published by Methuen Drama in 2011

A CIP catalogue record for this book is available from the British Library

ISBN: 978 1 408 15146 4

Designed by Janet m. Evans
Printed in Great Britain by Clays Ltd, St Ives plc

Dedicated to the memory of
Art Arthur and Jerry Hauge

ACKNOWLEDGMENTS

AS WITH THE INTRODUCTION THAT FOLLOWS IN A FEW PAGES, I WANT to leave the original list of acknowledgments from the first edition as it was. These people all contributed to this book in some way when I first wrote it more than twenty years ago, which means they are still a big part of this new edition. I have some new names I want to add to the list, but nobody gets taken away.

The wonderful thing about reading these acknowledgments from so long ago is the realization that most of these people are still an important part of my life. To all of you, I want to say how grateful I am for all the additional years you have blessed me with your guidance, your support, your friendship, and your love.

Of course, life being the way it is, some of the others have moved on—passed away or drifted away, so that we're no longer connected the way we used to be. But for whatever it was that brought us together way back when, you have my thanks.

So here is what I said then (except for the new last names I've added for Cisci and Nancy), and what I still feel . . .

—

SINCE I KNOW THIS IS THE SECTION OF THE BOOK YOU'RE GOING TO skip over anyway (unless you think you'll recognize one of the names), please bear with me while I give some words of thanks to some of the many people whose knowledge, inspiration, support, and guidance made this book possible.

To my parents: my mother, who always believed in me and gave me her love of learning and teaching and the written word, and my dad, who used to sell popcorn to the movie theaters (and got me into the movies for free), gave me his love and support (both emotional *and* financial), and always stood by me, even when I know he thought moving to Hollywood was a pretty crazy thing to do.

To the people whose faith, enthusiasm, and effort made this book a reality: Esther Newberg, my literary agent; Bobbi Mark, Elisabeth Jakab, Lucia Staniels, and Ann Craig at McGraw-Hill; Craig Nelson and Jenna Hull at HarperCollins; and especially my unofficial agent and good friend, Diane Cairns.

To Wendy Benjamin, Marty Chavez, John Deimer, Robert Mark Kamen, Lawrence Kasdan, Ivy Orta, Karen Rosenfelt, Jerry Weintraub, Jeremy Williams, and Wally Zavattero for their help and generosity in granting me permission to quote from *Body Heat*, *The Karate Kid*, and *The Sylmar Tunnel Disaster*.

To all those who have helped me in both my film and teaching careers, with particular gratitude to Gary Shusett and Sherwood Oaks Experimental College for getting me started; to producers Michael Jaffe, Zev Braun, and Robert Guenette for giving me the opportunity to learn; to Mona Moore, Steve Waterman, Stephanie Mann, and Michele Wallerstein for their career guidance at critical times; to the many schools throughout the country who have sponsored my seminars; and to my publicist, Vicki Arthur, who keeps getting my name in the paper and drawing people into my classes even if I am her toughest client. And a special thanks to those at the Writer's Program at UCLA Extension, who gave me the credibility to take my show on the road and who prove you can have a great educational program and still be fun to work with.

To the many producers, agents, executives, teachers, screenwriters, and filmmakers I have worked with and learned from over the years, who have all contributed to the information in this book. And to six talented screenwriters who are now close friends: Paul Margolis, Frederica Hobin, Don Buday, Jewel Jaffe, Jill Jaress, and Eric Edson.

To two of my own teachers: William Cadbury, at the University of Oregon, who was the first to teach me to appreciate the deeper levels of meaning that film can achieve, and Art Arthur, who knew more about screenwriting than anyone I ever met and who was my biggest supporter, my mentor, and my dear friend.

To the many students I have taught over the last seven years. You have brought me joy and helped me achieve my own inner motivation.

On a more personal note, to all the members of my family, for their unending love and support and for always laughing at my jokes, with a special thanks for always being there to my brother, Jim, Auntie Bon, Uncle Vince, Fritz, Jan, Bonnie Laurie, the Jacobsons, Jessica Arthur, and Pamela Steele.

To all my friends, with special thanks to Nancy Hicks and Cisci Deschaine for years of concern and caring; to Eugene Webb, Dave Grill, and Bruce Derman for helping me through the emotional obstacle course of writing a book; to Marty Ross, Mitchell Group, Art Silverblatt, Michael Firmature, Nancy Newman, and Dianne Haak for continued help and friendship; and most of all to Jim Hicks, John Hudkins, Earl Kamsky, Charles Moreland, and Bill Trezise, who for thirty years have been willing to go to the movies with me, even on sunny days in Oregon.

And finally, thanks to my wife, Vicki. Without her faith, support, commitment, inspiration, and love, I could never have written this book.

AND NOW . . .

Let me add to that list the people at HarperCollins who brought this new edition to fruition: Stephanie Meyers, my editor, for her invaluable input, support, and patience with my repeatedly postponed deadlines; my copy editor, Olga Gardner Galvin, for spotting all my mistakes and for being a movie lover; and Anthony Morias for designing a cool new cover.

To all my clients, everywhere, you are more than my livelihood: you let me live my passion. Without your talent and courage, the ideas in this book would never have emerged. And a special thanks to a handful of clients who have worked with me so long, and shared so much with me, that I see them as friends: Grace Boyett, Jacques Calixte, Robert Celestino, Loren Chadima, Shelley Evans, and Roger Stone.

Thanks to Will Smith and Jada Pinkett Smith, Ken Stovitz, Kim Wiethorn, Tracey Nyberg, Devon Franklin, and all the people at Overbrook Entertainment and Columbia Pictures who are so generous, such a joy to work with, and who have definitely raised the level of my A-game.

For giving me the opportunity to share my passion, thanks to Derek Christopher, Bill Donovan, and everyone else who has sponsored or attended one of my lectures, or e-mailed me with your questions or your gratitude. Anything I'm able to express in this book is because of you. And a particular acknowledgment to the Romance Writers of America chapters and members who have added so much fun to my work, and have helped me expand my ideas about story.

I also want to include associates who have helped my career immensely so they'll know how grateful I am for their unending support and friendship: Ginger Earle, Donna Jason, Steve Kaplan, Ken Lee, Heidi Roberts, Chris Vogler, Michael Wiese, Susan Wiggs, and especially my assistant Marissa Cerar, without whose help, patience, and understanding I'd simply be lost.

And finally (if this were an Oscar® speech, I'd have been played off the stage long ago), to Michael Fogel; John, Inger, Sabi, and Kelly Lofgren; Brian, Iraida, Lauren, and J. P. Mathews; and Jenn Hauge; all my love and gratitude for being those people in my life who I know will always be there with your friendship, love, and support.

Oh, and one more thing . . .

Two repeats actually, from that first set of acknowledgments: my brother, Jim, for whom I am more grateful than he could realize; and my wife, Vicki, who—amazingly—still loves me and believes in me after more than thirty-five years.

Still for Cookie

CONTENTS

INTRODUCTION
to the Second Edition

WHY READ THIS BOOK AGAIN?

It's been more than twenty years since the first edition of *Writing Screenplays That Sell* was published. In that time it's sold about 75,000 copies—not J. K. Rowling territory, but not bad. I like to think each of those 75,000 people read it and then passed it on to somebody else, making the total closer to 150,000. But that's probably not realistic, so let's just stick with 75,000.

If you are one of those people who liked the earlier edition, I first want to say thank you, for making this book one of the most rewarding experiences of my life. Thanks for all the letters and e-mails telling me it made you want to be a screenwriter, or that it helped you write your script. Thanks to all of you who have approached me at writers conferences or lectures or book signings to tell me how it was the first book on screenwriting you ever read, or that it's still your favorite, or that it inspired you to go after your dream, or that it helped you break into screenwriting, or that it helped you get your script produced.

I also want to reply to the question you're no doubt asking: "Since I already read the first edition, should I buy this one as well?"

My answer is yes.

It's a self-serving answer, I know. But here's why I think it's a good idea:

► In this new edition, I use as examples more than a hundred new movies released in the last twenty years.

► I also chose a new screenplay—*Avatar*—to analyze in detail, along with new scripts to illustrate character categories, character growth, and theme, and charting your screenplay.

► I've expanded the section on structure to include a lot more about the opening and setup of your script, the end of your script, and the use of such structural principles as anticipation, credibility, time, and powerful endings.

► I've added an entire chapter on exceptions to the rules, to examine successful screenplays that don't follow the traditional Hollywood model.

► When I originally wrote the book, no one used the Internet. Now everyone does, so I identify a bunch of invaluable Web sites for marketing your screenplay.

► I reexamined every single principle for writing and selling screenplays to make certain it was still appropriate in today's marketplace, adding new ideas and approaches that come from twenty more years of experience as a Hollywood script consultant and teacher.

But perhaps most of all, I think it's a good idea to revisit all these concepts you know, and many you don't (or might have forgotten), to reinforce your good writing habits, to get rid of any bad ones you've developed, and to get reinspired to go after your screenwriting dreams.

—

THERE ARE ALSO A FEW THINGS I DECIDED NOT TO CHANGE. THE first is the original introduction, which I've left more or less intact, starting on page xxv. I still like what I wrote twenty years ago. And it's all still true.

If you want to be a screenwriter, you'll still encounter lots of people who'll try to discourage you from your dream, and who'll tell you it's dumb or impossible. And the only way to overcome that is still to ignore them, stay with your passion, and hit the keyboard.

Technology may have improved, and the markets for your work may have changed a bit, but the principles of good storytelling have not. And the fact that Hollywood is desperate for good screenwriters is as true as ever.

I also kept some of the examples from the first edition, because they were just too good at illustrating the principles of great screenwriting to omit.

And I hope I've kept whatever clarity or simplicity or insight or humor or passion or whatever it was in the first edition that seemed to enlighten and inspire people.

This is where those of you who are brand-new readers come in.

I have been very blessed, and am very grateful, that this book has been helpful enough, and has meant enough, to writers and filmmakers and agents and development executives that it has stayed on the shelves for twenty-plus years. I hope you will find it as beneficial to your craft and to your screenwriting career.

Enjoy.

INTRODUCTION

WHY READ THIS BOOK?

Screenplays became, in the last half of the twentieth century, what the Great American Novel was for the first half. Closet writers who used to dream of the glory of getting into print now dream of seeing their story on the big or small screen.

That dream is by no means confined to Hollywood. People everywhere watch TV and think to themselves, "I could write better than that." Or they go to the movies, and they want to be a part of that magic or that glamour or that wealth that they see and read about. Or they just want to touch the pain and the wonder that comes from filling a blank page with something totally their own.

So they decide to give it a shot. And then they meet The Great Destroyers: Everybody's writing a screenplay. You can't learn creativity. It's impossible to get an agent. You've got to live in southern California. It's who you know, not what you know. They'll rip you off. They'll ruin your script. Nobody knows what sells. All they want are teenage sex comedies. All they want is macho violence. All they want are established writers.

And you don't have any talent anyway.

So the dream gets changed or diminished or vanishes altogether. Or those writers forge ahead in blind, confused ignorance, assuming that there *are* no standards in Hollywood, that it's just a crapshoot. Or they refuse to consider commerciality at all, because that's a sellout. Or they decide *just* to go after the bucks because you can't hope to say anything meaningful anyway. And so on.

I don't buy it. After working in Hollywood developing screenplays as a reader, a story editor, staff producer, and consultant for countless writers and production companies, and after listening to, talking with, working with, and interviewing writers, agents, producers, executives, and movie stars, I think all those notions listed above are myths. At the very least, they have grown way out of proportion to reality and need to be put in proper perspective.

The goal of this book is to destroy those common myths of failure and to replace them with the following ideas:

1. If screenwriting is a goal you wish to pursue, then you should go for it. And as long as you find the *process* of writing screenplays personally fulfilling, then you should keep at it, because anyone with talent who sticks around long enough will succeed.

2. Lots of us would like to *have written* a screenplay; what's important is whether you want to *write* a screenplay. If you get fulfillment out of the day-to-day work of putting a story to paper, then the additional rewards of money and success and fame can follow. But if it's those secondary rewards you're focused on, it probably won't happen, and success certainly won't be as golden as you think it will be if it does arrive.

3. Creativity is something we all possess. Your objective should be not to learn creativity but to stimulate it. This book is filled with methods of nudging, nurturing, and recognizing your own creativity, and funneling it into your screenplay.

4. No matter how much new technology can be thrown into a movie, and no matter what new stars or concepts or directors are hot, the foundation of any successful film will always be a good, well-written story. A bad movie can be made out of a good script but never the reverse. Hollywood will always need the screenwriter.

5. Hollywood does have standards, and it is possible to know what those are and write screenplays that meet them. The most straightforward way is to look at successful movies and TV shows to see what they have in common, and to listen to the stated desires and needs of the people who are in the position of buying screenplays. This book contains numerous checklists and outlines of those requirements and the methods for achieving them with your writing.

6. Commerciality and artistry are not mutually exclusive.

7. The screenwriting process can be broken down into a proven series of steps and stages, which will enable you to achieve a salable, emotionally involving screenplay.

8. You can be a working screenwriter and live anywhere in the world.

9. You can launch a career as a screenwriter even if you don't know anyone within a thousand miles of southern California.

And finally:

10. You can make a bundle of money doing all of this.

If you want to decide whether screenwriting is a career for you, then do it on the basis of the reality of the work involved and the fulfillment you will achieve with your writing, not just on the expectation of whatever delayed rewards may await you somewhere down the road. If you choose to pursue screenwriting because it is your passion and your dream, you can empower yourself to do so by developing your own creativity, knowing what is required and helpful at each stage of the writing and selling process, and intelligently focusing on methods that have proved successful.

That is what this book will teach you.

QUALIFICATIONS, DISCLAIMERS, AND EXCUSES

Finally, before launching into the meat of the book, a few words about my particular point of view in approaching this subject.

Even though working, experienced, living-on-the-beach-in-Malibu screenwriters can find value in the enclosed information and principles, I'm assuming that most of you reading these pages are beginning writers attempting to *launch* a career in feature films and television. Therefore the book is geared toward the screenwriter in the early stages of his or her career. Certainly the book will be helpful to anyone writing screenplays, even if you've sold a dozen.

But don't worry if you've never even *read* a screenplay, let alone tried to write one. By the time you finish the book, you will have sufficient information to know how to complete a screenplay, starting at square one, and how to market it when it's done.

Similarly, though the principles included (particularly the artistic ones) apply to nearly all films and screenplays, many of the commercial considerations do not apply to established filmmakers.

If you are, in fact, at the early stages of your screenwriting career, you must understand that principles that apply to Woody Allen, William Goldman, James Cameron, and Quentin Tarantino do not necessarily apply to you. Particularly in the arena of commerciality, there are certain criteria, standards, and restrictions to which you must adhere, restrictions that those established filmmakers can ignore.

Woody Allen can write any screenplay he wishes and get it made. *Zelig* is a terrific film. But it is not a screenplay that would serve a novice screenwriter well in attempting to launch her career. Usually, those groundbreaking exceptions to the principles and standards outlined here, those films on the cutting edge of cinematic achievement, were written by established writers. Until you are in that situation, and can call your own shots, you must give much greater consideration to the tried-and-true rules of screenwriting.

This book also assumes that you are pursuing the American (U.S. or Canadian) film market, so the rules and standards for screenwriters working for the markets in France, Germany, Japan, or India do not necessarily apply to you. If you are a screenwriter in England or Australia or Sweden, almost all of the writing principles will apply to your work, but some commercial considerations will differ, and you will need to research the current screenwriting market in your own country in choosing your story concepts and marketing methods.

To illustrate the principles I outline, I will be using American movies and television series made within the last two or three decades. Even though *Casablanca* can still turn everyone to mush, my assumption is that if you are reading this book, you are pursuing a screenwriting career today, and principles and commercial considerations apply to you that might not apply to screenwriters writing in other countries, or who wrote in other eras.

The book outlines screenwriting for what I call "mainstream film and television": narrative feature films that are distributed nationally, prime-time (network and cable) TV movies and episodic series, and short fictional films. We're not talking about documentaries, industrials, Saturday animation, daytime soaps, commercials, news, sports, or weather. But again, the goal of *all* of those forms is to create an emotional response in the audience, so many of the principles will overlap.

I will talk a lot about Hollywood in this book. By *Hollywood* I do not mean the city in southern California that could make Sodom and Gomorrah blush. Rather I mean the power structure and purse strings of the film industry. So, if you're pursuing Hollywood, it could mean that you're approaching an investment group in Ocala, Florida.

Finally, this book is filled with personal opinions. The principles that constitute good screenwriting can be verified by looking at those movies that have been commercially and financially successful by virtue of their box office returns or Nielsen ratings, or by looking at films that have garnered awards, strong word of mouth, cult standing, etc. But emotional response is purely personal, and in talking about how movies have succeeded in creating emotion, I'm obviously talking to a great extent about how they created an emotional response in me. So don't be overly concerned with your agreement or disagreement with my evaluation of a film. Focus on using the examples to increase your understanding of how the principles involved apply. And, in turn, you should repeatedly verify the principles I outline by using your *own* favorite movies, those that created a positive emotional response in you.

Use and enjoy this book in whatever way is most helpful to you. Read it through once and then focus on the sections where you're feeling weakest. Or use the checklists after you have done one or two drafts of that facet of your own script. Or read the book just to decide if screenwriting is for you. Or lay it on your coffee table to convince the woman down the hall that you really *are* in show business. Or put it under the short leg of your desk to keep it from wobbling.

But at some point, put the book away. Screenwriting books, like screenwriting classes, run the risk of becoming a substitute for writing rather than a supplement to it. It's better to attempt your own screenplay, then go back to this book and its checklists after each draft. Then read other screenwriting books or take a writing class to get additional points of view prior to each screenplay you write.

In other words, somewhere along the line you've got to trust that you have enough information. Then you must call on all your courage, get out some paper, dig into your soul, and start writing.

PART ONE

DEVELOPING THE STORY

ONE

THE GOAL OF THE SCREENWRITER

PEOPLE DO NOT GO TO THE MOVIES SO THEY CAN SEE THE CHARACTERS on the screen laugh, cry, get frightened, or get turned on.

They go to have those experiences themselves.

The reason that movies hold such a fascination for us, the reason the art form has been engrossing and involving audiences for more than a century, is because it provides an opportunity to *experience emotion*. Within the safety and isolation of a darkened theater or in the privacy or comfort of one's own home it is possible to leave the real world behind or at a safe distance and experience emotions, thoughts, feelings, and adventures that would not be encountered in everyday life. In watching a movie or television show, we can feel the love, the hate, the fear, the passion, the excitement, or the humor that elevates our lives, but in a safe, controlled setting.

All filmmakers, therefore, have a single goal: to elicit emotion in an audience. Every director's, every actor's, every gaffer's, and every production assistant's ultimate objective is to create a positive emotional response in the audience. When the movie or TV episode does that, it is successful; when it doesn't, it fails.

THE PRIMARY GOAL OF THE SCREENWRITER

The screenwriter's primary goal is even more specific: *The screenwriter must elicit emotion in the person who reads the screenplay.*

The effect of a screenplay on a reader must be the same as the effect of the movie on the audience: a positive emotional experience. All of the stated considerations of commerciality, big stars, hot topics, low budgets, high concepts, and strong demographics go out the window if this single objective is not achieved.

If the producer, executive, agent, manager, or star who can get your movie made doesn't smile, laugh, cry, get scared, get excited, or get turned on while reading your screenplay, then your script will never reach a real audience.

In other words, for the screenwriter, the term *reader* and the term *audience* are synonymous.

HOW TO WRITE A SCREENPLAY
IN ONE EASY LESSON

Knowing what a screenplay needs to accomplish is simple; I can tell it to you in one sentence: *Enable a sympathetic character to overcome a series of increasingly difficult, seemingly insurmountable obstacles to achieve a compelling desire.*

That, in nineteen words, is what almost every successful feature film has ever done. The few exceptions are those films where the character *fails* to achieve the compelling desire, as in *Brokeback Mountain* or *No Country for Old Men*, or a film where the hero realizes that his compelling desire is a mistake, as in *Rain Man* or *An Education*. But the essence of all successful movies is still the same.

The difficulty is not in understanding what you must accomplish as a writer. The tough part is actually accomplishing each of the facets of that objective. How do you make a character sympathetic? How do you establish a compelling desire? How do you create and arrange the series of hurdles that must be overcome? How do you write this in such a way that the emotional involvement of the reader is ensured?

And finally (and probably the reason you bought this book), how do you get rich doing all of this?

THE FOUR STAGES OF ANY SCREENPLAY

Every aspect of writing your screenplay will be contained in one of the following four stages:

1. **The Story Concept:** the single sentence or two that identifies the hero of the story and what he or she wants to accomplish.

2. **The Characters:** the people who populate the story.

3. **Plot Structure:** the events of the story and the order in which they occur.

4. **The Individual Scenes:** the way the words are laid out on the page and the kind of action, description, and dialogue that will increase the reader's emotional involvement.

This book will outline each of those four facets in detail, in the above order. You should note that beginning with a single-sentence story concept and developing that into a full, 115-page screenplay is one way to write your screenplay. It is very organized, logical, and left-brained, and it allows each expanded phase of the screenplay to grow out of the previous one. Its big advantage is in its safety, so to speak.

However, this logical, step-by-step approach is not the *only* way to write a screenplay. Of equal value, depending on what works for you, is the more free-form, right-brained method of writing FADE IN, and then simply seeing where the story takes you. In other words, letting the story "write itself."

Like any other journey of unknown destination, what you sacrifice in safety and security you may get back in surprise and excitement. This approach may enable you to tap into your unfettered creativity more easily and provide a more effective, fulfilling screenwriting experience.

The key is to use whichever method, or combination of the two, works for you.

Regardless of the approach you choose, the outcome must be a screenplay that effectively elicits emotion because the story concept, characters, plot structure, and scene writing are all outstanding.

This book is going to give you a foundation from which you can depart in whatever direction improves your ability to get the screenplay written. If something's working, keep using it; if it's not working, find something better. My goal is to give you a method that prevents you from getting blocked at any stage of the process.

BRAINSTORMING, EDITING, AND WRITER'S BLOCK

Throughout the process outlined in this book, you will repeatedly encounter the word *brainstorming*. This refers to the periods of creativity that require you to go for quantity and not quality, when you want to give your creativity free rein to extend its limits without fear of censure or criticism.

It is only after you have allowed your creativity to blossom through the nonjudgmental brainstorming phase that you enter the editing phase of screenwriting. This is the critical, evaluative phase that will determine which of the multitude of ideas that your brainstorming generates will best serve your screenplay.

Art Arthur, who was a successful screenwriter for more than forty years, used to say that there are two secrets to success as a writer. Secret #1: *Don't get it right, get it written.* (Sorry, but you'll have to wait until the end of the book to get the second one.)

If you wait for your writing to be perfect, it's never even going to be good. You'll become so frozen with fear and judgment that you'll eventually give up on the entire process and start buying books on real estate investment. In other words, you'll become *blocked*.

Writer's block is the flip side of brainstorming. *Brainstorming* gives the mind freedom to go in whatever direction it chooses, holding back criticism and judgment so the writer can freely tap into her own creative source. *Block* is when the mind isn't going in any direction at all because of some fear—of failure, of success, of change, of criticism, or of imperfection.

Writer's block doesn't mean that you're staring at the page for fifteen minutes until you find the line of dialogue that works best. Block is when you haven't worked on your screenplay in two weeks, and now you're watching *Jeopardy!* and eating Hostess Snowballs instead of writing. Writer's block feeds on itself, so the longer it continues, the less the chance of escape.

So even if you choose to follow the logical, ordered, step-by-step process outlined in this book, you will still need to depart from it occasionally and move around a bit.

For example, there might be situations where you are working on the character development stage of your script, but you just can't get a handle on your villain. Instead of waiting for perfection and blocking yourself, a better solution would be to jump over to the scene-writing stage. If you know there's going to be a terrific confrontation between your hero and the bad guy, and you know how that scene should look, then go ahead and write it. Writing the scene will then reveal to you things about each of those two characters that you can take back to the character development stage in order to re-prime your pump and keep the story flowing.

Writers often fear that the use of formula (of which I am an unapologetic advocate) will stifle creativity. But a formula is simply a method for consistently achieving the same result. If you consistently want to elicit emotion with the way you structure your story, or reveal your characters' inner lives, and there are formulas for that, then it only makes sense to try them out to see if they work for you. A formula never tells you *what* to write—it only reveals the storytelling tools and patterns that have worked for decades of successful movies and television.

And a formula can actually enhance your brainstorming. If an element of your script might seem contrived or unbelievable, but you know that there are proven methods for overcoming that problem (which there are, by the way—they're revealed in chapter 5), then you can start brainstorming ideas for creating those prescribed actions and dialogue.

Eventually, the four stages of your screenplay will only form a general pattern, and you'll be jumping all over the map in order to ensure the flow of ideas and creativity, alternating between your nonjudgmental brainstorming and your selective editing. This will both prevent writer's block and maximize your ability to elicit emotion in the reader and the audience.

THE FORGOTTEN STEP TO SCREENWRITING SUCCESS

Just one more major step before diving into your screenplay: *you've got to see movies.*

There was a time when I would have thought it obvious that screenwriters should see lots of films. But in my travels around the world, I am repeatedly astounded by how many people pursuing this career hardly ever bother to visit a movie theater or even rent a DVD. And when they do, it's some classic film from the forties or fifties, a cartoon to watch with their kids, or something with subtitles.

There's nothing wrong with art-house fare or animation, and it's certainly helpful to have a broad knowledge of film history. But no matter what profession one is pursuing, knowing the marketplace is essential.

You wouldn't want to be represented by a lawyer who hadn't been to law school or who didn't keep abreast of recent legal decisions and statutes. Well, the film industry isn't looking for screenwriters who don't know what's being produced or who don't know which of those recent releases have been successful.

As a serious screenwriter, you can no longer regard movies as something you only do when you have a date on a Saturday night, or as something the whole family must enjoy together. Your MINIMUM quota of movies should be a hundred a year: at least two visits to movie theaters or two video rentals or downloads every week.

If your immediate reaction to this advice is "I can't possibly watch that many movies," it's usually for one of three reasons:

1. **You don't have time.** I'm only talking about four hours a week here. If your life is *truly* so full and hectic you can't find any spare time at all, you're probably too busy to pursue a second career as a screenwriter until your kids are in school, you find an easier job, or you rearrange your priorities.

2. **You can't afford it.** A movie is cheaper than a new book, two six-packs, or most restaurant meals. Netflix is less than ten bucks *a month*. And remember: now that you're a screenwriter, every movie ticket is a write-off.

3. **You have children.** Tell your spouse or significant other that every Wednesday is his night for quality time with the kids. Or, if you're a single parent, find another single parent in your writers group, neighborhood, or twelve-step program, and swap babysitting nights.

I know that families can sometimes become obstacles to your screenwriting pursuits. You must sit down with them and explain how important this dream is to you, and that going to see movies isn't just for fun and entertainment anymore; it's as important as taking classes would be if you were a real estate appraiser or an architect. At first they'll look skeptical and whine about being neglected. But the more seriously you take your career, the more seriously they will.

They must also accept that sometimes you'll be watching movies by yourself, when they're not of interest to, or appropriate for, the rest of your family. They'll survive.

———

ONE OTHER ISSUE ABOUT YOUR VIEWING REGIMEN: I'VE JUST GIVEN you permission to see two Hollywood movies every single week. If

you're not excited by that prospect, if it doesn't sound like fun, then are
you certain this is the right path for you?

If you aren't going to the movies or watching television because you
don't *like* what Hollywood's producing these days (a comment I hear
frequently), then why do you want to be a screenwriter? Is it really wise
to pursue a career in the film industry if you think that the stuff that
Hollywood produces is crap? If that's your belief, then your screenplay
is likely to be so strikingly different from current mainstream films that
it will be impossible to sell.

This doesn't mean you have to like everything you see. One of the
advantages of this process is that no movie you ever see will be a waste
of time—it can still serve as a good "bad example."

HOW TO WATCH A MOVIE

To make the process of watching films as informative as possible, approach them in the following way:

1. **Avoid reviews, trailers, and previews.** The best way to see a film is
   with as little knowledge as possible about what will happen, so
   you can fully experience whatever surprises and emotional peaks
   the writer intended. Save any reviews or publicity articles until
   after you see the movie, so you can enter the theater as receptive
   as possible.

2. **See movies uninterrupted.** Whether in a theater or at home, the
   key is to be able to totally focus on your movie-watching experience. If you can, see movies at a conscientious theater delivering
   great pictures and sound with a minimum of talking and texting
   patrons and unruly kids. If you can't, a Blu-Ray player, premium
   channel cable system, and HD TV make watching films at home
   superior to many theatrical situations.

   However, if you do watch a movie at home, you've still got to
   treat it like a movie, and not like some TV talk show or local news

broadcast that plays in the background while you visit on the phone, chat with your family, raid the refrigerator, or hit the john.

3. **See it the first time for fun.** Don't take notes, don't read along with the script, and don't even think about the screenplay when you first view a film. Ride the roller coaster the filmmaker created. You can figure out how the movie worked after it's over. (In a really good film, this rule is unnecessary; you'll be swept up in the emotion in spite of your intention to analyze the work.)

4. **See the good stuff twice.** When a movie touches you deeply, watch it a second or third time to thoroughly analyze all the details of story, character, structure, dialogue, and theme. This is especially important for any movie similar to your own screenplay in terms of plot, setting, or genre. You can reexperience all of the highs and lows, and can now appreciate much more deeply the ways the screenwriter and filmmakers elicited your emotion. And you'll *always* discover things you didn't catch the first time.

5. **Analyze your emotional reaction.** Whenever you become engrossed in a film, ask yourself why. What kept you on the edge of your seat? Fascinating characters? Hilarity? Suspense? Big action? Sex? Romance? Sadness?

   When you find yourself distanced from the story, determine the cause of that as well. Is it illogical? Too predictable? Repetitive? Boring? Why? And what would make it more emotionally involving?

6. **Did it follow the rules?** Every movie you see should reinforce the principles of screenwriting contained in this book. Which methods did this screenwriter employ for creating character identification, anticipation, surprise, curiosity, believability, conflict, character growth, and theme? Was the story concept simple, original, and commercial? Did the structural turning points occur as

expected? Was the dialogue unique, varied, and interesting? Was the ending satisfying?

Did the film intentionally "push the envelope" in any way, and violate traditional structure or character development? If so, was the film more effective as a result? Could this departure from the norm be duplicated (especially by a writer trying to break into the industry) or was it an approach that would only be new and different once?

7. **Pitch the movie.** If you had to sell this story to a Hollywood executive, how would you do it? How would you express the story concept in a single sentence? What would you emphasize to maximize your chances for selling the script? Which companies would you have pursued with it? How would you have packaged it? If you had been an executive, would you have given it a green light? Why or why not? (Be honest; checking the box-office returns isn't fair.)

8. **Research the production.** Check the box-office success of the film, domestically and internationally. Read any articles and watch any interviews you can that reveal how the movie got made. This research will not only sharpen your commercial sensibilities, it will give you a much greater working knowledge of the people in power, what they're looking for, and the avenues for marketing your own scripts.

9. **Write a scene.** Pick a scene from a movie you enjoyed, watch the scene two or three times, and then try writing it yourself. How vividly and succinctly can you describe the settings and characters? How would you describe the action as simply as possible without losing its emotional impact? How would you convey what's shown on the screen without resorting to camera directions? (Skip copying the dialogue, unless you want to try writing the scene using different, more effective language.) When you're finished,

compare your version to that of the original screenwriters when you . . .

10. **Read the script.** You can't possibly hope to improve your craft and improve your own writing style without reading lots of examples of scripts that have successfully done what you're trying to do.

Screenplays for most Hollywood movies are now available online (usually at no cost, at sites like scriptstork.com, script-o-rama. com, simplyscripts.com, scriptcity.com, and dailyscript.com) or in printed or published form (at thewritersstore.com and sites such as scriptshack.com and scriptcity.com).

In addition to reading scripts for your favorite films, read as many as you can from the genre of the script you're working on. And include scripts for movies you haven't yet seen, and then watch the movie versions of those scripts to see how they were transformed into film.

After reading a screenplay, ask yourself how effective it was at eliciting emotion, and how closely it followed the principles presented in this book. Did the written version of the movie create an emotional experience as effectively as the film did? Why or why not? How did the style of the script match the tone of the film itself— was it fast-paced for action, humorous for comedy, etc.? And if you were an agent or an executive, would you have wanted to represent this writer or produce this project based on the screenplay?

If you want to write for television, this process (minus the movie theater stuff) applies to you as well. See at least one episode of as many dramatic series or sitcoms as you can. Then select a series for which you will write a sample episode, watch every episode of that show, and see one or two additional episodes of every series similar in genre to the one you've picked. Then ask yourself the same questions, and do the same exercises listed above.

Once you've mastered the art of watching movies and TV shows, you'll be ready to move on to the other essential aspects of screenwriting: HOW TO SHARPEN A PENCIL; HOW TO STARE OUT THE WINDOW; and HOW TO TAKE A NAP.

SUMMARY

1. The primary goal of any filmmaker is to elicit emotion in the audience.

2. The primary goal of the screenwriter is to elicit emotion in the person reading the screenplay.

3. In order to succeed, your screenplay needs to accomplish the following objective: enable a sympathetic character to overcome a series of increasingly difficult, seemingly insurmountable obstacles and achieve a compelling desire.

4. The four stages of any screenplay are:

       Story concept

       Characters

       Plot structure

       Individual scenes

5. The great pitfall of screenwriting is writer's block, which is rooted in fear of failure and desire for perfection. To prevent block, alternately brainstorm for a quantity of ideas and edit those ideas for quality.

6. Seeing movies or TV shows and reading screenplays are essential steps to screenwriting success:

▶ See at least two recent Hollywood movies a week—a hundred movies a year

▶ See the good ones twice or more

▶ Analyze your emotional reactions and relate them to the principles in this book

► Purchase or download screenplays for successful films and episodic series—particularly those within the genre you're writing—and read at least one of those per week

► Watch and read all of the episodes of any television series you're attempting to write

TWO

STORY CONCEPT

MY FIRST JOB IN THE FILM INDUSTRY WAS AS A READER (AKA STORY analyst) for a major Hollywood literary agent. This meant that it was my responsibility to read, evaluate, and write synopses for the numerous screenplays and novels that had been submitted to the agent for representation or for one of his acting clients.

When I reported for work on my first day, the agent told me, "Ninety-nine out of every hundred screenplays you read won't be worth considering. I just want you to find that one out of a hundred."

When I heard this, I thought the guy was either joking or awfully cynical. Being new to the business and just off the turnip truck from Oregon, I naively assumed that at least half of the people who would go to all the trouble of writing a screenplay would have *something* that had potential or showed writing talent, even if the screenplay wasn't fully realized. Giving the agent the benefit of the doubt, I figured at least 25 percent would be decent or worth further consideration.

I was wrong.

I discovered, after I had read a few hundred scripts myself, that, if anything, the agent had been too generous. It was a rare day indeed when I could give a screenplay even a mild recommendation.

Of the ninety-nine out of a hundred screenplays that can't be recommended, ninety fall apart in one very basic way: the story concept sucks. Repeatedly, after reading a screenplay, I would ask myself in amazement how the author could possibly think that the story *idea* would be of interest to anyone besides him and maybe his mom. Had the writer even chosen a *concept* that had the slightest degree of interest, uniqueness, or artistic and commercial potential, he would have already elevated his screenplay into the top 10 percent!

In this chapter, we will discuss those qualities that give a story idea both commercial and artistic potential, and how you can create, discover, acquire, or select such an idea.

THE POWER OF DESIRE

Every story begins with the question *What if . . . ?* The writer thinks of a character, situation, or event and begins to ponder: What if such and such happened?

What if everything we accept as real were actually a hallucination created by computers that have taken over the world? *(The Matrix)*

What if a boy discovered he was actually a wizard? *(Harry Potter and the Sorcerer's Stone)*

What if a newspaper tycoon's mysterious dying word was investigated after his death? *(Citizen Kane)*

Even in true stories, there is the same implied question: What if a poor young man from the South had to overcome an abusive childhood, imprisonment, and drug addiction to become a legendary country singer and win the love of his life? The fact that such a situation actually occurred provides the writer with a specific answer, but it is still the provocative nature of the *question* that gives *Walk the Line* its artistic and commercial potential.

Your *What if . . . ?* pondering will lead you to one of two places: a plot situation (the prophesied end of the world in *Knowing* and *2012*, the Battle of Thermopylae in *300*, the bank heist in *Inside Man*) or a character (a drunken, nasty superhero in *Hancock*, a man who ages backward in *The Curious Case of Benjamin Button*, a pregnant teenager in *Juno*). Then you will begin looking for either a character that will enhance your plot, or the plot situation that will best bring out the qualities of your character.

These examples all describe characters that find themselves in unique and captivating situations. But it's not really the situation that drives a great story concept; it's the desire that grows out of it. Without giving your hero or protagonist some compelling goal to pursue, your story will have no forward movement, your audience will have nothing to root for, and your reader will have no compelling reason to keep turning the pages of your script.

OUTER MOTIVATION

In the vast majority of Hollywood movies, the heroes aren't simply pursuing something they want: the desires that define their stories are *visible*. If you go to boxofficemojo.com and look at the top ten money-making films for the last twenty years, you won't find a single movie where the hero isn't pursuing a goal with a clearly defined finish line. In other words, for significant commercial potential, and to stand a chance of getting your script produced by mainstream Hollywood, defining a visible objective for your hero is close to essential.

So when we learn that the hero's goal in *Monsters vs. Aliens* is to unite with a group of monsters to defeat an alien invasion, we can easily imagine what that will look like on the screen: the aliens will be imprisoned or dead, and our hero and the monsters will be victorious and alive. We don't know if this is how the movie will actually end, but we can envision what success would look like.

This visible finish line is what I term the hero's *outer motivation*, because achieving it will be outwardly apparent to the audience, as opposed to *invisible* desires such as acceptance, belonging, revenge, and fulfillment. If I tell you my script is about a hero who wants to fulfill his destiny, you have no idea what is actually going to happen on the screen, or what success for my hero will look like.

But if I tell you that *Slumdog Millionaire* is about a hero who wants to reunite with the love of his life and rescue her from a gangster, you now know exactly what you're rooting for. The fact is that achieving this outer motivation will indeed fulfill Jamal's destiny. But until you learn the visible finish line that we're rooting for him to cross, you don't know what the movie is really about.

Any workable story concept can be expressed in a similar single sentence: It is a story about a _____ who wants to _____. For example: It is a story about a greeting-card writer who wants to win—and keep—the love of a coworker (*(500) Days of Summer*). Or: It is a story about a congressman who wants to help the Afghans defeat the Russians (*Charlie Wilson's War*).

The same principle applies to episodic television. The episode of *The Middle* titled "The Fun House" is about Frankie wanting to prevent a motivational consultant from getting her fired.

This all sounds simple, doesn't it? Just give your hero/protagonist a visible goal to pursue, and you have the story concept for your movie. *It is* that simple, but it's far from easy to achieve. Even experienced screenwriters struggle with this basic principle again and again, resisting the fact that it is essential to creating a successful commercial screenplay.

Why is that? Why, if it has been shown to be a consistent element of almost every commercially successful movie in the last fifty years, is it so hard to accept? The answer is, *because the outer motivation is not what gives the story its power and artistry*. The things that grab us, inspire us, move us, or change us are a film's action, dialogue, conflicts, character arcs, originality, style, themes, and deeper levels of humanity. And the qualities of story that inspire us as writers and filmmakers are more than just simple story concepts. We want to touch people widely and *deeply*, with rich, layered characters, provocative themes, strong emotions, and meaningful insights into the human condition. So we resist thinking of story in terms of a clear, simple, visible outcome.

Few people leave *Good Will Hunting* talking only about Will's pursuit of Skylar, even though that desire forms the foundation of the film. Without that visible objective, the movie would just be a series of therapy sessions with no end in sight.

So even though your hero's outer motivation alone won't give your script its power, without it you'll have nothing on which to build your unique vision, nothing to keep an audience in the theater or the reader immersed in your screenplay.

Of course, this isn't true for every single movie made. In many biographies or independent or foreign-language films like *Ray*, or *Precious*, or *The Maid*, there is no visible finish line the hero is trying to cross. (These exceptions to the rule will be discussed at length in chapter 7, which is brilliantly titled "Exceptions to the Rule.")

Here are the qualities that distinguish effective outer motivations. These will help ensure that your story concepts will create a satisfying (and commercially viable) emotional experience:

I. **The desire must be visible.** I use the term *outer* motivation because it is outwardly apparent to the audience as they watch the action on the screen. Whether it's stopping the bad guys in *Air Force One* or the *Mission: Impossible* movies, putting on a strip show in *The Full Monty*, or saving Private Ryan in that film, the heroes of those films are *doing* things to achieve their desires, not simply revealing themselves through dialogue.

In the movie *In the Line of Fire*, the hero wants desperately to make up for a moment of hesitation and failure early in his career. But this need doesn't give the story a plot; it only justifies the actual outer motivation: to stop the assassin from killing the current president.

Stating an outer motivation must immediately conjure a specific image of what that would look like on the screen. And the image must be the same for anyone who hears it. If you tell me your hero's outer motivation is to be a success, or even to be a successful football coach, I won't know exactly what that looks like. *Remember the Titans* is about a coach who wants to win the state football championship. Because my image of his team going to the playoffs and ultimately winning the championship game is essentially the same as anyone else's, it's a properly defined outer motivation.

2. **The desire must have a clearly implied endpoint.** When you write a screenplay, you are taking the reader on a journey with a specific destination in mind. Or think of your movie as a race. Your hero is trying desperately to reach the finish line before some other character or force of nature can stop her. If you don't tell the audience where the finish line is, how will they know what to root for? How will they even know when the movie's over, other than the end credits coming on?

3. **Your hero's outer motivation must seem impossible to accomplish.** If the desire is easy to achieve—if it isn't the most difficult thing the hero has ever had to do—your story simply won't be emotionally involving or entertaining enough.

4. **Your hero must pursue his outer motivation until the end of the story.** Your hero's goal cannot be resolved until the climax of your screenplay. So don't think just in terms of initial desire. In *Rain Man*, Charlie Babbitt wants to kidnap his brother. This goal is visible, and creates a clear, consistent image. But it only takes us into act two of the movie. The movie won't be over until he achieves his ultimate outer motivation: to get his half of Raymond's inheritance. Kidnapping Raymond is just one of the means he will use to try to accomplish that goal.

5. **Your hero must desperately want to achieve the desire.** If your main character is only mildly interested in achieving his outer motivation, how can you expect the audience to care whether he wins?

   Maximus's desire to destroy the emperor in *Gladiator*, and Batman's desire to stop the Joker in *The Dark Knight*, are so powerful that these heroes do whatever is necessary to achieve those goals.

6. **Your hero must actively pursue the desire.** Your characters can't simply sit around talking about how much they'd like to have

money, success, or the love of a beautiful woman. Your hero must take control of his life and use every ounce of strength, courage, and intelligence he has to rob the bank, stop the serial killer, or win the love of the prom queen.

Your protagonist can be passive at the beginning of your script, as in *Knocked Up* or *The 40-Year-Old Virgin*, but before too long, he has to declare, "I WANT THAT!" and go after it with everything he's got.

7. **It must be within your hero's power to achieve her desire.** Never create a hero who waits to be rescued, in any sense of the word. If she's pursued by a killer, trapped in a mine shaft, or threatened by dinosaurs, she can't just wait helplessly for the Mounties to arrive.

The exception to this principle is the courtroom drama or comedy, where a judge or jury ultimately decides whether the hero wins or loses. But notice that in films like *A Few Good Men*, *A Time to Kill*, or *Liar Liar*, the verdict is preceded or supplanted by a scene where the hero confronts an antagonistic witness, reveals key evidence, or makes an impassioned summary that transforms the outcome into a foregone conclusion.

8. **Your hero must put everything on the line to achieve his desire.** The more passionate, determined, and courageous your hero is in pursuit of his quest, the greater the audience's own emotional involvement, and the greater their elation when he succeeds. This principle is fairly obvious in movies like *Star Trek*, *3:10 to Yuma*, or *National Treasure*, where the heroes put their lives on the line to stop the bad guys, make their escape, or get the loot. But it's also true in any successful love story or comedy. In *The Birdcage*, Armand risks embarrassment, humiliation, self-esteem, the loss of his lover, and the loss of his own son's love and happiness in his attempt to convince the future in-laws that he's a straight man.

In romantic comedies and love stories like *My Best Friend's Wedding*, *Brokeback Mountain*, and *As Good As It Gets*, the heroes must take the greatest emotional risk of all: exposing themselves to rejection, fear, and pain as they struggle with identities that have brought them a lifetime of protection.

Think of outer motivation as the foundation upon which the rest of your story will be built. From this simple but powerful principle—to which we will return repeatedly throughout this book—will emerge plot structure, character arc, theme, action, dialogue, and even your marketing plan and the ultimate success of your screenplay.

FINDING ORIGINAL STORY IDEAS

As you've probably figured out, expressing a story idea in a single sentence is no big deal. Creating the character and desire in the first place is a big deal.

On rare and glorious occasions, the muse will be sitting on your shoulder and a story idea will blossom full-blown into your mind. When that happens, take full advantage of the situation. But don't be discouraged when this fails to occur. Most of the time, creativity is not so spontaneous.

To originate story concepts for your screenplays, it is almost always necessary to stimulate your own thinking by observing, recording, and reacting to all of the potential material that confronts you every day, and to use that material as a jumping-off point for your own brainstorming and creativity.

I strongly recommend keeping a small notebook, a recorder, or a cell phone with a notepad feature with you at all times. Whenever you are confronted with a potential plot idea, character trait, or situation, write it down. The more you develop the habit of regarding *all* your experiences and *all* outside information as possible story material, the better you will ultimately be at "creating" story concepts.

Notice that you are not to find and record only good story ideas, but any possible ideas at all. This is the brainstorming phase of story concept, and you're going for quantity, not quality. We'll discuss evaluating the concepts later, but at this stage you don't want to block the process in any way by judging your ideas. Just start noticing, pondering, and recording everything.

Besides recording ideas, characters, and situations as they present themselves to you, you must also actively search for story ideas. Here are a few reliable sources to stimulate your own thinking and originate potential story concepts:

1. **Personal Experience.** The first piece of (usually misused) advice most writers get is, "Write about what you know." An old joke in the film industry is that 90 percent of all screenplays are about someone who has just come to Hollywood to break into the movies, because that is what all of those screenwriters know.

   There is a real danger in writing from personal experience, because most of us don't have lives that are all that exciting or interesting. The autobiographical screenplay, unless your life story puts Jason Bourne to shame, is best avoided. Likewise with screenplays based on traumatic events from your past. Screenwriting holds many rewards, but journal writing is a far better choice for working through your own emotional issues.

   An added difficulty in writing about personal experience is objectivity. I repeatedly read scripts that have severe problems with logic and audience interest, and the writers' excuses are often that the events really occurred. Sacrificing dramatic and artistic truth for historical fact is a great pitfall of the autobiographical screenplay.

   There is a much more effective and productive way to write about what you know. Use your personal knowledge and experience as a basis for a *fictional* story concept that gives you the freedom to meet all the criteria of an effective screenplay.

   An excellent example of this principle is *The Hurt Locker*. *The Hurt Locker* is not the true story of screenwriter Mark Boal's tour of duty in Iraq. In fact, he wasn't a member of a bomb squad, but rather a journalist embedded with a bomb squad unit. The depth, richness, believability, and emotional impact of his fictional screenplay are obviously increased because the writer drew on his own personal experiences reporting on that war.

2. **Headlines.** Story topics from newspapers, magazines, TV, and radio can provide an excellent springboard for creating your own fictional story concepts. Remember, at this brainstorming stage you're looking for any ideas, no matter how unlikely or terrible or absurd, that will get the creative juices flowing.

The original screenplay for *The Karate Kid* is an excellent example of how this process can work. The film's producer, Jerry Weintraub, saw a newscast about a boy in the San Fernando Valley who stopped getting picked on by the school bullies after he learned karate. The eventual screenplay that Robert Mark Kamen created from these few facts included a love story, an aging Okinawan instructor, a transplanted high school student, and a climactic tournament. These elements probably had nothing to do with the true story. But the newscast served to stimulate the producer's thinking, eventually resulting in a movie that met all of the criteria for an effective concept.

Episodic television abounds with fictional stories that grew out of real events and headlines. These have been the foundation of the multitude of *Law & Order* series for two decades, and have provided *Grey's Anatomy*, *House*, *HawthoRNe*, and innumerable other medical series with untold diseases and crises.

An equally effective use of headlines can result when you stimulate your thinking by trying to combine two totally unrelated story topics. Some time ago, a headline in a Honolulu newspaper read GRAY LINE DRIVERS THREATEN STRIKE. This might lead you to a story about a tour bus driver who goes on strike and the effect on her and her family, or to a comedy about all of the bizarre jobs the driver must obtain to support herself during a strike. Letting your creativity roam, you may be led to a story about economic hardship and its effect on children, which has nothing to do with strikes or bus drivers. Or you might pursue a strike story from the point of view of a museum that was one of the stops on the tour. The further you wander from the original source, the better you are doing.

The same Honolulu newspaper also provided a good opportunity for combining two headlines. Another headline from that same day read: HARE KRISHNAS SUED FOR $1 MILLION. Suppose you tried to connect it to the earlier story.

The result might be a totally fictional comedy about a woman who inherits a small tour bus company. Because the drivers don't want to work for a woman, they go out on strike. At the same time that our hero is looking for bus drivers to save her company, a local religious cult must raise a lot of money for a pending lawsuit, so the members agree to go to work driving the tour buses, with hilarious results. (If anyone out there is interested in pursuing this obviously high concept, please give me a call and we'll talk option.)

The point of these examples is that the *process* of using headlines as a starting point for your own brainstorming and lateral thinking is the real goal. As long as you don't block, edit, or restrict yourself at the outset, the result can be a number of original ideas that have strong potential.

3. **Other Movies.** It should be fairly obvious that Hollywood is a clone factory, with producers and studios repeatedly trying to replicate the success of unexpected blockbusters by duplicating elements of their genres and story concepts. (Really, would *Percy Jackson & the Olympians: The Lightning Thief* have ever been made had it not been for the success of the Harry Potter franchise?) So why not use the same approach in brainstorming your own ideas? Don't try to duplicate successes; instead, combine two concepts or situations that seem completely different in genre or story line. This can often result in new, original ideas that haven't been explored, but which still fall into commercially viable genres and story lines.

Consider two successful films from 2009: *Zombieland* and *District 9*. Rhett Reese and Paul Wernick's script for *Zombieland* took two *very* familiar genres, the zombie movie and the road comedy, and combined them to create something that (to my knowledge) had never been done before—a story about a group of strangers who join forces to battle a world overtaken with zombies as they make their way from Texas to Los Angeles, and en route create a kind of surrogate family.

This horror film version of *Little Miss Sunshine* (Abigail Breslin even stars in both) was no pale imitation; the two genres were blended only as a jumping-off point. The characters, the nature of the zombies, the specific situations, the humor, and the underlying theme of love and connection were all original and emotionally involving.

District 9, an even bigger blockbuster worldwide, and an Oscar® nominee for both best original screenplay and best picture, took a similar approach by combining the alien-from-outer-space movie with a handheld, real-time documentary style. This had already been done successfully in the more traditional creature-feature *Cloverfield*. But Neill Blomkamp and Terri Tatchell's screenplay *District 9* used these elements to create a more complex portrait of an unlikely hero, a government conspiracy, misunderstood aliens, and ultimately a buddy action film and an allegory of apartheid.

So make a list of your favorite successful films and then randomly combine any two of them. Or take any one of the stories on your list and change just one element: turn a drama into a comedy, or a suspense thriller into a science fiction thriller; change the age, gender, and/or occupation of the hero; turn the villain into a hero. A lot of the ideas that result will be nonsensical, but a few will spark your interest, and serve as starting points for story concepts with real commercial and artistic potential.

ADAPTATIONS

Other than original story concepts, the most obvious source of story material is the adaptation of other fictional forms—novels, plays, and short stories. These have the advantage of providing you with an already created plot, as well as the added commercial strength that may come from identifying your screenplay as an adaptation of a published or produced work. If you think your weakness is in originating plots out of whole cloth, but your strength is in your ability to mold a story into screenplay form, then adaptations can be a good starting point for your material.

If you find a piece of fiction that you want to adapt, you must then track down the author or publisher (or their representatives) and negotiate for the film rights to their creation. Your ability to do that will depend on what you are offering: how much money (up front and upon production of the film); how much talent and experience you bring to the table; how much respect you have for the original material.

Unless you have googobs of money, you're probably not going to get the rights to adapt J. K. Rowling's next fantasy series. (If you do have that kind of money, give me a call and we'll discuss the meaning of the term *coproducer*.) But since not all books and plays are big best-sellers, fictional and dramatic works can be a good source of material for even the less experienced screenwriter of modest means. It could be that the material you have found never achieved a great deal of commercial success, or that it is ten or fifteen years old, and all of the interest and enthusiasm that accompanied the work's initial appearance has now faded.

The original source material might not even be very good. But since you are using it only as a starting point for your own screenplay, it still might be appropriate for you to pursue the rights to it. Most of Alfred Hitchcock's career consisted of turning lesser-known works of fiction into great movies.

―――

BECAUSE BOTH NOVELISTS AND SCREENWRITERS USE CHARACTERS TO tell fictional stories, it may seem logical to assume the transition is a natural one. But pause to consider the wide gulf that separates these two forms of fiction.

Screenwriters must conform to very narrowly defined rules and parameters, while novelists have much greater latitude in the ways they can tell their stories. Novels *may* follow the structure that movies do, and the fiction-to-film transition in those cases might be fairly straightforward. But no matter how much you love an original work of fiction, *you must eliminate all those elements that do not conform to the rules of screenwriting.* This can be painfully hard, but the process is essential to creating a movie that will ever reach a mass audience.

So here are some crucial principles you must keep in mind if you are considering adapting a work of fiction into a screenplay, or even if you're a novelist considering crossing over to screenwriting with an original idea:

1. **Great literature doesn't mean great cinema.** This is a lesson Hollywood never seems to learn. Those elements that usually bring a novel critical acclaim include rich, textured writing, lots of interior thoughts, feelings, and descriptions, an expansive, convoluted plot, and an abundance of symbol and allegory. None of these translates readily to the screen.

   As a screenwriter, you are getting only three things from your original source material: character, plot, and sometimes dialogue. Your screenplay must have a style, mood, texture, and structure of its own. Don't assume that just because you love reading a certain book, an audience will also love seeing the movie.

2. **Your allegiance is to your screenplay, not to the original source.** If, in order to fulfill the requirements of film structure and character, you have to alter or eliminate parts of the original material, then do it.

3. **Adapting your own novels and plays is seldom wise, particularly if your original work is unpublished or unproduced.** If you originally wrote the story as a novel or play, it's probably because that is how you envisioned it, and that is the best format for the story. If you want to write a screenplay, find *another* concept, which is best suited to film.

I can usually recognize within five pages whether a screenplay is adapted from the writer's own novel or play. The play adaptations are consistently "talking heads" scripts (with a few outdoor scenes thrown in), and the novel adaptations lack the structure of a well-written screenplay. Books are books and movies are movies, and with your own original work, you should keep it that way.

4. **Movies must conform to a budget.** When the Mongol hordes come sweeping over the mountains in your novel, all you've added is excitement. When the same thing happens in your screenplay, you've added $3 million to the budget of the film.

5. **Commerciality is the major concern of film financiers.** Though publishers are obviously also in business to turn a profit, there are hundreds of publishing houses turning out thousands of titles a year, while only about a hundred movies a year are released by the major studios, with an average production and distribution budget in excess of $100 million a picture. Such a huge cost creates a demand for movies that will reach the widest possible audience.

6. **Genre is critical.** While novels can portray characters in just about any time or place, there is a strong prejudice in Hollywood that favors action movies, thrillers, and comedies over musicals, period pieces, Westerns, and dramas.

7. **Movies have a prescribed length.** While novels can range from the almost-a-novelette size of *Animal Farm* to the epic sprawl of *War and Peace*, most movies last between ninety minutes and two hours, and their corresponding screenplays between 105 and 119 pages. This means if you're considering adapting a 300-plus-page novel (not an unusual length for fiction), you're facing a massive job of editing and streamlining the story.

8. **Movies portray a condensed period of time.** Most Hollywood movies take place over a period of hours, days, or weeks—rarely months or years. The epic saga may work fine in fiction, where a reader can return to a book as often as necessary, but when an audience is there for a single sitting, they don't want to watch characters grow old together.

9. **Screenplays may only reveal what the audience will hear and see on the screen.** Novels can include illustrations, footnotes, maps, fancy fonts, and chapter headings. They can offer asides from the author, reveal the characters' thoughts and feelings, and give the reader any historical or background information the author considers helpful or interesting. None of these things can be included in a script, unless it is revealed through action or dialogue.

10. **Style is nearly irrelevant in screenwriting.** The screenwriter's goal is to create a movie in the mind of the reader by making the script as fast, easy, and enjoyable to read as possible. Qualities usually present in highly acclaimed fiction—an extensive vocabulary, a rich, textured style, a unique use of language—should be avoided when writing a script.

TRUE STORIES

Similar to converting literature into film is the adaptation of true stories and historical events. Many of the most effective true stories depicted on film are not about legendary or well-known figures, but rather about everyday individuals caught up in situations that bring out their courage and humanity. Think of John Nash in *A Beautiful Mind*, Coach Herman Boone in *Remember the Titans*, Chris Gardner in *The Pursuit of Happyness*, or Leigh Anne Tuohy in *The Blind Side*. Few people were familiar with any of these heroes until the movies were made.

In other words, the possible sources for true stories are unending. Most historical events, at least those from many years ago, fall in the public-domain category: When all of the principal characters in your dramatization are deceased, there is no need to obtain rights to the story. However, using a single book as a source for a historical adaptation means going through the same process of obtaining rights as you would for a novel. If there is some question about the need to obtain rights, as when some of the characters in the story are still alive, then it is advisable to get legal help.

The strongest and most effective historical screenplays are those that involve some contemporary issue, theme, or plot situation placed in a period context. Contemporary issues of poverty, human dignity, and personal courage are explored in *Cinderella Man*, even though the story takes place during the Great Depression.

Unfortunately, like novels and plays, true stories also come with a number of artistic and commercial pitfalls:

1. **A story isn't appropriate for adaptation just because it's true.** Real life seldom conforms to the neat, single-thrust story concept and structure of a movie, with the appropriate positive or uplifting outcome. In the real world, events and situations usually just go on and on, evolving or dissolving rather than resolving. So unless you've found a true story about a hero pursuing a clearly defined outer motivation, and which meets all the other criteria already presented in this chapter, I'd move on.

2. **A true story is often more effective as a documentary film or a news item.** Many times a true story achieves its most dramatic and effective portrayal as a segment of *60 Minutes* or as an article in *Rolling Stone*, and adapting it to a feature-length screenplay means stretching it too thin.

3. **You must be truer to the screenplay than you are to the original source.** Just as with adaptations of novels, your commitment must be to creating an emotionally involving screenplay for the reader and audience, even if that means altering the facts of the original

story. Unfortunately, you have much less leeway to do this with a true story than you do with fictional sources. Even to maintain that your screenplay is *based* on a true story requires some allegiance to the actual events.

4. **Period pieces are much more difficult to sell.** Stories that aren't set in the present or future can be nearly impossible to get produced in Hollywood—or even to get read. Audiences simply don't line up for period drama the way they do for contemporary comedies, love stories, action movies, and thrillers.

Of course there are exceptions, but very, very few. Of the top fifty box office hits for each year from 2005 to 2009, only eleven were based on true historical events. That's eleven out of a list of *two hundred and fifty* successful movies. Is it any wonder that Hollywood shies away from this category?

This is why your best use of true historical events is almost always as a jumping-off point for a fictional story. You still face the commercial obstacles that come with a period piece, but at least you have more latitude for giving the story both proper structure and contemporary application. *Titanic*, *The Last Samurai*, and *There Will Be Blood* all grew out of such historical events and characters.

If you've gotten the idea that just about anything can be used as a source of possible story ideas, then you're right. Movies have been written that grew out of video games, songs, song titles, myths, jokes, ads, board games, and amusement-park rides. The essential rule is that you never edit, judge, or block yourself as you search for, and record, ideas.

SELECTING THE BEST STORY CONCEPTS

Searching for and recording *What if . . . ?* situations and characters should be an ongoing process that begins immediately and continues uninterrupted throughout your screenwriting career. But at some point you're going to need to select the single story idea that you will then begin developing into a complete screenplay. It is at that point that you will need to evaluate which ideas possess real *artistic* and *commercial potential*.

Commercial potential is a fairly easy term to define. Generally it means that the motion picture based on your screenplay will earn more money than it costs to make it, promote it, and exhibit it. More appropriate for you as a screenwriter, commercial potential means that enough Hollywood agents, producers, stars, and investors *think* that the movie of your script will turn a profit, thereby increasing the chances that this particular story concept can lead to a screenwriting deal for you.

Artistic potential is tougher to define. On one level, it means that the screenplay will succeed on its own terms and will fulfill whatever internal goals you set out to accomplish. Artistic potential implies the possibility of awards, critical acclaim, and strong acceptance by some select audience. In other words, if a movie wins the New York Film Critics Circle award and makes $40 at the box office, it achieved artistic potential. If it cost $40 million to produce and made $400 million worldwide, it achieved commercial potential. Artistic success is a matter of opinion; commercial success is a matter of dollars and cents. *Stranger than Fiction* was (in my opinion) an artistic success; *Paranormal Activity* was (without question) a commercial success.

STORY CONCEPT CHECKLIST

The following checklist contains those criteria you can use for evaluating a story concept at periodic intervals throughout the writing of the screenplay. The first five items on the list are *essential* for both artistic and commercial success. *No movie can succeed without these five qualities:*

1. **A hero.** The story must have at least one hero—a main character or protagonist who is on screen most of the time, whose motivation drives the plot, and with whom the audience is deeply in-

volved. The hero can be a man, a woman, a boy, a girl, or an android, as long as this character (or characters) is the central focus and driving force of the story.

2. **Empathy.** The reader must put herself inside the hero emotionally; she must experience emotion *through* that character. This does not mean that the hero is without flaws, shortcomings, or strongly negative qualities; often the opposite is true. It only means that there is sufficient identification with the hero to elicit emotion. (How you create empathy with your hero will be discussed at great length in chapter 3.)

3. **Desire.** There must be at least one clear, specific objective that the hero hopes to achieve by the end of the story. Without some goal for your hero to achieve, without some motivation to carry your hero through to the climax of your screenplay, your reader and audience will have nothing to root for, and the story will fail. Desire is equally important to character development, plot structure, and each individual scene. Even if your hero's motivation doesn't have a clear, visible end point—if it's simply to get through or resolve some new situation or relationship (as in *One True Thing*, *Driving Miss Daisy*, or *The Hurt Locker*), the hero still has to want *something*. Passive, unmotivated heroes won't work on any level—commercially or artistically.

4. **Conflict.** Desire drives your story forward, but it is the *conflict* your hero must overcome that elicits the emotion. The peak moments in any movie are always those where we anticipate the conflict to come, where the hero faces a huge hurdle, or where the hero is rewarded for having conquered it.

5. **Risk.** In facing these challenges, hurdles, and obstacles in pursuit of his motivation, your hero must ultimately put everything on the

line. He must find the physical or emotional courage to risk things of vital importance to him (his life, his reputation, his emotional protection). Whether your hero ultimately *finds* whatever courage is necessary remains to be resolved by your screenplay; this is what the audience will stick around to find out.

The next items on the checklist are not essential, but they can add significantly to the success of your screenplay and to the likelihood that it will get financed or will get you other work. The more of these criteria are met by your story concept the fewer the hurdles you will have to overcome in order to sell it.

6. **A high concept.** *High concept* is a film-industry term that gets tossed around fairly frequently and seems to take on a variety of definitions. Basically, it means that the story idea alone is sufficient to attract an audience, regardless of casting, reviews, and word of mouth. High-concept movies are those whose titles, ads, newspaper descriptions, or online blurbs promise a peak emotional experience: big action; sex; violence; humor.

    If the single sentence describing your concept (It is a story about a _____ who wants to _____.) is enough all by itself to get a huge number of people to see it, then it has a high concept.

    Speed epitomizes a high-concept movie: "A lone cop has to save the people on a Los Angeles bus that will blow up if it drops below 50 mph." *Precious: Based on the Novel* Push *by Sapphire* is the antithesis: "In Harlem, an overweight, abused, pregnant, illiterate teen wants to attend an alternative school." It was the promotion of the story idea alone that accounted for most of the initial audience for *Speed*; it was the awards, the reviews, and the word of mouth that led to the eventual success of *Precious*.

7. **A commercial goal.** More than 95 percent of all Hollywood movies are about heroes pursuing one of only five visible objectives. These are:

► *To win*—this is by far the biggest of these categories, because it not only encompasses all competition movies (*Friday Night Lights*, *Kicking and Screaming*, *Akeelah and the Bee*), it also includes all love stories and romantic comedies, where the hero's desire is to win the love of another character (too many examples to mention).

► *To stop*—here the hero's desire is to stop something bad from happening, whether it's a suspense thriller (stopping the hit man in *Collateral*), an action thriller (stopping the assassination and bombing in *Eagle Eye*), a horror film (stopping that creepy girl from the well in *The Ring*), a disaster movie (stopping the meteor in *Armageddon*), or a science fiction thriller (stopping the enslavement and experimentation in *District 9*).

► *To escape*—this simply means to get away from a threatening situation, as in *Panic Room* or *The Truman Show*.

► *To deliver*—in these films, the hero must take something of value to some faraway, or at least well-protected, destination. *Up*, *The Book of Eli*, and *The Lord of the Rings* (the entire trilogy) are all delivery stories.

► *To retrieve*—the desire here is to get to something of great value, and then either to get away with it, as in *The Thomas Crown Affair* and *The Bank Job*, or to bring it back to safety, as in *The Da Vinci Code* and *Ransom*. In other words, retrieval movies include all heist movies, kidnapping movies, and Indiana Jones knockoffs.

Clearly, many movies combine two or more of these basic desires. In *Taken*, the hero must stop the kidnappers and retrieve his daughter. And winning a character's love can become a part of any genre—romantic comedy, romantic adventure, romantic thriller, etc. The key is creating a desire for your hero that falls into at least one of these categories.

8. **Originality and familiarity.** Mentioning originality at all as a quality for acceptance by Hollywood seems ludicrous in light of what is currently produced. Just look at the schedule of programs for any new TV season and *try* to find a wholly original concept. Or remove the sequels, remakes, adaptations, take-offs, rip-offs, and clones from any feature-film production list, and it becomes evident that total originality scares Hollywood to death.

Nonetheless, "lack of originality" is consistently a stated reason for the rejection of screenplays and story concepts by producers and studios. And it is true that while audiences seem to support "more of the same," people still line up and tune in to see something they've never seen before. This unique or original element to an otherwise familiar story idea is often referred to as its *hook*. This is the startling, seductive idea that makes people hear about a movie and say, "Wow—I've got to see *that!*"

You have to give executives and producers some precedent for the potential success of your script: motivations and character traits that have proved successful before. *Then* you can add the necessary elements of originality that will separate your screenplay from all the others.

But these unique elements can't just be different; they must be different in a way that will grab an audience. When selecting a story concept, research any films that have ever drawn on a similar plot situation, so that when discussing your story idea, you can justify both its familiarity and its originality. And when you rip something off, rip off a winner. Saying that your story idea is the next *Amelia* is probably not your best sales pitch.

This is where the idea of *antecedents* can be extremely helpful. As you originate and evaluate your story concepts, ask yourself,

"What successful movies from the recent past can I point to and say, 'Because *that* movie made money, mine will make money?'"

This doesn't mean you have to find movies or TV shows with the same story line or character. But if you can't come up with any recent hits within the same genre, and with a similar tone, style, key plot element, and/or marketing demographic to your own idea, you should know your concept is going to be a very tough sell.

Hancock is an excellent example of a film that successfully combines familiarity and originality. Hollywood has been cranking out superhero stories for decades, going all the way back to the days of *Superman* on the radio. But to this very familiar genre, screenwriters Vincent Ngo and Vince Gilligan added a superhero who's a misanthropic drunk, unloved by society, who engages a PR person to improve his image, and who is attracted to that man's wife. These original elements provide the movie's hook, while still drawing on the familiarity of all the blockbuster superhero antecedents that came before it.

9. **Character arc.** If your story concept contains the potential for your hero to become a more evolved, individuated person, then both the commercial and artistic potential of your story increase. Creating powerful arcs for your characters will be discussed at length in chapter 4. For now, suffice it to say that character arc means finding not just the physical courage to achieve the outer motivation, but the emotional courage as well.

10. **Theme.** Closely related to growth for the hero is the notion of theme: the universal statement the screenplay makes about the human condition. This is a level of meaning that goes beyond the plot of the film and is instead a prescription for living that any member of the audience can apply to his or her own life. The theme is not the same as the "message" of a movie. A message is a more political

statement that connects directly to the plot but has no obvious application to the average person's own actions. The message of *Hotel Rwanda* addresses the issue of African genocide, and in particular the grossly immoral neglect of that situation by the Western world. The theme of *Hotel Rwanda* is, on the other hand, universal. It is the idea that to live better lives, to be more fully evolved, we must find the courage to do what is right, even at the risk of our comfortable existence, and even at the risk of our own lives and those of our families. This is a principle that can apply to anyone—whether or not they have some direct experience of genocide.

ARTISTRY VERSUS COMMERCIALITY

It's pretty easy to become discouraged and antagonistic toward Hollywood's pursuit of the dollar and the rating point. Movies and television are often a cavalcade of slick mediocrity, attempting little and achieving less. And the big-budget splurges on stars, special effects, and "sure things" always seem to be at the expense of story and screenplay.

Because the movies and TV shows coming out of Hollywood so often fall short of becoming anything moving, original, or meaningful, there is a prejudice among many writers against *any* commercial considerations. I repeatedly encounter the belief that any movie that strives for, or attains, commercial success is a superficial sellout.

This attitude is understandable but unrealistic and unfortunate. It is certainly possible (as *Avatar, The Sixth Sense, Slumdog Millionaire, Brokeback Mountain, Up, Seinfeld, The West Wing, Modern Family, The Good Wife,* and countless other movies and television programs illustrate) for a work of art to be both a commercial hit and succeed marvelously on its own artistic terms. It is intellectual hogwash to maintain that any original or meaningful movie must be obscure, subtitled, or a financial failure.

As a screenwriter, you must accept this fact: if you want a *career* in screenwriting, you have to write movies and TV shows that people want to see. Otherwise you're writing only for your own personal satisfaction, with no realistic career goals in mind.

At the same time, striving solely for big bucks is just as unrealistic and unfulfilling as disregarding commerciality altogether, because screenplays based on "hot" concepts, which are devoid of any emotional involvement on the part of the screenwriter, will almost never get sold or produced—the topic won't stay hot and the screenplay won't be that good. *My Babysitter's a Stripper!* and *Ice Pick in the Eye* might sound like sure bets to make millions, but if you don't have any real love for such movies, then they won't make millions coming out of *your* computer.

To decide if any story concept contains the right combination of commercial and artistic potential, I recommend asking yourself the following questions:

1. **Do I want to spend at least the next year of my life working on this story idea?** If the answer to this question is no, no matter how commercial the concept might seem, go on to another idea. Otherwise you're in for a year of misery, with little hope of a payoff. But if the answer to this first question is yes, then go on to question 2:

2. **Does this story have commercial potential?** This should be fairly easy to answer simply by using the Story Concept checklist above. So if the answer to this question is also yes—if it's a high-concept idea with a clear outer motivation that falls into one of the win/stop/escape/deliver/retrieve categories, *and* you have a passion for it, then start developing the story. But if the answer to question 2 is no, then go on to question 3:

3. **In spite of the fact that I know this story is commercially difficult, am I so passionate about it that I'm determined to write it anyway?** In other words, is this the story you were born to write, the one that's burning a hole in your soul and costing you sleep until you get it made? If the answer to this question is also no, then you should go on to another idea. Without that level of passion, it would be wiser to find a more commercial story to launch your career.

But if the answer is yes, if the story truly does mean that much to you, then you should go for it. Writing should above all else be personally fulfilling, and you will gain the most pleasure and satisfaction from a story that holds your greatest emotional commitment. And if you do a good enough job of writing a screenplay that grows out of your own passion for the story, then eventually you can find others who will share that passion, and the film can get produced.

If you were to remove all the sequels, and all the movies based on phenomenal best-selling books and products (like *The Da Vinci Code*, the Harry Potter films, the *Twilight* series, and the *Transformers* films), from the list of all-time box-office champs, almost every remaining film took years of struggle and setbacks, as well as rejection by at least some of the major studios, before getting financed. Each eventually got made because its creators would not let their passion and determination die.

MODIFYING YOUR STORY CONCEPT

The criteria for story selection and development must be used very gently when first considering ideas, because at the initial stages, your concepts will of course seem ordinary or absurd. But as you continue to use them, these principles will be useful throughout the screenwriting process in helping you modify and develop your story.

Certainly you must, from the outset, turn your idea into a concept that meets the first five items: hero, empathy, desire, conflict, and risk. You can then mold and modify your idea with regard to many of the other considerations, such as giving it a more original hook, or adding elements of winning, stopping, escaping, delivering, or retrieving, or developing more of an arc for your hero. If you keep returning at all stages of the writing process to these checklists, you can continually modify and build on the ideas and concepts you have selected until they become commercially and artistically successful screenplays.

SUMMARY

1. Every story begins with the question *What if . . . ?* This will lead to either a unique, compelling character, or situation—or both.

2. The vast majority of Hollywood movies are about characters pursuing *outer motivations*—visible goals with clearly defined finish lines.

3. Any workable story concept can be expressed in a single sentence: It is a story about a _____ who wants to _____. The first blank identifies the hero/protagonist of the story, the second states that hero's outer motivation.

4. Effective outer motivations share these qualities:

► It is visible

► It has a clearly implied endpoint

► The hero will pursue it until the end of the story

► The hero must desperately want to achieve it

► The hero must actively pursue it

► It's within the hero's power to achieve it

► The hero must put everything on the line to achieve it

5. The primary sources of story ideas are:

► Personal experience

► Headlines

► Other movies

► Adaptations of books, plays, and short stories

► Contemporary true stories and historical events

6. The principles and pitfalls of adapting fictional stories are:

- ► Great literature doesn't mean great cinema

- ► Your allegiance must be to your screenplay, not to the original source

- ► Adapting your own novels and plays is seldom wise

- ► Movies must conform to a budget

- ► Commerciality is the major concern of film financiers

- ► Genre is critical

- ► Movies have a prescribed length

- ► Movies portray a condensed period of time

- ► Screenplays may only reveal what the audience will hear and see on the screen

- ► Prose style is nearly irrelevant in screenwriting

7. The principles and pitfalls of adapting true stories are:

- ► A story isn't appropriate for adaptation just because it's true

- ► A true story is often more effective as a documentary film or a news item

- ► Reality rarely conforms to the principles of a well-written screenplay

- ► Period pieces are much more difficult to sell

8. Commercial potential means the ability to convince the people in power that producing the screenplay will result in profits or high ratings.

9. Artistic potential means the ability to do something meaningful that's of deeper value to humanity than simply entertaining the audience.

10. The five essential elements of any film story are:

- A hero
- Empathy
- Desire
- Conflict
- Risk

11. Five story elements that will greatly increase commercial potential are:

- A high concept
- A commercial goal:

  To win

  To stop

  To escape

  To deliver

  To retrieve

- Originality combined with familiarity
- Character arc
- Theme

12. The three questions to ask before developing any story concept, in order to resolve any conflict between artistry and commerciality, are:

- Do I want to spend at least the next year of my life writing this screenplay?
- Does this story concept have commercial potential?
- Even if it lacks commercial potential, am I truly so passionate about the story that I'm determined to write it anyway?

THREE

CHARACTER DEVELOPMENT

ONCE YOU HAVE SELECTED A STORY CONCEPT FOR DEVELOPMENT INTO a screenplay, you must create and develop the characters that will populate your story. As with all facets of screenwriting, your goal is to elicit the maximum emotional involvement from your reader and audience. While your initial story concept is evaluated on the basis of its *potential* for creating emotion and attracting an audience to the movie in the first place, it is *through* the characters that your reader will experience emotion.

As with story concept, the cornerstone for the development of your characters is the hero's visible outer motivation. This chapter will give you the various components of effective characters; provide more specific methods of developing identification, motivation, conflict, and theme; and show you how to use those principles to create original, emotionally involving characters.

THE FOUR FACETS OF CHARACTER

Movie and television characters consist of four basic facets:

Physical makeup: age, sex, appearance, disabilities

Personality: intellectual and emotional makeup

Role: whatever situations and attachments define the character's situation at the beginning of the script: job, family, friends, affiliations, finances, ethnicity, religion, living situation

Background: everything that happened to the character prior to his appearance in the screenplay

It is easy to see how these are crucial to your story. If you compare Alex Hitchens, the hero of Kevin Bisch's screenplay *Hitch*, to Andy Stitzer, the hero of *The 40-Year-Old Virgin*, written by Judd Apatow and Steve Carell, you can see how each story would be changed and diminished if the characters did not differ as they do—even though both movies are romantic comedies.

Hitch and Andy are about the same age, but Hitch is smooth, handsome, and a ladies' man in every way. He's charming, outgoing, and smart, and shrewdly helps others fall in love. His background—having his heart broken in college—led to his determination to help others avoid all the romantic and sexual mistakes he has learned to overcome. It even led to his job and well-to-do financial status. It also led to the superficiality of his own relationships with women—he refuses to allow himself to fall in love, out of fear of suffering the pain he felt long before. So his living situation is comfortable and affluent but rather isolated—he seems to have only one friend in the film; everyone else is either a client or a sexual conquest.

Andy, on the other hand, is anything but smooth. He's so awkward around women that he has completely resigned himself to remaining a virgin forever. He's an average-looking guy who dresses and acts like a child, playing with model action figures and even hiding from women at work, preferring to repair electronic equipment in the safety of the back room rather than risk interacting with people out on the sales floor. This has determined his financial situation (his apartment is far less expensive and modern than Hitch's). His background has been filled with painful experiences with women, but instead of combating and overcoming them, as Hitch claims to have done, he long ago surrendered to them and gave up on love altogether. On the other hand, he seems to be more connected to the people around him (his coworkers and his neighbors) who show real affection for him—taking him under their wing and looking out for him, as one would a child or a younger sibling.

The physical makeup, personalities, roles, and backgrounds of these two heroes are so critical that if they were to be switched, neither story would even make sense.

DEVELOPING THE HERO

The *hero* of your story is that character whose motivation drives the plot, who is the central focus of the story, who is on screen most of the time, and with whom the audience most closely identifies. Since creating emotion in the audience is your goal, your hero must be the vehicle for leading your audience through that emotional experience. Your entire story must revolve around this character.

In creating the hero who best suits your story concept, you must first determine those qualities the character should possess to suit the logic and reality of the basic plot. Then you must establish the necessary empathy with the hero for the reader, and finally you must add those individual facets to the character to make him or her original and compelling.

Creating a Rough Outline of Your Hero

You will certainly have some general idea of who your hero will be, based on your story concept alone. There are certain qualities that are going to be dictated by the plot itself. If your basic concept concerns a woman gymnast, then the logic of the concept has already necessitated a certain sex, age range, and general physical makeup. If your concept is an adaptation of a true story, you will begin with an even more fully defined hero.

Let's assume, though, that you have no idea who your hero will be, and you have to create a character from scratch. What do you do?

First ask yourself, What limits are placed on this character by the plot situation itself? Must the character possess a certain age, sex, background, appearance, level of intelligence, or personality?

Then go to all of the sources outlined in chapter 2 (headlines, true stories, personal experience), this time as a stimulus for developing character traits in your hero. As with story concepts, the key is to brainstorm rather than edit; open yourself to lots of possibilities, no matter how seemingly ludicrous, before narrowing the focus of your potential hero.

Finally, *research* the area of your story concept. Whether you're doing a story about outer space, the Old West, or a barbershop, read the appropriate literature and talk to people who have been involved, either directly or through research and study, in your story arena. Observing, interviewing, and researching can stimulate your own thinking and help you create and develop characters who suit your story concept and jump off the page for the reader.

Creating Empathy

Empathy means that audiences and readers identify with a character and experience emotion *through* her: if the character is in danger, the audience feels frightened; if the character suffers loss, the audience feels sad.

The three most powerful methods for establishing this identification are listed below in order of priority. (Though your primary concern is with their application to the hero, these principles can apply to any other character in your screenplay as well.)

1. **Create sympathy for the character.** This is by far the most effective and widely used method of creating reader empathy with the hero. If you can get the reader to feel sorry for your hero by making her the victim of some undeserved misfortune, you will immediately establish a high degree of identification with that character. Our first shot of Sam in *Sleepless in Seattle* shows him standing by his son at his wife's funeral; Jenna in *13 Going on 30* is exploited and rejected by the cute, popular girls in school; and in

Little Miss Sunshine, Richard Hoover is introduced giving his rather lame motivational speech to a nearly empty auditorium of unresponsive listeners.

Undeserved misfortune can originate either with a specific event (such as Dewey Finn getting kicked out of his band in *School of Rock*), or with a hero's basic situation at the opening of the film (as in *Erin Brockovich*, who is immediately revealed to be a poor, unemployed, single parent with no visible career skills). The sooner you can employ this principle, whether as background for your hero or as an early event in the plot of your screenplay, the more effective and stronger the empathy with your hero will be.

2. **Put the character in jeopardy.** Closely aligned to creating sympathy for the character is getting the reader to *worry* about your character by putting her in a threatening situation. The Indiana Jones movies are prime examples, as each opens with a scene in which the hero's life is in great danger.

   The jeopardy you create doesn't have to be life-threatening. Danger of exposure, embarrassment, or loss of a job can be similarly effective, depending on the tone of your film. *Night at the Museum*, *Juno*, *Michael Clayton*, and *Rain Man* open with physical, financial, or emotional threats to their heroes, thereby increasing our empathy.

3. **Make the character likable.** Getting the reader to like your hero will further strengthen empathy. There are basically three ways to get a reader to like your hero, which can be used singly or in combination:

   ► Make the character a kind, good-hearted, and generous person, as with the heroes of *While You Were Sleeping*, *Enchanted*, and just about any Tom Hanks movie. (Even when Tom Hanks played a mobster and hired killer in *The Road to Perdition*, his character was first introduced as a loving husband and father, to establish empathy before the dark side of his nature was revealed.)

▶ Show your hero as well-liked by other characters. If you introduce your hero surrounded by family or friends who care about her, readers will be drawn to that character as well, just like those popular kids in high school that everyone wanted to be friends with, or at least noticed by. The openings of *Good Will Hunting*, *Legally Blonde*, and *Ocean's Eleven* all include scenes of their heroes hanging with, and supported by, their best friends.

▶ Make the character funny. Even if your hero is not at all big-hearted or even moral, we will still like him if he makes us laugh. Melvin Udall in *As Good as It Gets* is a racist, homophobic, and misogynistic misanthrope who is introduced throwing a dog down a garbage chute. (In all fairness, the dog did pee in his lobby—undeserved misfortune.) And although the heroes of *Bad Santa* and *Wedding Crashers* lie and take advantage of women just to get what they want, these characters are hilarious enough that the audience will forgive their nastiness and dishonesty.

You must employ at least one of these three methods of establishing empathy for your hero. Otherwise your reader won't care enough about your hero to remain emotionally involved in the story. And if you can use two or all three of the above principles, identification with your hero will be even stronger.

In addition to these three essential devices for creating empathy, several other qualities or situations will strengthen our identification with your hero even further:

1. **Make the character highly skilled.** We are naturally drawn to people who are talented, who are masters at what they do. When we

immediately see Frankie skillfully fix his fighter's cut in *Million Dollar Baby*, Charlie Croker lead a brilliant art heist at the opening of *The Italian Job*, or Hitch help three dorky guys win the women of their dreams, we want to become these characters—which is the essence of identification.

2. **Show the character in touch with his own power.** Closely related to the quality of skill is that of *power*. Powerful heroes hold a fascination for an audience and elicit empathy on an almost fantasy level.

Power can take four forms in a character:

► *Power over other people.* This is illustrated by characters like Charles Foster Kane in *Citizen Kane*, Don Corleone in *The Godfather*, or Miranda Priestly in *The Devil Wears Prada*. Such characters connect with an audience not because they are likable but because their wealth, clout, and control exert a deep fascination, and there is a satisfaction in aligning oneself emotionally with the power they possess while distancing oneself from the evil or amoral actions they employ in gaining or exercising their power.

Notice, though, that in only one of these examples is the powerful character the hero of that film (and that example is seventy years old). Watching the great and mighty topple from their positions of power is more the stuff of Shakespearian tragedy than of Hollywood blockbusters. The mass audience is far more likely to empathize and root for everyday heroes who come up against powerful bosses, dictators, and crime lords—and win.

► *Power to do what needs to be done, without hesitation.* The popularity of heroes like James Bond; John McClane in the *Die Hard* films; and the Clint Eastwood characters in the *Dirty Harry* movies, most of his westerns, and, more recently, *Gran Torino*, grows out of the fact that these characters experience little or no ambiguity about their actions. They see what needs to be done, and they do it, regardless of the danger, the odds, or the political and moral implications. They possess a power over their own and others' destinies that the rest of us sorely lack.

When Bryan Mills learns of his daughter's kidnapping in *Taken*, his response is simply, "She has to be rescued, and I'm on my way." He doesn't care about politics, danger, or body count; he simply exercises his power. To an audience that feels increasingly helpless in the face of war, crime, corruption, climate change, the economy, bosses, political leaders, natural disasters, and the Internal Revenue Service, this hero's power becomes irresistibly seductive.

► *Power to express one's feelings regardless of others' opinions.* This principle is often tied to the character's humor, and is illustrated by many of Jack Nicholson's roles besides Melvin Udall. When Bobby orders the wheat toast in *Five Easy Pieces*, when McMurphy stands up to Nurse Ratched in *One Flew Over the Cuckoo's Nest*, or when the devil expresses his desire for the women in *The Witches of Eastwick*, these characters are exhibiting the power of their undiluted emotions. Such power is irresistibly seductive to all of us who worry about even raising our voices.

► *Superpowers.* This fantasy level of empathy and identification can also apply to superheroes—archetypal characters who always do what is necessary to save the world.

But in almost all superhero movies, the hero begins as an everyday person who is then transformed into a powerful character. We immediately empathize with Peter

Parker not because he is the Spider-Man, but because we feel sorry for this shy but good-hearted orphan who gets teased and pushed around, who lives with his grandparents (who love him deeply), who longs for the girl next door (who barely notices him), and who gets bitten by a spider. Eventually he'll do whatever it takes to save the world, but when introduced, this character is a great example of the first three items on this list.

3. **Place the character in a familiar setting.** The time in which a character lives, the place where she works, and her home and family situation all contribute to greater empathy. For example, Julie in *Julie and Julia* is a young wife living and working in Manhattan. Obviously, this doesn't mean that everyone who identifies with the character has been in that situation, but rather it means that the audience is likely to have known or heard a lot about people who are in such a setting—and has repeatedly seen similar situations on the screen. This would not be true for characters in a movie about a caveman or a Russian count.

   In a similar way, high school and college students, cops, doctors, secretaries, parents, and working stiffs are all easier to identify with than, for example, the characters in *Blood Diamond* or *Minority Report*. Those two films depended on the other devices for establishing empathy.

4. **Give the character familiar flaws and foibles.** This is closely related to both undeserved misfortune and creating a character who is funny. If your hero walks into walls like we all do from time to time, then identification increases.

   This is particularly true in the arena of social and sexual awkwardness. When Woody Allen's early comedies were achieving their success, I used to hear guys that looked like *Playgirl* centerfolds say how much they identified with his characters. I couldn't imagine how some six-foot hunk could relate to the schlemiels

Woody Allen portrayed, but I later realized it's because we've all felt awkward around the opposite sex or in high-pressure social situations, so we identify with any hero who suffers some of the same nervousness and embarrassment we have.

5. **Make your hero the eyes of the audience.** Identification is sometimes strengthened when the audience *only* learns information as the hero learns it. In a mystery, for example, the reader might only be given the clues as the detective gets them. *Body Heat* is an excellent example of the hero serving as the eyes of the audience, for we become aware of what's really going on only as Ned Racine does.

On occasion, a screenplay will include a character who is not the hero but who serves as the eyes of the audience. In *The Road to Perdition*, the story is told from the point of view of the narrator, an adolescent who is accompanying his father, the hero of the movie. And in *Sophie's Choice*, the hero is clearly Sophie, but the young man Stingo serves as the initial point of identification for the audience and the source of the gradually revealed truth about Sophie. The advantage of this device is to create immediate identification with the more familiar character and then *transfer* that identification to the hero through the course of the film.

You must combine these methods to create empathy with your hero *immediately*—as soon as possible after your hero is introduced. Only then can you begin to reveal flaws in the character. In *Tootsie*, Michael Dorsey, the hero of the movie, is actually a jerk, an actor who has little concern for the feelings of others, whose only interests are acting, picking up women, and saving face when caught in a lie. Yet the audience is clearly made to sympathize and identify with him and overlook or accept his dishonesty and his self-centeredness.

The very first scenes of Michael show him rejected for a series of auditions, not because he is a poor actor but because he is too short, too conscientious, or they don't pay attention to him (undeserved misfortune). We see immediately that he is a respected acting teacher (highly skilled), and is willing to help both Jeff and Sandy (likable). He is also funny, lives and works in a familiar situation, and is in jeopardy of permanent unemployment.

The combined use of all these devices within the plot is a sterling example of how a character can possess shortcomings, weaknesses, and negative characteristics but can still be the focus of reader and audience sympathy and identification.

Making Your Characters Original

After ensuring that your reader will identify with a character (particularly your hero), you must give the character qualities that will add to her originality. A reader enjoys encountering characters he feels he has never seen before, who jump off the page and are not carbon copies of countless other characters from movies and television.

Of course, just as with your story concept, your hero will draw on qualities that we have seen before in real life or on the screen; you don't want to create a hero who isn't grounded in some way in the reader's previous experience.

Indiana Jones is a literary and film descendant of Sam Spade, Robin Hood, and Jason (the Argonaut Jason, not the *Friday the 13th* Jason). But these qualities are combined and modified in order to make the character something more than all of those others; Indy's hat, whip, job, knowledge, and relationships with women and children give him layers of originality that make him a unique, three-dimensional character.

Think of a clay sculpture. First the armature and the clay will identify the figure as human; then the details will be added that will identify the sculpture as a *particular* person. In the same way, when you create a character, you will draw on familiar qualities and identification devices to establish a common bond with the audience; then you will add the background material, personality traits, habits, speech patterns, attitudes, occupations, and appearance that will make that character original, unique, and entertaining.

There are several methods that will help you lay on these unique qualities for your character:

1. **Research.** The best device for fine-tuning your characters is extensive research of your subject area. If you are writing a movie about firefighters, then you should talk to lots of real-life firefighters, not only to get plot ideas but to observe individual personality traits as well. I have seen average heroes become unique and three-dimensional when the writers gave their characters the qualities observed in their real-life counterparts.

2. **Go against cliché.** Look at all of the traits you have assigned to your character and change each to its opposite. If your private eye is a thirty-five-year-old, tough, good-looking, working-class male, make the character a nine-year-old rich girl who is blind.

   Again, the purpose of this device is to facilitate brainstorming; you're not looking for good ideas, only ideas—quantity, not quality. You are altering your character to the point of absurdity in order to force yourself to be creative.

   You will probably decide that a rich nine-year-old blind girl is totally inappropriate for your screenplay. But what qualities would such a character possess that could be incorporated into your hero, to make the character more original and interesting?

   Perhaps the private eye could be a woman or come from a wealthy family or collect dolls or build doll houses or be blind or wear thick glasses or have some other disability or have a nine-year-old daughter or work part-time in a day-care center or have a wife or husband who is blind or be hired to protect the blind nine-year-old witness to a murder. Once your brainstorming kicks into gear, the possibilities for originality are much more apparent.

   A wonderful example of violating cliché was a TV cop who lacked almost all of the typical traits of that genre. He was married, polite, talkative, scared of guns, not particularly attractive, never got into fights, and genuinely liked other people. Of course, I'm describing Lieutenant Columbo. One of the main reasons for the long success of *Columbo* is the way Richard Levinson and William Link broke the mold in creating their hero.

TV crime series have always placed a premium on finding at least one unique trait that separates their main characters from all the other cops on television: a mystery writer in *Castle*, a former fake psychic in *The Mentalist*, a real psychic in *Medium*, an obsessive compulsive in *Monk*.

3. **Play off other characters.** You can often bring out unique and unexplored facets of a character by pairing him with another character, who is far different. If the next James Bond movie showed Bond teaming up with Harry Potter, we'd probably see facets to both characters that hadn't emerged before.

   Often, the story concept itself involves opposites being thrown together, which results in greater depth and originality for the entire film. *The Bridges of Madison County*, *The Rock*, and *Analyze This* all employ this device in their basic concepts.

4. **Cast the character.** Imagine a particular actor playing the role of the character you're developing. If your story is about a character in jeopardy after witnessing a murder, your hero will take on far more individualized traits if you imagine Gerard Butler, Michael Cera, or Penélope Cruz in the role. This device can also be used to create effective dialogue.

   Never target your screenplay for only one possible actor, however. Putting all of your eggs in one casting basket will severely limit the possibilities of selling the script. Rather, you should imagine specific stars portraying a character merely to help make the character more unique, and then flesh out the character so that a wide range of possible stars could play the role.

Motivation

Whatever your story concept, each of your characters must *want* something. These goals, desires, and objectives are what drive your story. This is the specific way, as is often stated, that character determines plot.

Motivation is my term for whatever a character hopes to accomplish by the end of the movie or TV episode. More important, it is your *hero's* motivation that determines your basic, one-line story concept. This is the spine on which the entire plot, each of the other characters, and each individual scene will be built.

In other words, what your hero desires determines what the story is about. *Ghostbusters* is a story about a former university professor who *wants to earn money by getting rid of ghosts*. *The Terminator* is about a waitress who *wants to escape a cyborg from the future who is trying to kill her*. And one episode of *In Treatment* was about Paul *trying to convince one of his patients to begin chemotherapy*. The story concept for *any* film or TV episode can similarly be expressed in terms of what the hero visibly hopes to achieve within the context of the movie.

The visible motivation for your hero is the most important element of your entire screenplay. Every single facet of your script, from original concept to final draft, hangs on how clearly and effectively you create and develop the motivation for your hero. The problem with unsalable screenplays can almost always be traced back to poorly chosen, confusing, or nonexistent motivations for the heroes.

Motivation is not limited to the hero of your screenplay; as we will discuss, every character in your movie wants something. But I will first focus on the hero because that character's motivation forms the spine of your story and drives the plot. Then I will examine how the other characters all fall in line in relation to the hero.

Notice that the definition of motivation includes the phrase *by the end of the movie*. Characters can want all sorts of things in your screenplay, but their specific motivation is whatever they hope to gain by the time the story ends. Thus, in *An Officer and a Gentleman*, Zack keeps saying how he wants to someday fly jets. But that is not his motivation, because the movie is not about him attempting to do that. Rather, his motivations for that film are to become an officer, to have an affair with Paula, and to gain a sense of belonging. Those are the objectives that determine the plot and thrust of the film.

As discussed earlier, motivation exists on outer and inner levels:

Outer motivation is the answer to the question *"What does this character want to accomplish* by the end of the film." And, as I've purposely stated repeatedly, to the point of tedium, it is the hero's outer motivation that drives the plot of the story and determines the basic story concept.

Solving a murder, winning the love of a beautiful woman, and holding a rich man's wife for ransom are all visible, plot-oriented outer motivations.

Inner motivation is the answer to the question *"Why does the character want to do that?"* And the answer is always related to gaining greater feelings of self-worth. Inner motivation is the path the character thinks will allow him to feel better about himself. Since this level of motivation comes from *within the character*, it is invisible, and is revealed primarily through dialogue. It is also more closely tied to theme and character growth than to plot.

Comparing the two levels of motivation reveals the following qualities for each:

OUTER MOTIVATION	INNER MOTIVATION
Visible	Invisible
Desire for outward accomplishment	Desire for self-worth
Revealed through action	Revealed through dialogue
Answers question, What does this character want to do?	Answers question, Why does she want to do that?
Related to plot	Related to character growth and theme

There is nothing particularly mysterious about this notion; real life works the same way. We all want to accomplish certain things, and those desires determine our actions: going to work, going to school, writing, playing golf, collecting string, or spending time with a loved one. These are all visible outer motivations. But the *reasons* we go after these things can differ for each of us.

For example, your outer motivation right now is obvious: to read this book. This is the visible desire that determines your actions at this moment.

But your inner motivation, the *reason* you are reading this book, is impossible for me to determine without asking you. It could be to educate yourself; to become a better writer; to be able to make a lot of money; to cure insomnia. Whatever your inner motivation, though, it must be related to greater feelings of self-worth. Somehow, you believe that reading this book will enable you to feel better about yourself.

The process works the same way for the characters of your screenplay. For example, in Pete Chiarelli's screenplay for *The Proposal*, Andrew wants to marry his boss Margaret and convince the INS agent that they are legitimately in love. That is Andrew's outer motivation. But the *reason* he wants to marry her (and receive the promotion she has promised him) is to achieve a new level of success at the publishing company, and be out from under her control. Success and independence are his inner motivations, the ways his visible actions will make him feel better about himself, and give him greater feelings of self-worth.

In the course of the movie, Andrew genuinely begins to fall for Margaret, so eventually winning her love becomes an equal outer motivation. And in any love story or romantic comedy, love is an inner motivation, because we always believe we'll feel better about ourselves when we win the love of the person we're in love with.

Characters are often unwise in choosing their inner motivations—they frequently take the wrong path to achieving self-worth. In *Doubt*, Sister Aloysius believes that if she can rid the parish of Father Flynn, she'll feel righteous, superior, and vindicated. By the end of the film, she feels none of these things, and now has her own doubts. But as long as she *thinks* that her rigid and narrow-minded judgment is the path to self-worth, it qualifies as her inner motivation.

Similarly, many films are about heroes who believe that their inner motivations of revenge, greed, or power are paths to self-worth, and who learn otherwise in the course of the movie.

Outer motivation for your hero is an absolute necessity. It determines the story concept for your film; it is the cornerstone of your entire screenplay. Without a clear, visible outer motivation for your hero, you will have no screenplay and no movie.

Exploration of your hero's inner motivation is optional. All of your characters, including your hero, will have reasons for doing whatever they do, but you may choose not to examine their particular desires for self-worth.

Many successful films, including the James Bond and the Indiana Jones movies, don't explore their heroes' inner motivations. We get a sense that these heroes like the excitement and are driven to do a good job, but the movies do not really examine this level of motivation in any significant way.

Conflict

Motivation alone is not sufficient to make your screenplay work. If Luke Skywalker says, "I want to overthrow the Empire," and Darth Vader immediately replies, "Okay. We give up," you've got no movie. There must be something preventing the hero from getting what he wants.

Conflict is whatever stands in the way of a character achieving her motivation. It is the sum of all the obstacles and hurdles that the character must try to overcome in order to reach her objective.

Always remember that your primary goal as a writer and storyteller is to elicit emotion. And *emotion grows out of conflict*, not desire. The most emotionally involving scenes in any script or movie are those involving the overwhelming obstacles the character must face. These might be direct confrontations with a villain or a force of nature, anticipation of major obstacles to come, a character wrestling with their inner conflicts, or even those moments when a hero is rewarded for having found the skill or courage to overcome some obstacle. But desire is really there just to move the story forward; it's the size, depth, and originality of the conflict that keep readers turning the page.

Conflict, like motivation, exists on both an outer and inner level. *Outer conflict* is whatever stands in the way of a character achieving his outer motivation.

Outer conflict will be provided either by other characters (*Crash, Ratatouille, Up in the Air*) or by characters combined with forces of nature (*Groundhog Day, Jaws, Twister*).

Inner conflict is whatever stands in the way of a character achieving real self-worth as she pursues her inner motivation (if you have chosen to explore that aspect of your character). Until the character can overcome her inner conflict, she will never be able to achieve the feelings of self-worth that are her objective.

Once again, consider the truly great script by Murray Schisgal and Larry Gelbart (and about a dozen uncredited writers) for *Tootsie*. It is a story about an out-of-work actor who wants to successfully work as an actress on a soap opera and win the love of one of his costars. "Working as an actress" and "winning the love of his costar" are Michael Dorsey's outer motivations, because they are visible, they drive the plot, and they are revealed through the action of the film. The hero's outer conflicts, which stand in the way of his achieving his outer motivation, are that he is really a man (conflict with nature), and if the other characters, including his costar, find this out, he'll lose his job and the possibility of winning her love (conflict with other characters).

The hero's inner motivation, the *reason* he wants to pose as an actress, is to achieve success as an actor; that is Michael's means of feeling better about himself and gaining greater feelings of self-worth. Posing as Dorothy Michaels will earn him the money to do a play, and more important, it will show what a great actor he is. Michael's inner conflict is that he doesn't know when to stop acting. When Jeff, his roommate, asks him why, if he can be a great actor and a great teacher, he can't just be himself, his response is, "What's my motivation?" Obviously, he sees no value in being himself, only in playing roles. This continually leads him to be dishonest with people he cares about.

He will never gain self-worth through the means he has chosen (acting), until he can become aware of and overcome his inner conflict. It is only when Michael (through Dorothy) learns the value of honesty that he is able to win Julie's love and friendship and thereby experience real feelings of self-worth.

DEVELOPING THE OTHER CHARACTERS OF YOUR SCREENPLAY

At this point in the development of your story, you have at least outlined the physical makeup, personality, and background for your hero; found the means to create audience identification with the hero; and added qualities and character traits to make your hero unique. You have also determined the hero's outer motivation and outer conflict and perhaps have begun to explore inner motivation and conflict.

But there is no such thing as a one-character movie, so now you must develop your other primary characters and your secondary characters. And their relationships to your hero's outer motivation will define all of them.

The Four Categories of Primary Character

In creating the other primary characters of your screenplay, you will be in one of two situations:

You may already have a cast of characters in mind to populate your story because you've already thought it through, you're adapting a story from another source, or the logic of the plot dictates certain character types. In such instances, your characters will involve the reader most effectively if you know the basic function each fulfills in relation to your hero.

Or you may have your hero worked out but have no idea who the other characters in the story will be. Knowing the basic categories of primary characters is then helpful, because you know you must originate people for your story who will fulfill specific functions.

The four basic categories for primary characters in your screenplay are as follows:

1. **Hero.** This is the main character, whose outer motivation drives the plot forward, who is the primary object of identification for the reader and audience, and who is on screen most of the time. As with all the primary characters, the hero must possess some outer motivation and conflict, while an inner motivation and conflict may or may not be revealed and explored.

2. **Nemesis.** This is the character who most stands in the way of the hero achieving his or her outer motivation. A nemesis can obviously be a villain but might also be an opponent, a rival, or even a good guy, as long as the character is somehow standing in the way. While the serial killers in *Silence of the Lambs*, the hijacker in *Air Force One*, and the emperor in *Gladiator* are obviously nemeses, so are Apollo Creed in *Rocky*, Walter in *Sleepless in Seattle*, and even Mozart in *Amadeus*, although those latter characters are not villains.

   The stronger and more formidable your nemesis, the more effective the story. Apollo Creed isn't just another palooka from down the block. The fact that he is the heavyweight champion of the world gives *Rocky* its emotional impact, because the challenges and hurdles he creates for the hero are so formidable. In the same way, Darth Vader's effectiveness as the nemesis of *Star Wars* arises from his ability to use the Force as powerfully as Obi-Wan. And Lord Voldemort is an emotionally involving nemesis in the Harry Potter films because he is seemingly indestructible.

   The nemesis must be a visible and specific character, not a collective noun ("the Mafia"), force of nature ("cancer"), or quality of life ("the evil in the world").

The reason conspiracy stories are very difficult to write effectively is that the audience can't get its mind around a nemesis like "the CIA" or "the KGB" or "the government." One reason the conspiracy story *Shutter Island* is emotionally involving is that the nemesis is a specific individual, Dr. Cawley. If your hero is coming up against "terrorists," then create a *specific* terrorist to represent the overall threat.

Making your nemesis visible does not necessarily mean that the reader knows the identity of the person. In a murder mystery, for example, the audience may not know which character the hero is up against, but they know by the results of the nemesis's actions that there *is* a specific individual providing the obstacles to the hero's ability to solve the crime or stay alive.

You must also *show* the final confrontation between your hero and nemesis. Think about a Western in which the entire film has been leading up to a gunfight between the sheriff and the bad guy. Then all at once the sheriff runs into the saloon and declares, "You should have seen it! I shot him!" Nobody would sit still for that.

In most screenplays, this final confrontation is the climax of the entire movie, because it is at this point that the hero either succeeds or fails to achieve his outer motivation. Even when this final confrontation occurs prior to the climax, as in *Body Heat* (where the murder of the nemesis occurs halfway through the movie) or *Jaws* (where the mayor is last seen before the three good guys head out to sea to find the shark), the confrontation remains a necessary element to the story.

3. **Reflection.** This is the character who supports the hero's outer motivation or at least is in the same basic situation at the beginning of the screenplay. The reflection can be a friend, mentor, sidekick, trainer, coworker, spouse, lover, or any other character who adds support to the hero's objective.

Examples of characters who serve as reflections would be the Morgan Freeman characters Ned Logan in *Unforgiven* (who wants to help hero William Munny get the reward), Scrap in *Million Dollar Baby* (Frankie's best friend, who wants to help him lead Maggie to the championship), and Lucius Fox in the Batman movies (who wants to help Bruce Wayne do whatever Bruce Wayne wants to do). What can I say? Morgan Freeman makes a great reflection.

There are three main purposes for creating a reflection character in your screenplay. First, it adds credibility to your plot if your hero has help in overcoming the outer conflict (it would be impossible for Erin Brockovich to win the case against PG&E if she didn't have the help, expertise, and legitimacy provided by her boss Ed Masry). Second, it gives the hero someone to talk to, making it easier to reveal background, inner motivation, inner conflict, and theme, or to create anticipation ("Now here's my plan, Tonto . . ."). The third reason relates to the hero's character arc, but we'll talk about that shortly.

4. **Romance.** This is the sexual or romantic object of at least part of the hero's outer motivation. When your hero's outer motivation includes as its objective winning the love of, or getting into bed with, another character, then that other character is the romance. Jessica Biel, Maggie Gyllenhaal, and Jake Gyllenhaal play romance characters in *The Illusionist*, *Crazy Heart*, and *Brokeback Mountain*, respectively.

Further, a romance must always alternately support, then oppose, the hero's outer motivation. At first they might share the outer motivation of wanting to be together; then some conflict arises, and the romance doesn't want to be with the hero; finally, they get back together and are again sharing the same outer motivation.

A character is not classified as a romance just because there is sexual or romantic involvement between that character and the hero. In *Iron Man*, there is a clear sexual attraction between Tony Stark and Pepper Potts, but she is a reflection, not a romance, because the movie is not about the hero trying to win her love. The same holds true for the spouses, sidekicks, friends, and loved ones in *Julie and Julia*, *Marley and Me*, and *The Station Agent*. A character serves as a romance only if the hero's outer motivation is to win that character's love.

In creating characters to fill these four primary categories, there are certain ground rules and qualifications you must understand:

1. **Characters must be people.** The characters we're discussing must be human or humanoid; a nemesis can't be an animal (unless it's an anthropomorphized creature like Remy in *Ratatouille*), a situation (like war, famine, or a bad economy), or a force of nature (like a disease, a man-eating shark, or sunspots).

2. **Inner motivation and conflict may or may not be explored for any of the primary characters.** Usually, if your screenplay explores those levels of character development at all, it will be for your hero, adding inner motivation and conflict for the other primary characters as needed.

3. **It is not necessary to have a character in each category.** The hero is the only *essential* category. There is no nemesis in *Julie and Julia*, no reflection in *Amadeus*, no romance in *Up*. You will always want to create at least one of the categories of primary character in addition to your hero; creating additional primary characters is optional and depends on the needs of your story.

4. **A character cannot occupy more than one category.** If you say that your hero is "her own worst enemy," you are really indicating an inner conflict; she can't also be the nemesis. And a reflection can't also be a romance—one category per character only.

You may be thinking, "What if the reflection becomes the romance, then turns out to be the nemesis?" But the purpose of all the terms, principles, rules, and methods in this book is to *simplify* the process of writing your screenplay. And to think of a romance also being a reflection, or a hero being his own nemesis, does just the opposite.

Certainly the hero will be in conflict with the reflection at times (particularly over the hero's inner conflict—see chapter 4). And the hero and romance will move in and out of conflict throughout a love story (see above). Either the reflection or romance might even be revealed to be the killer at the end of a mystery or thriller.

But when creating your characters, think of their *primary* function in relation to the hero's outer motivation. Make sure they fulfill that purpose in a clear, emotionally involving way. Then you can play around with added dimensions to their relationships for the sake of depth and originality. To place a character in two separate categories simply makes it harder for you as the writer to employ all the principles that follow, principles that I guarantee will increase the reader's emotional involvement in your screenplay.

The exception to this rule is when you have more than one hero in your screenplay (see below). In these cases, each hero will usually serve as one of the other three roles for the second hero. So in *Catch Me if You Can*, both Frank Abagnale and Carl Hanratty are heroes of the movie, and each serves as the nemesis for the other. And in two-hero love stories like *Pretty Woman*, *Shakespeare in Love*, and *The Proposal*, each is the other's romance character.

5. **A character cannot change categories.** Characters are defined by the way they function in the *beginning* of the film. When primary characters are introduced, their relationship to the hero *at that time* determines whether they are nemesis, reflection, or romance characters.

It may turn out that the reflection ultimately opposes the hero, or that a nemesis isn't such a bad guy after all, but that doesn't alter the roles they play and the functions they serve in the film.

Just as with the issue of a character inhabiting two categories, I get asked again and again if the nemesis can't become a reflection by turning into a good guy at the end of the movie. The answer is no, because thinking along those lines serves no purpose—the function of these categories is to simplify the writing process and to bring your primary characters into focus so they will function more effectively. If you start worrying about switching categories, you're only going to muddy up the clarity and thrust of your story. Whatever the characters do in act three, their categories remain the same, because this tool has already done its job. And because the categories are also important in revealing character growth and theme (as we will discuss in chapter 4), it is essential that each character fall into only one category.

When an audience sees a movie, they subconsciously ask themselves, "Who am I rooting for and what is she after?" (hero and motivation), "Who is she up against?" (nemesis), "Who is going to help her?" (reflection), and "Who will she fall in love with?" (romance). The purpose of these four categories is to guide you in creating and introducing characters that will meet those expectations.

6. **It is possible to have more than one character in any of the categories.** Dual heroes are fairly common in buddy movies (*Lethal Weapon, The Bucket List*) and romantic comedies (*Just Like Heaven, Knocked Up*). In each of these examples, we empathize with both characters, both are in a majority of scenes, and both possess outer motivations that drive the plot.

Similarly, there are two nemesis characters in *Silence of the Lambs*, three reflections in *Monsters vs. Aliens*, and two romance characters in *While You Were Sleeping, Shopgirl*, and *It's Complicated*.

The Big Chill, American Graffiti, Crash, Traffic, and *Valentine's Day* are examples of *multiple* hero stories. And, of course, dual or multiple heroes abound in episodic television: every episode of *Modern Family, Grey's Anatomy,* and *Mad Men* contains two or more equal heroes.

My strongest advice to those considering writing a multiple-hero feature film is simply *don't.* Such a screenplay is extremely hard to pull off, because multiple heroes tend to diffuse the focus of your story and make it confusing. It is also tough to sell such a screenplay, because it is often difficult for a reader to keep all of the characters straight in written form. For newer writers in particular, the best approach is to stick to a single basic hero—or perhaps two heroes if your script is a buddy movie, a love story, or a romantic comedy.

Secondary Characters

Secondary characters are all the other people in your screenplay, the characters you create to add logic, humor, complexity, depth, and reality to your screenplay after delineating your primary characters. Most should add either greater conflict for the hero or greater support for the hero in pursuing her outer motivation.

Let your secondary characters serve as many of the above functions as possible in order to keep each one as rich, unique, and emotionally involving as you can. But employ them only as needed in terms of your hero's outer motivations. You don't want to overload your screenplay with an abundance of walk-on characters who diffuse and complicate the plot.

I've never seen a script that had terrific primary characters and then got rejected because the secondary characters were too weak. Create primary characters that function to maximum effectiveness and then create additional secondary characters as needed, and the overall character development of your screenplay will be fine.

CHARTING CHARACTER, MOTIVATION, AND CONFLICT

Now I will illustrate these principles of character, motivation, and conflict by filling in the chart below with regard to each of the primary characters in *Shrek*, written by Ted Elliott & Terry Rossio, Joe Stillman, and Roger S. H. Schulman:

	OUTER MOTIVATION	OUTER CONFLICT	INNER MOTIVATION	INNER CONFLICT
Hero				
Nemesis				
Reflection				
Romance				

Shrek is a story about an ogre who wants to rescue Princess Fiona and win her love. That is the story concept.

The hero is Shrek. He is the main character, he's on screen more than any other character, he is the one with whom the audience most empathizes, and it is his outer motivation that drives the plot forward.

Shrek's outer motivation is to rescue the princess (first from the castle, then from Lord Farquaad) and win her love. Those desires are visible; they have clearly defined finish lines that we can envision as soon as we hear them; the desires are revealed through the action; they determine the plot; and they answer the question, "What does this character want?"

Shrek's outer conflict is that he must overcome a fiery moat and a fire-breathing dragon to rescue Fiona; Fiona has been cursed to be a princess by day and an ogre by night; and he will have to overcome the powerful Lord Farquaad and his army. These situations meet the definition of outer conflict by providing the obstacles Shrek must overcome to achieve his two outer motivations.

To determine which characters meet the definitions of nemesis, reflection, and romance, always look at the hero's outer motivation.

The nemesis is the character that most stands in the way of the hero achieving his outer motivation. So ask yourself, "Who provides the greatest obstacle to Shrek winning Fiona's love?"

The curse is certainly an obstacle, but that's a force of nature, not a character. So the answer would, of course, be Lord Farquaad. Lord Farquaad's outer motivation is to marry Princess Fiona. In other words, he wants what Shrek wants, which puts him at cross-purposes with the hero. As is always the case, the nemesis's outer motivation provides the outer conflict for the hero, and vice versa.

Lord Farquaad's outer conflict is that Fiona is falling in love with Shrek, and Shrek will ultimately try to get her back.

The reflection is Donkey, the character who supports the hero's outer motivation—Donkey leads Shrek to Duloc to meet Lord Farquaad; he helps Shrek rescue the princess; he encourages both Shrek and Fiona to pursue each other; and he persuades Shrek to go after Fiona before she marries Lord Farquaad.

Donkey's outer motivation, then, is to help Shrek rescue Fiona and win her love. His outer conflict is the same as Shrek's: the fiery moat, the dragon, the curse, and Lord Farquaad.

Finally, the romance character is the one who is the object of the hero's outer motivation, sexually or romantically: Princess Fiona. She further meets the requirements of a romance character by alternately supporting and being at cross-purposes with Shrek's outer motivation. Fiona wants to get away from the castle, and ultimately wants to win Shrek's love (supportive). But when Shrek fails to fit her image of "Prince Charming," when she doesn't want to get close to him because of the curse, and when she agrees to marry Lord Farquaad, she and Shrek are at cross-purposes.

Fiona's outer motivation is ultimately to win Shrek's love. Her outer conflict includes the curse, Shrek's misunderstanding of her resistance, and Lord Farquaad.

If this sounds a bit simplistic, it should. These categories should be easy to define, and the characters' visible desires obvious. Successful screenplays aren't successful because they're complicated and confusing, they're successful because the unique nature of the specific characters, desires, and conflicts are emotionally compelling.

Those, then, are the four primary characters in the story, and the chart would now look like this:

	OUTER MOTIVATION	OUTER CONFLICT	INNER MOTIVATION	INNER CONFLICT
Hero SHREK	Rescue Princess Fiona; win her love	He's an ogre; she's protected by a dragon; she's cursed; Lord Farquaad wants her		
Nemesis LORD FARQUAAD	Marry Princess Fiona	Shrek and Princess Fiona fall in love; Shrek tries to get her back		
Reflection DONKEY	Help Shrek win the princess	Fiona is protected by a dragon; she's cursed; Lord Farquaad wants her		
Romance PRINCESS FIONA	Win Shrek's love	She's cursed; Shrek misunderstands; Farquaad won't allow it		

Keep in mind as you examine the chart that in a love story, the hero and romance characters may not be *consciously* trying to win each other's love right away. In *Shrek*, the two don't even meet until almost the midpoint of the screenplay. But as long as the audience is rooting for the two to end up together, and as long as the two are gradually falling in love as the story moves forward, their outer motivations can be defined as winning each other's love.

The right half of the chart, dealing with inner motivation and conflict, becomes a bit more complicated, since these are often revealed through subtle bits of dialogue. In *Shrek*, determining these levels necessitates digging deeper into the characters' comments and attitudes to find the paths they have each chosen for achieving self-worth.

Shrek agrees to retrieve Princess Fiona for Lord Farquaad in order to get rid of the fairy-tale creatures that have invaded Shrek's swamp. His swamp is more than just a piece of property—it represents solitude for Shrek—protection from anyone getting close enough to interact with him, to make demands on him, or ultimately to reject and hurt him. Besides his reaction to the fairy-tale creatures, we have as evidence all of Shrek's initial encounters with Donkey. Though Donkey wants nothing other than to help Shrek and be his friend (and maybe have some waffles), and though Donkey accepts Shrek for who he truly is, Shrek repeatedly insults him and tells him to go away.

So Shrek's inner motivation is *isolation*. This is what he thinks will lead to greater feelings of self-worth.

But then he meets Fiona and falls in love with her. So from that point forward, Shrek's inner motivation for wanting to win Fiona's love is the same as in all romantic comedies: *love*. As in real life, where we all feel better about ourselves when we win the love or desire of the person we love or desire.

Inner conflict is whatever within the character prevents him from achieving self-worth. For Shrek, it's the fact that deep down, he's chosen the wrong path to self-worth. He'll never truly feel better about himself, never truly be fulfilled, as long as he cuts himself off from others. And he certainly won't win Fiona's love, or experience love of any kind, living behind a barbed-wire fence that says KEEP OUT.

This inner conflict is also revealed in Donkey's dialogue with Shrek. "You've got a problem, Shrek," Donkey tells his friend, encouraging him to get closer to Princess Fiona. (Challenging the hero in this way is a primary function of the reflection character, as you will see in the next chapter.)

"It's not me who has the problem," replies Shrek. "It's everybody else." Whenever they see him coming, they turn and run the other way. Shrek will do anything to avoid experiencing that pain yet again—even if it means losing out on true love.

Lord Farquaad's inner motivation has nothing to do with love. For him it's all about power and lust, as we see repeatedly in his conversations with the magic mirror (the closest thing Farquaad has to a reflection of his own). It's Fiona's status he's after, not her love.

Farquaad's inner conflict is his ruthless, wicked nature. Because of this he will never attain real self-worth—or even the external power he lusts for.

Donkey's inner motivation, the reason he wants to help Shrek, is also self-worth. His path to self-worth is through friendship and connection. And his inner-conflict square on the chart is blank. Donkey has no inner conflict, and nothing blocks his path to self-worth; his genuine love and friendship are a legitimate path to feeling good about himself, and he does.

This is perfectly acceptable, and typical for lots of movies. The reflection character is an enlightened, emotionally mature (at least compared to the hero) character who is there to support the hero on his inner and outer journeys, but who has no inner conflict or character flaw of his own to overcome. It may seem odd to describe Donkey as emotionally mature, because he's such a goofball. But he falls into the same archetype as the fool in *King Lear*, Dory in *Finding Nemo*, or Olive in *Little Miss Sunshine*.

While not the same kinds of naive innocents as in the previous examples, the priest in *Gran Torino*, Scrap in *Million Dollar Baby*, and Juno's father in *Juno* are all examples of emotionally evolved reflection characters. Remember, it is not necessary to take all your primary characters through growth and transformation. You may choose not to explore this level of character at all, or if you do, it can be for the hero alone.

Romance character Fiona's inner motivation is eventually love, but at the outset, her path to self-worth is in fulfilling all of the rules laid out for her in countless fairy tales. She's upset when Shrek won't kiss her to awaken her; she is taken aback (though not at all repulsed, as he expected) when she discovers he is an ogre and not her image of Prince Charming, and she is mortified at the possibility of anyone learning she's an ogre by night—the antithesis of the beautiful fairy-tale princess that she believes she must be.

And like Shrek's, her inner conflict grows out of a misguided path to self-worth. Fiona is so locked into the "rules" set down by fairy tales that she can't be herself. She's not just imprisoned in a castle tower; she's imprisoned by her fear of not living up to her image of a fairy-tale princess. Just as Shrek would give up real love to retain his isolation, Fiona would sacrifice her real destiny in order to marry Lord Farquaad merely because he is royalty, and closer to what she thought her Prince Charming should be. When she finally is given "love's true kiss" and it releases her from the curse, she's as surprised as anyone that she turns back into an ogre. She had to learn that the real path to self-worth and fulfillment isn't through being beautiful or marrying Prince Charming or living in a castle, it's through being true to yourself, and opening and trusting your own heart.

Again, it is not necessary to take your romance character through his or her own arc. In many love stories (*Titanic*, *A Beautiful Mind*, *Stranger than Fiction*), the romance is an evolved character with no inner conflict, and it is only when the hero recognizes and overcomes his own inner conflict that he reaches the level of his romance, wins her love, and achieves his outer and inner motivations.

The completed chart of motivation and conflict for *Shrek* would therefore look like this:

	OUTER MOTIVATION	OUTER CONFLICT	INNER MOTIVATION	INNER CONFLICT
Hero **SHREK**	Rescue Princess Fiona; win her love	He's an ogre; she's protected by a dragon; she's cursed; Lord Farquaad wants her	Isolation; love	He's cut himself off from any kind of connection, friendship, and love
Nemesis **LORD FARQUAAD**	Marry Princess Fiona	Shrek and Princess Fiona fall in love; Shrek tries to get her back	Power	Ruthless; lusts for power
Reflection **DONKEY**	Help Shrek win the princess	Fiona is protected by a dragon; she's cursed; Lord Farquaad wants her	Friendship	N/A
Romance **PRINCESS FIONA**	Win Shrek's love	She's cursed; Shrek misunderstands; Farquaad won't allow it	Live up to her image of a fairy-tale princess; love	Imprisoned by the rules of fairy tales

An excellent exercise is to attempt to complete the above chart for other Hollywood movies, particularly films such as *Working Girl*, *The Matrix*, and *Wedding Crashers*, which have clear outer motivations for characters in all four categories, and inner conflict for at least their heroes. Chapter 8 of this book, which analyzes *Avatar* in detail, should further clarify these principles.

SUMMARY

1. The four facets of character are:

- Physical makeup
- Personality
- Role
- Background

2. The three essential methods for creating immediate empathy with your hero are:

- Sympathy—a victim of undeserved misfortune
- Jeopardy—in danger of losing something of great value to the hero
- Likability—possessing one or more of these qualities:

  Kind, good-hearted, and generous

  Well-liked by other characters

  Funny

3. Qualities for strengthening empathy and identification are:

- A high level of skill
- In touch with his own power
- Power over other people
- Power to do what needs to be done, without hesitation
- Power to express one's feelings regardless of others' opinions
- Superpowers
- Living or working in a familiar setting
- Familiar flaws and foibles

➤ Serving as the eyes of the audience

4. The primary methods for ensuring *original* characters are:

➤ Research

➤ Go against cliché

➤ Play off other characters

➤ Cast the character

5. The two levels of motivation are:

➤ Outer motivation: What the character visibly hopes to accomplish by the end of the movie

➤ Inner Motivation: The reason for the outer motivation, which the character thinks will lead to self-worth

6. The sources of conflict are:

➤ Outer conflict: Obstacles created by nature or other characters

➤ Inner conflict: Obstacles coming from within the character

7. The four categories of primary character are:

➤ Hero: The main character, whose motivation drives the plot and with whom we most strongly empathize

➤ Nemesis: The character who most stands in the way of the hero's achieving her outer motivation

➤ Reflection: The character who most supports the hero's outer motivation or is in the same basic situation

➤ Romance: The sexual or romantic object of at least part of the hero's outer motivation, who must alternately support and be at cross-purposes to the hero

8. Additional ground rules for creating primary characters:

► Characters must be people or anthropomorphized animals, creatures, or cyborgs

► Inner motivation and conflict may be explored for any or all of the primary characters, or for none of them

► It is not necessary to have characters in all four of the primary categories

► A character cannot occupy more than one category

► A character cannot change categories

► More than one character can occupy any of the categories

9. Secondary characters are added for logic, credibility, greater conflict for the hero, greater support for the hero, or more complexity to the story.

FOUR

THEME AND CHARACTER ARC

I GET FRUSTRATED EVERY TIME I HEAR SOMEONE IMPLY THAT ONLY foreign films say anything of significance and that Hollywood movies are too slick, too commercial, and too superficial. The greatness of the best Hollywood movies is that they *can* be slick, entertaining, and appeal to the masses and, underneath, convey ideas, principles, and universal truths that reach audiences on an entirely different level. This underlying level of morality is explored through the film's *theme*.

Theme is the universal statement the movie makes about the human condition. It is the screenwriter's underlying prescription for how one should live one's life in order to be a more evolved, more fulfilled, more individuated, more moral person. It's the filmmaker's way of saying, "This is how to be a better human being." Theme is universal; it applies to any individual in the audience. Beyond the hilarity, clever plot, terrific dialogue, and sexual shenanigans, the theme of *Wedding Crashers* has nothing to do with crashing weddings or getting laid. It speaks to the need for honesty and emotional risk.

Whatever universal prescription for living you want your screenplay to deliver, it must be illustrated by your hero's growth and inner transformation through the course of the story. In other words, *theme grows out of character arc.* If your theme is about how we must connect with, and give to, others to live a fulfilling life (as in *Rain Man*, *Shrek*, *Good Will Hunting*, *Hancock*, *Bruce Almighty*, *Lars and the Real Girl*, and countless other films), then this is a lesson your hero must learn through the course of the story.

Only by learning to live by whatever principles or morality your theme espouses does your hero earn the right to achieve his *outer* motivation. The outer motivation becomes his reward for finding the courage to overcome his inner conflict, to change and grow, and do what is right. Because we empathize with your hero—because we become that character on a psychological and emotional level—your movie gives us the direct experience of transforming, and of living by that principle.

As with inner motivation and inner conflict, this is an arena you may choose not to explore with your own screenplay. It is perfectly acceptable to write a screenplay that elicits emotion only at the level of outer motivation and outer conflict and doesn't get into deeper thematic levels. Many immensely successful movies do just that.

RECOGNIZING THEME

In the previous chapter, I kept saying that the four categories of primary character were also critical to developing character arc and theme. Here is why: *theme emerges when the hero's similarity to the nemesis, and difference from the reflection, are revealed.* When we recognize how the hero, at any point in the movie, is like the character he opposes and unlike the character with whom he is aligned, we begin to see the screenplay's broader statement about how we should live our lives.

Similarly, *character growth begins when the hero recognizes his own similarity to the nemesis and difference from the reflection.* Theme is recognized (and vicariously experienced) by the audience; growth is experienced by the hero of the movie (and, perhaps, by other characters as well). The character's transformation from someone stuck in his inner conflict to someone who has found the courage to overcome it is his arc. It's an arc from fear to courage, from inner conflict to true self-worth.

Here is the primary-character chart from the last chapter, this time using the screenplay for another commercially successful and artistically acclaimed film, *Working Girl*:

	OUTER MOTIVATION	OUTER CONFLICT	INNER MOTIVATION	INNER CONFLICT
Hero **TESS MCGILL**	Put together a deal; win the love of Jack	She's a secretary, not a broker; Katharine wants to steal her idea, get Jack back	Success; love	Afraid she's not really good enough
Nemesis **KATHARINE PARKER**	Steal Tess's idea; win back Jack Trainer	Tess is putting the deal together; Jack is falling for Tess	Success	Dishonesty
Reflection **CYN**	Help Tess make the deal and win Jack's love	Tess is a secretary posing as a broker	Friendship	N/A
Romance **JACK TRAINER**	Put together the deal; win Tess's love	He doesn't know Tess is lying; Trask & Co. resist the idea	Success; love	Insecurity; won't take risks

The hero of *Working Girl* is Tess McGill, a secretary from Staten Island whose outer motivation is to put together a radio station buyout deal by posing as a broker, as well as to win the love of Jack Trainer, the broker she's working with on the deal. Her outer conflict is that she's just a secretary, her boss Katharine Parker wants to steal her idea, and Katharine is already romantically involved with Jack.

This makes Katharine the nemesis and Jack the romance. Tess's reflection is her best friend, Cyn, the fellow secretary who is most closely aligned with her at the beginning, and who helps Tess execute her plan.

So far this is all pretty simple and straightforward. Kevin Wade's screenplay for *Working Girl* is a sterling example of a movie that can follow all the "rules" of structure and character and still be wonderfully original, emotionally involving, and commercially successful.

To discover the theme of *Working Girl*, we must ask how Tess, the hero, is like her nemesis, Katharine. Both are women who work on Wall Street, both want to get credit for the Trask deal; both have the hots for Jack Trainer. But on a *thematic* level, their similarity lies in their inner motivations and conflicts. Both women want to succeed. More important, *both lie to get what they want.* Katharine tries to steal Tess's idea, and when that doesn't work, she falsely claims that Tess stole the idea from her. Similarly, Tess lies when she tells everyone she's a broker, when in reality she's just a secretary.

But it's a little too simplistic to say that the theme is just "honesty is the best policy." We realize Tess is justified in attempting the imposture, since the rules are stacked against her. She's only turning the tables on Katharine's own dishonesty, and (unlike Katharine's lying) no one is really being hurt by Tess's pretense: the deal she's proposing is legitimate, and will benefit everyone.

So we must dig deeper, and look more closely at Tess's inner conflict: *she doesn't think she's good enough.* Deep down, she doesn't really believe she belongs in that inner circle of brokers—she sees herself as just a Staten Island secretary who will always be riding that ferry to the Promised Land. *And this is exactly how Katharine sees her.* Katharine exploits Tess because she can, because she sees herself as superior and entitled to whatever she can coerce or steal from Tess. She looks down on Tess as inferior, just the way Tess sees herself as inferior.

In addition, both Tess and Katharine are alike in their emphasis on image. When Tess first goes to work for Katharine and asks for any wisdom she can share, Katharine's only response is "You might want to rethink the jewelry." To Katharine, it's all about looks and presentation.

And as Tess pursues her goal, she starts turning herself into Katharine. She cuts her hair shorter, wears Katharine's clothes, lives in Katharine's apartment. After becoming Katharine's new secretary, Tess, like Katharine, believes the success she desires will come not from her intelligence and skill but from how she appears, whether it's genuine or not.

So the theme of *Working Girl* is related to honesty and image. To refine it further, we need to see how our hero is *unlike* her reflection.

Tess and Cyn also have much in common: they are best friends; they're both from Staten Island; they are both secretaries for the same company. But they differ in one key way: throughout the movie, Cyn represents honesty and self-acceptance. Though Cyn is willing (as a reflection character must be) to help Tess pull off the imposture, she repeatedly chides Tess for believing she actually is the false person she's created. "Just because you walk like a broker and talk like a broker doesn't mean you're a broker," she says. And later, when Tess won't give her ex-boyfriend a chance to explain—when she's cut herself off from her Staten Island life—Cyn declares, "That's not like you."

This is a typical statement from a reflection character—telling the hero that the way they're behaving is not who they truly are. (It's not that different from Donkey telling Shrek he has a problem.) For Cyn, it's not just about Tess pretending to be a broker; it's about Tess forgetting who she really is. Tess is unlike her reflection in that she won't stand up for who she truly is. Only in the climax, when Tess finally reveals how she came up with the idea for the radio network buyout, is she acting out of her truth rather than out of some image of herself. And only then is she able to achieve her outer motivation, because that is when she has found the courage to complete her arc.

Putting this all together, the theme of *Working Girl* is: *To be the best person you can be, you must stand up for who you truly are, not for some false image of who you think you should be.* This theme is universal. We may not be secretaries or brokers, we may not even know where Wall Street is, but we all can achieve greater fulfillment in life by standing up for the person we truly are. And this is what makes *Working Girl* such a great film. Not only is it a hugely entertaining and commercially successful romantic comedy, it's a movie that says something deeper by developing a very insightful theme, and one that can truly elevate people's lives if they find the courage to practice it.

Notice how once you recognize the character arc and theme, so many other elements of the script support and enhance it. Consider, for example, setting and description. The movie opens with Tess riding the Staten Island Ferry, sailing past the Statue of Liberty to (in the words of the Carly Simon theme song) the "new Jerusalem"—Manhattan is the Promised Land for Tess. She has "big hair," wears big hoop earrings, and walks off the boat in tennis shoes, which will be replaced with heels when she gets to the office. She is the image of a secretary in every way.

We will see her ride that same ferry from Staten Island to Manhattan two other times in the script, in a wonderful example of *echoing*, a structural device that will be explained in the next chapter. The second time is late at night, after she has refused her old boyfriend Mick's very public proposal, disappointing all of her old friends. She is now the image of the Wall Street broker—short, well-styled hair, Katharine's expensive clothes and jewelry—but she looks forlorn, knowing she is leaving behind the "Staten Island Tess" for good.

The third and last time we see Tess on the ferry is after she's been fired. The truth has come out, and Katharine has won. Tess has lost the deal, her job, the love of her life, and her future. The ferry now represents no-man's-land for her. Tess had already ended her Staten Island life, and now she has no Wall Street life either. This time she's not the image of anything. She has no makeup, her hair is sort of mussed, and she's wearing jeans, a sweatshirt, and sneakers—with no heels to replace them. Everything she was ever attached to is gone.

But, we shall see, this is a good thing. Thematically, it's *always* a good thing when a hero is stripped of his attachments; it means that all of his emotional protection is gone, and he must find the courage to live his truth in order to prevail, get what he wants, and complete his arc.

On this final ferry ride of the film, Tess is carrying an empty cardboard box (again, representing no possessions, nothing to fall back on but herself) to go clean out her desk. But when she arrives at the office, she encounters Katharine, Jack, and Trask. This time she is ready to stand up to her nemesis and stand up for herself. She finds the courage to be completely honest, which empowers her to complete her arc, make the deal, and get the guy.

This device, using clothing and makeup to reflect a character's arc, can be very effective. Notice how the heavy dresses that symbolize the existences that weigh down both Rose in *Titanic* and Elizabeth Swann in *Pirates of the Caribbean: Curse of the Black Pearl* almost kill them at critical points in those two films. Or, in *Thelma and Louise*, look for the moment when Louise, who has had her whole life defined by men's expectations of her, starts to put on lipstick, then changes her mind and throws it to the ground. It is precisely at this moment in the movie that heroes Thelma and Louise start controlling their own destinies.

This is not to say that the people who came out of the theater after seeing *Working Girl* were declaring, "I loved that movie! I, too, believe we must stand up for who we truly are." But just because an audience doesn't verbalize a theme doesn't mean they didn't internalize it.

Theme grows out of the writer's unconscious (creativity), is delivered through the characters' unconscious (inner motivation and conflict), and is received by the audience's unconscious. It is, if you will, a soul-to-soul communication between screenwriter and audience.

DEVELOPING THEME
IN YOUR SCREENPLAY

So how does all of this help your own writing? How are you going to use all of this complex information to develop a theme in your own screenplay?

Again, you can't impose a theme on your script. It's kind of absurd to think you could begin with the idea of needing to stand up for who you truly are and from that conclude, "Guess I'll write *Working Girl*!"

Begin with a story concept that meets the criteria outlined in chapter 2. Then focus on the outer motivations and outer conflicts for your primary characters. After that, begin exploring those characters' inner motivations and conflicts. Only then are you ready to see what more universal theme and character arcs may be emerging.

If you try to impose a theme on your story, it may not be true for either you or your screenplay. I've had conversations with writers who insist that their themes are elevated messages for the world, when what was actually emerging from their stories and characters was something quite different. That's why it is best to develop your *plot* and then see what underlying principles come to light.

Once your theme begins to emerge, applying these principles can help you reveal and enhance the theme by clarifying the differences between your hero and your reflection, and the similarities between your hero and your nemesis. Then, in successive drafts, you can lay in situations, action, description, and dialogue that strengthen the arc and theme you have discovered in your own story.

THE METHOD OUTLINED ABOVE IS NOT THE ONLY WAY TO APPROACH A movie's theme. There are other definitions of theme and other ways to find deeper levels of meaning in any film or screenplay. But this process is a very effective way of giving greater depth to your own screenplay, and of finding added substance to the movies you see.

There can also be deeper levels of meaning beyond the theme and message of a screenplay: symbol, allegory, archetype, etc. *Stand by Me*, adapted by Bruce A. Evans and Raynold Gideon from Stephen King's novella, develops a theme of recognizing one's own gifts and pursuing them regardless of others' opinions or approval. But beneath that, it explores the terrifying but necessary death of one's childhood that precedes passage into the unpredictable world of adulthood if one is to realize one's own gifts. And beneath that allegorical level, the film is a quest story, a Holy Grail myth portraying the journey from childhood to maturity, power, and individuation.

Whatever the layers of meaning in your screenplay, your primary concern must always be your hero's outer motivation. It is only from that foundation that the depth and complexity of your screenplay can emerge.

SUMMARY

1. *Theme* is a universal statement the movie makes about the human condition, which goes beyond the plot. It is the screenwriter's prescription for how one should live one's life in order to be more fulfilled, more evolved, more individuated, or a better person.

2. Theme emerges when the hero's similarity to the nemesis and difference from the reflection are revealed.

3. *Character growth* begins when the hero recognizes her own similarity to the nemesis and difference from the reflection.

4. Theme grows out of the writer's unconscious, is developed through the characters' unconscious, and is received by the audience's unconscious.

5. Theme must grow out of the story concept; it must never be imposed on it.

FIVE

STRUCTURE

THINK OF YOUR MOVIE AS A ROLLER COASTER AT AN AMUSEMENT PARK: your story concept is the way the experience appears initially—does it look like a ride that has the potential to be emotionally involving? In other words, is it a ride that will attract people in the first place? Your characters (particularly the hero) are the vehicles through which the audience experiences emotion, like the cars on the roller coaster. The structure involves the sequence of events in the story—the curves and turns that will determine whether or not the ride is exciting and memorable.

Plot structure consists of the specific events in a movie or TV episode and their position relative to one another. In a properly structured story, the right events occur in the right sequence to elicit maximum emotional involvement in the reader and audience. If the events of your story lack interest, excitement, humor, logic, or relevance, or if they occur in an order that fails to create suspense, surprise, anticipation, curiosity, or a clear resolution, then the structure is weak.

Structuring your story effectively involves two stages of development: dividing your plot into three acts and making use of specific structural devices.

THE THREE ACTS TO ANY SCREENPLAY

Any film story, of any length, can be divided into three acts. This division constitutes the first level of plot structure and is necessary to create an effective screenplay. These acts must satisfy the dramatic requirements of film and are not necessarily related to the acts of a play or the commercial breaks of a TV show, although there is often a close connection. The three acts of a film story can be defined in several ways, which will also help explain how to effectively divide your own screenplay.

The first method of defining the acts of a screenplay is in terms of the screenwriter's *objective* within each act. The goal of act one is to *establish* the setting, characters, situation, and outer motivation for the hero. The goal of act two is to *build* the action, suspense, pace, humor, character development, and character revelations. The goal of act three is to then *resolve* everything for both your hero's inner and outer journey.

The next means of defining each act is in terms of the *outer motivation for your hero*. As discussed, the hero's outer motivation determines your story concept and serves as the cornerstone of your entire screenplay. So it is with structure; the three acts of the screenplay correspond to the three stages of the hero's outer motivation.

This hardly differs from your own three objectives for the story. In terms of the hero's outer motivation, *it will require all of act one just to establish that visible goal*. More accurately, your hero cannot begin pursuing the outer motivation until the beginning of act two.

Act two will then consist of building the emotion—and since emotion grows out of conflict, this primarily means building up the hurdles and obstacles the hero must overcome as she desperately pursues her goal. This act must always end with some major crisis or setback—some huge hurdle the hero is unable to overcome, so it seems like the hero is certain to fail.

Then, in act three, the hero will make one final effort to reach the finish line, where she will either achieve her desire or not, with no ambiguity.

The final way the acts of your screenplay can be defined corresponds to length: *Act one is always the first quarter of your screenplay; act two is always the next half; Act three is always the last quarter.* In a properly structured two-hour movie, act one should last about a half hour, act two one hour, and act three a half hour. The same holds true for episodic television. In a twenty-four minute sitcom, the three acts should be about six minutes, twelve minutes, and six minutes. In a one-hour episode . . . well, you get the point.

A larger consideration in episodic television is to leave the audience with a feeling of anticipation so they won't change channels during the commercial. Getting the audience to wonder, "What's going to happen next?" so they'll sit through the commercials (or at least zip through them on their DVR) is more important than getting the commercial breaks to correspond to the three acts of the story. But the necessary stages of the hero's outer motivation must still be there, following the quarter-half-quarter formula.

The acts of your screenplay must also conform to this formula in terms of page count. The basic formula in Hollywood is that one page will equal one minute of screen time. If your screenplay is 120 pages long, then act one should end around page 30, and act two should end around page 90. The same formula (quarter-half-quarter) holds true regardless of the length of your screenplay.

The acts are the organic structural changes in your story, not in your written format. *Never label the acts of a screenplay, as you would for a play.*

In Michael Arndt's screenplay for *Little Miss Sunshine*, the outer motivation for the hero, Richard Hoover, is to get his daughter, Olive, to Los Angeles and help her win the Little Miss Sunshine pageant. This is his visible goal, which has a clearly defined finish line (winning the contest), and as soon as we hear it, we can imagine what that would look like on the screen.

An argument could be made that *Little Miss Sunshine* is actually a multiple-hero story, with six equal main characters: Olive, her father, her mother, her grandfather, her brother, and her uncle—the entire family that has piled into the van to get Olive to the competition. Since we empathize equally with each of them, and since each one is on screen an equal amount of time (at least until Grandpa dies), this makes sense. But it makes no difference to the structure of the plot. As is typical for many multiple-hero stories, the heroes share the same outer motivation, which they work together to achieve.

Either way, act one of the movie establishes the characters—the entire family of six—and their individual situations, and culminates with Richard announcing that they will all go to Los Angeles together. And it is *precisely* at the 25-percent mark of the screenplay and film that they climb in the van and start their journey.

Now begins act two, where they are finally pursuing their outer motivation. And now, just as it should, the conflict starts to build. The van breaks down. Dick loses his book deal. Grandpa dies. The hospital won't release the body or let them leave. A cop stops them. And Dwayne discovers he's color-blind. Finally, at the end of act two—the 75-percent mark—they face the biggest obstacle of all to the goal of winning the competition: they arrive at the pageant four minutes late, and Olive is not allowed to register.

The actual shooting script for *Little Miss Sunshine* is 109 pages long, and the moment they are told it's too late to enter the competition occurs on page 80—73 percent of the way into the script. Close enough, I'd say—this is art, not accounting.

Now, in act three, the heroes do everything they possibly can to overcome this obstacle, get Olive into the pageant, and help her win. In the end, she loses the competition, but structurally that doesn't matter—the outer motivation is resolved, along with the arcs for these characters.

Any properly structured episode of a tv series can be broken down in the same way. For example, a past episode of *Lie to Me*, titled "Secret Santa," is about hero Cal Lightman going to Afghanistan to help U.S. soldiers determine if an American they've captured is a member of the Taliban. In act one of the script by Alexander Cary (the series was created by Samuel Baum), Lightman is approached by a government agent, asked to help, told he must go there, and is forced to say good-bye to his daughter without her learning the truth about the danger he'll be in. All of this establishes the situation and builds up to the moment when the hero actually begins pursuing his goal. Because this is an episode of a series, there is no need to establish the everyday life of the main characters—only to show their opening situation in *this* episode—getting ready for a Christmas celebration.

Act two begins when Lightman arrives in Afghanistan and begins interrogating the prisoner. The conflict builds as a unit on a rescue mission is ambushed; a new, mysterious government agent shows up; and Lightman realizes that the captured soldier isn't the only one keeping secrets.

Act two ends with the news that the Taliban is now attacking the bunker where Lightman is questioning the prisoner, and they are all likely to be killed. Act three is about his final effort to get to the truth, and to escape.

Episodic television won't always follow these acts and percentages so closely. More serialized shows—like *Lost*, *Mad Men*, *In Treatment*, and *Nurse Jackie*, or shows that create their own structure, like the *Law & Order* franchise, often take more liberties with the locations of the act breaks. But almost every series, even those, will take the audience through the three stages of establishing a goal for that episode alone, building up the conflict, and then resolving it.

SETUP AND AFTERMATH

In addition to the three acts of a properly structured screenplay, two elements must be used *within* act one and act three: the *setup* and the *aftermath*. These two stages of your story mirror each other. Each gives a glimpse of the hero's everyday life, one at the very beginning of the screenplay, before the hero begins his forward movement, and one at the very end, after the hero has completed his journey.

A well-structured story gives us a "before" and "after" picture of the hero. At the level of the outer journey—the hero's pursuit of his outer motivation—the hero begins the movie lacking something he will try to obtain by the end of the movie (or possessing something that will be threatened or taken away, which he will then have to protect or recover). But the audience needs to see the life the hero has been living prior to the beginning of the script, so they can compare it to the life he will begin living at the end of the screenplay, after having achieved his goal (or not, if he fails in the end or changes his mind).

This before and after picture becomes even more critical when you develop an arc for your hero. You must introduce your hero by showing how he is emotionally stuck, mired within his inner conflict. He may believe himself to be happy and content, or he may wish for something better in life, but his emotional fears will always prevent him from pursuing real growth and fulfillment. He is torn between the emotional safety of his limited existence and the vulnerability and emotional risk that change and courage would entail.

In the aftermath, you will reveal your new, emotionally evolved hero, reaping the rewards of having found the courage to change (or condemned to living the life of a tragic hero if he didn't).

About a Boy, the adaptation of the Nick Hornby novel written by Peter Hedges, Chris Weitz & Paul Weitz, opens with Will, the hero/narrator, watching *Who Wants to Be a Millionaire* and refuting John Donne's claim that no man is an island. Will declares, "All men are islands. And what's more, this is the time to be one. This is an island age."

We can see in this setup that all of this is true, not just from the dialogue but from Will's actions and environment. He lives in a modern but sterile flat filled with metal furniture and modern appliances, but devoid of anything like a photograph or memento implying human connection. He listens to, and deletes, a voice mail from a Swedish flight attendant thanking him for their night together and leaving her number, which he writes down, then promptly discards in his metal wastebasket.

Will compares himself to Ibiza, a lovely, isolated island in the Mediterranean known (according to Wikipedia) for its summer parties. When he refuses to become godfather for his friends' new baby, one of them says she always thought he had hidden depths. "No, no," he answers. "You've always had that wrong about me. I really am this shallow."

She later tells him he will end up childless and alone. "Well," Will replies, "fingers crossed, yeah."

So this is the "before" picture of Will in *About a Boy*: he claims from the opening line to be happy, and his life to be perfect, but the audience knows better. All this sterility makes it clear that something is missing from his life: it's devoid of any real love or human connection.

Then the young boy Marcus enters Will's life, and at the beginning of act two, Will begins protecting Marcus from all the people who are making his life miserable (both the bullies and Marcus's mother), and starts using Marcus to pick up women (and eventually one in particular). He first pursues these goals just to get rid of Marcus and to find his next one-night stand. But in order to achieve them, he is forced to get closer to Marcus, and then he starts to fall in love with one of the women he's pursuing. He can't help but leave his island existence, and as a result, he begins connecting with others, for the first time putting their well-being above his own. This is his arc.

In the aftermath, we again see Will in his flat, again watching television. (This is a common, and very effective, structural device—placing the aftermath in the same location as the setup, so the contrast, and the hero's transformation, become very clear.) But this time he is surrounded by his new friends and loved ones. Will the narrator once again describes his island existence: "Every man is an island. I stand by that. But clearly some men are island *chains*. Underneath, they are connected."

The universal theme of *About a Boy* is now also clear: to be fully evolved/realized/fulfilled/individuated, we cannot live as emotional islands; we must risk connecting with others.

This "before" and "after" picture applies even when a film portrays a tragic hero. We are first introduced to Ennis in Larry McMurtry and Diana Ossana's screenplay for *Brokeback Mountain* as the epitome of the isolated loner. He is a penniless hitchhiker, dropped off in a desolate stretch of Wyoming, carrying everything he owns in a small paper sack. He even has to save his cigarette butt after a couple puffs, since he can't afford a new pack. And when he first meets Jake, he doesn't say a word. He, like Will in *About a Boy*, is cut off from any human connection.

We will come to realize that his inner conflict comes from living a lie, terrified of acknowledging even to himself that he is gay. But through the course of the movie, he will begin to connect with Jake. His outer motivation is to win Jake's love, and to have a permanent, committed relationship with him. But ultimately, Ennis is unable to overcome his fear of declaring and living his feelings for Jake, and in the end, he loses him. While we understand and sympathize with Ennis's terror, especially given the setting of the story, he is a tragic figure nonetheless. He failed to achieve his outer motivation because he couldn't find the courage to overcome his inner conflict.

So in the aftermath we again see Ennis alone, clutching an empty flannel shirt—the only remnant of the love and fulfillment he lost. This is the new life he will now live, having failed to achieve his inner or outer motivations.

THE OPENING

You've no doubt heard the timeless Hollywood maxim, "You've got to grab the reader in the first ten pages."

Ignore it.

While the first ten pages of your screenplay are critical to getting it read, represented, optioned, packaged, and produced, no one likes to be grabbed. It's a jarring, unpleasant experience. A far better way to approach the opening of your script is to realize you've got to *seduce* the reader in the first ten pages. Everybody likes to be seduced; it's a gradual, enjoyable and emotionally involving experience that thoroughly captures our attention.

I've read hundreds of bad scripts that were doomed to rejection by page 10—not because there was no action but because the action was too immediate and abrupt. Without any real introduction of character or setting, with nothing but a scene heading and a character name, the hero was battling an alien monster, winning a big game, or declaring, "I love you!" on page 1. The only "grabbing" involved would be that of an agent or executive picking up the script and tossing it into the rejection pile.

If you can't immediately plunge the reader into the plot of the story, how *do* you open your screenplay effectively? How do you structure the setup of your screenplay to seduce the reader while still giving us a glimpse of your hero before she has begun pursuing her goal, before the story has even begun moving forward? And how do you show your hero living her everyday life, emotionally stuck, without your script immediately becoming static and boring?

Your ultimate objective for the opening ten pages is the same as for the rest of your screenplay: to elicit emotion. And emotion grows out of conflict. So as you show us your hero's everyday life, and present all of the other necessary elements of the setup, you can do so in a way that brings out conflict for your hero.

I. **Transport readers from the world they occupy into the world you've created.** Consider the situation agents and development executives are in when they read your screenplay. They are far too busy during the week with meetings, phone calls, negotiations, and screenings to also have time to read scripts. So it's the weekend, and your script is somewhere in the pile of a dozen or so they've had to lug home and get through by Monday morning. By the time they open yours, they're thinking about all their friends who *don't* work in the film industry, who get to spend the day with their kids or playing tennis or watching football. Somehow you've got to get these readers out of their heads and into your story.

This is one reason that you've got to *take your time.* Seducing the reader in the first ten pages means that *you get ten pages.* You don't have to shock a reader into submission in the first paragraph. So you start with a vividly described setting, then introduce vividly described characters, and *then* begin detailing some action and dialogue to get things moving. You've got to create images of what we're seeing on the screen, so that a picture begins forming in the reader's mind. Once they occupy your fantasy world, important stuff can start happening.

There are four basic opening sequences you can employ and combine to pull a reader into your screenplay, or an audience into your movie:

► *Broad to narrow.* The most common style for the opening shot of the film is to begin with a broad or panoramic shot or series of shots, then gradually to move into the specific location for the first scene. You might begin with a shot of a city skyline, then cut to a shot of a specific skyscraper, then a single window in the skyscraper, then finally inside that room, where the initial action occurs. This is the exact opening of *Psycho*, and is also used in *Star Wars*, *American Beauty*, and *I Am Legend*.

► *Narrow to broad.* Here you do the opposite. Begin with a close-up, or a shot with a limited view, then pull back to reveal the bigger setting in which this object or action occurs. This opening shot has the effect of creating curiosity, immediately focusing our attention, and providing variety from the standard big-to-small opening. *Dangerous Liaisons* opens this way, with a tight shot of the Marquise's face in a mirror, followed by a full shot of her and her surroundings.

Avoid using extensive camera directions when employing this sequence (or anywhere in your script). Simply describe what we see on the screen, beginning with that single item and then adding the words "We pull back to see . . ."

► *Black screen. Slumdog Millionaire* and *About a Boy* both open with a black screen and the sounds of *Who Wants to Be a Millionaire?* Revealing the sounds of the scene before the sights has a similar emotional effect to the narrow-to-broad opening: it focuses the audience's attention by limiting what they are allowed to perceive.

► *Narration.* This device can be used in combination with any of the others. Narration helps seduce the reader by re-creating the effect of the words "Once upon a time . . ." Our attention is immediately piqued if we hear that someone is going to tell us a story.

Two additional elements to keep in mind are:

► *Title cards.* Title cards can be used to supplement any of those four basic openings. If you want the audience to know the specific time (if it's a period piece or set in the future) or location (if it's a specific city or locale that isn't obvious from what we see on the screen), you must superimpose that information on the screen. It's usually indicated in your script by writing

```
SUPER: Salem, Oregon
       1959
```

or whatever the place and date are. You can't simply put this information in the scene heading, because it doesn't tell the reader how the *audience* will know where we are.

► *Credits.* Never, never, never mention where the opening credits of your film should occur. It's not your job, and it only distracts the reader from the story you're telling.
　　I'll go into a lot more detail about writing description, action, and dialogue, and the other rules for what you can and can't include, in chapter 6, when I discuss the principles of scene writing. For now, just understand the

necessity of immediately projecting your movie inside the reader's head.

2. **Introduce your hero.** Your hero must appear in the opening ten pages of your screenplay. Usually your hero will be the first character on the screen in the opening scene.

3. **Create empathy with your hero.** As soon as your hero is introduced, you must employ at least two of the methods for creating empathy described in chapter 3.

4. **Show the hero living her everyday life.** Again, we need to see the "before" picture of your hero. In the setup, you're saying to the reader, "This is who my hero was yesterday. In fact, this is who she has been for some time."

5. **Begin revealing the hero's inner conflict.** Even though you won't announce it yet through dialogue, and probably won't reveal the source of it, your hero's everyday life must hint at her inner conflict. This is the beginning of her arc, and we need to see how she is emotionally stuck in some way—living with some unconscious fear, even if we don't yet know what that fear is.

    In *The Bridges of Madison County*, our first glimpse of Francesca shows her as a wife and mother, seemingly content but afraid to break out of the emotional shell her marriage has created. She is clearly needed and even loved, but all independence and passion are gone from her life. This is where she is stuck. And we get glimpses of this immediately, before anything new or exciting happens to her, and before the story begins its forward movement.

6. **Present the hero with some opportunity by page 10.** At the end of the setup—10 percent of the way into your screenplay—

something must happen to your hero that has never happened to her before. Some new event must occur that will take her into some new situation, out of which will emerge her specific outer motivation. This is the opportunity that will begin the hero's journey, which will shift the story out of neutral and into first gear. Remember, the hero can't begin pursuing her outer motivation until the beginning of act two—at least fifteen more pages into your screenplay (if it's a feature-length script). But your hero can, and must, begin pursuing some initial desire to leave her everyday life and move into new territory.

In *Get Shorty*, the opportunity occurs when Chili Palmer is sent to Las Vegas to find Leo Devoe. In *The Firm*, this is when Mitch takes the job with Bandini, Lambert and Locke, and he and Abbie head to Memphis. And in *While You Were Sleeping*, this is when Lucy rescues Peter, the man of her dreams, and takes him to the hospital, where she enters her new situation: becoming part of Peter's family.

Notice that in all of these examples, the opportunity actually takes the hero to a new location. This is a common and effective device—let geography match your structure. But it isn't a necessity; in *Spider-Man*, Peter is bitten by the spider at the 10 percent mark. He'll remain in the same location where he began the story but he will still move into his new situation: transforming into the spider-man.

In films that exceed two hours, the opportunity may come past page 10, since 10 percent of a 150-page screenplay is 15 pages. In *Titanic*, Rose doesn't board the ship and set sail until about twenty minutes into the film. But if you're trying to *launch* your career, don't let your screenplay exceed 120 pages, and make sure your hero's opportunity occurs by page 10. Save your own epic for when you become an established Hollywood screenwriter.

THE SEVEN TYPES OF SETUPS

There are at least seven different approaches you can take to the setup of your screenplay, which can be used separately or combined. I'm not referring just to the opening *shots* of the movie, outlined above, which can be used with any of the methods listed below. Here I'm talking about selecting the style for the entire opening 10 percent.

1. **The action hero introduction.** Because emotion grows out of conflict, and because sympathy and jeopardy are powerful tools for establishing empathy, introducing your hero within a thrilling action sequence can instantly captivate your reader and audience. After the now-legendary opening of *Raiders of the Lost Ark*, Indiana Jones could probably have read an insurance policy for the next twenty minutes and the audience would have stuck around. This approach is also used in *Saving Private Ryan* (big battle sequence), *The Fast and the Furious* (big car chase), and *The Negotiator* (exciting shootout and rescue).

   Unfortunately, unless your hero is a soldier, spy, car thief, or cop, it's unlikely his everyday life will logically involve some high-adrenaline confrontation. Since most movies are about everyday people thrust *into* extraordinary circumstances, this kind of setup, as powerful as it can be, isn't all that common.

2. **The everyday hero introduction.** Here you immediately introduce your hero, living her everyday life, *before* she is thrust into the extraordinary circumstances that will begin with the opportunity. The initial emotion in these films comes from forms of conflict other than big action: the undeserved misfortune or jeopardy used to create empathy with the hero; the inner conflict for the hero; the anticipation of conflict to come; humor.

   In *The Proposal*, Andrew Paxton is living his everyday life, working as Margaret's assistant at a publishing house. Far from a big action sequence, it seems as if nothing happens at all. Yet it successfully draws us into the character and the story, thanks primarily to the conflict and humor. Andrew seems like a nice guy, well-liked by others in the office. But Margaret is a monster (undeserved misfortune for Andrew), and everyone is visibly apprehensive when they realize she's arriving early (anticipation of conflict to come). Andrew is stuck in this awful job, allowing her to exploit him in return for the promotion he's been promised, but which is way overdue because Andrew won't stand up for himself (inner conflict). By the time the opportunity arrives (Margaret and Andrew learning she's going to be deported), the conflict has become even greater, we fully empathize with Andrew, and we are emotionally involved in the film.

3. **The new arrival.** Ever notice how many movies open in airports? When you introduce your everyday hero just as his plane is landing or as he's walking down the concourse, you're subtly signaling the audience, "Don't worry, you didn't miss anything—we just got here." This opening sequence also makes it easy to provide exposition—if we learn what's going on as the newly arrived hero does, what could be a boring, "talking heads" scene becomes more natural and emotionally involving.

   Julie and Julia begins with a shot of Julia and Paul Child's car arriving in Honfleur, France, where Julia immediately emerges and says to the waiting landlady, "*Je m'appelle Julia Child*" (which feels a lot more natural, I think, than if she had introduced herself to her husband). We then cut to Julie Powell, the other hero of these parallel stories, as she and her husband, Eric, arrive at *their* new home in Queens.

   The new arrival is not always the hero of your screenplay. *Collateral* opens at LAX, with the arrival of Vincent, the contract killer who will serve as hero Max's nemesis.

4. **Outside action.** This familiar and very effective approach combines elements of both #1 and #2 above. It creates immediate emotional

involvement with an action sequence that does *not* involve your hero, followed by the introduction of your hero living his everyday life. In *A Few Good Men*, we see the attack on Private Santiago before we are introduced to Lieutenant Kaffee as he nonchalantly plea-bargains a deal for a soldier he's never even met. In *The Matrix*, a big action sequence involving Trinity precedes our introduction to Neo, the hero, living his "ordinary" life working in a cubicle and peddling black-market computer programs. And in *The Da Vinci Code*, the introduction of Robert Langdon is preceded by a suspenseful pursuit and murder in the Louvre.

Often, as in those last two examples, the outside action involves the hero's nemesis doing something bad, which creates anticipation of the obstacles our hero will eventually face.

Not only is the outside action setup a staple of science fiction (*Déjà Vu*), horror (*The Ring*), disaster movies (*2012*), animated films (*Monsters vs. Aliens*), and thrillers (*Live Free or Die Hard*) in which everyday people are thrust into situations of great danger, it can also be witnessed just about any night of the week on television—on police procedurals, fantasies, and mysteries, such as the *Law & Order* franchise, the *CSI* franchise, *Lie to Me*, *The Mentalist*, *Fringe*, etc., etc.

5. **The prologue.** This opening may or may not involve the hero, but it always begins with an event that occurs significantly prior to the main story. It serves to create anticipation, and reveals some event that will later provide either outer or inner conflict for the hero. In *Star Trek*, we see the death of Captain George Kirk at the hands of Nero. Nero will be the nemesis who will later confront Kirk's son Jim, thus creating the hero's outer conflict. This event also provides the basis for Jim's inner conflict (cynicism, isolation, and lack of respect for authority).

Similarly, we see heroes as children in the prologue openings of *Contact*, *Up*, *Walk the Line*, and *The Departed*. These events will all affect the heroes' later actions, and the conflicts they will encounter.

Prologue openings don't have to involve the hero's childhood—
The Sixth Sense shows us Malcolm Crowe being shot by a former
patient, an event that occurs just a matter of months before the
main story. Nor does the prologue have to involve the hero at all—
The Mummy reveals a curse and a cause for revenge that occurred
centuries prior to the hero being born.

Following the prologue, the screenplay will then jump to the
time and place of the story, and will introduce the hero living his
everyday life before encountering the 10 percent–mark opportunity.

6. **The flashback.** Here you open with a scene taking place somewhere in the middle of your story, then cut to a scene that occurs
significantly prior to that first event, one that shows your hero living his everyday life. An excellent example is *Mission: Impossible III*,
where arch-villain Owen Davian is holding a gun to hero Ethan
Hunt's head, demanding information Ethan claims not to have.
Ethan's new fiancée, Julia, is brought in; Ethan is given to the
count of ten to reveal the information; and at "zero," Davian
shoots her. Then we immediately smash-cut to Ethan and Julia at
their engagement party, which obviously occurred prior to that
opening scene.

The advantages of this kind of opening should be obvious: immediate action, huge conflict, and high emotion, followed by anticipation and curiosity about how this happy couple will end up in
such a horrific situation—and how Ethan can possibly prevent it
or escape from it. This opening also allows you to begin at just
about any peak emotional moment in the story, making it much
easier to hold the reader's attention through the setup and introduction of your hero. *The Hangover* uses this device for more comedic effect—opening at a moment of great crisis for the three
men who have lost their best friend just a few hours before his
wedding hundreds of miles away.

Just as with a prologue, when you employ this opening you
should follow it with the everyday introduction of your hero. But

the opportunity must still occur at the 10-percent point of the script.

7. **Bookends.** Very similar to the flashback setup, here you open with a sequence, then flash back to introduce your hero. But this opening begins after the end of the story you're telling. We then flash back to see the entire story, then return to the situation that opened the film before fading out.

These two "bookends" usually involve a narrator who will then tell us the story as we witness it. *Out of Africa* opens with an older Karen Blixen writing, "I had a farm in Africa . . ." Then we meet her as a young woman in Denmark before she heads off to Africa (her opportunity). Similarly, *The Princess Bride* introduces us to a young boy who is sick in bed, and his grandfather, who will begin reading him the story of Westley and Buttercup. *Gandhi, Lawrence of Arabia*, and *No Way Out* employ the same kind of opening, but without a narrator.

A more complex version of the bookend opening can be used to begin a screenplay that tells two parallel stories, as with *Fried Green Tomatoes* or *Titanic*, where we open on a narrator who will tell us a story from her past, but who is also part of a contemporary story. In *Titanic*, we are first introduced to "old" Rose, and we eventually flash back as she narrates the story of what happened in 1912. But intertwined with the flashback is the present-day story of the search for the Heart of the Ocean, the priceless gem believed to still be in the sunken ship.

THE ENDING

All commercially successful movies have two things in common: good word-of-mouth and repeat viewers. You won't achieve either if the audience doesn't find the ending of the movie satisfying and emotionally fulfilling. Choosing the best ending for your story is absolutely essential to its artistic and commercial success.

An effective ending involves two elements: the *climax* and the *aftermath*.

Just as the aftermath contrasts with the setup at the beginning of a screenplay (see above), the climax of the story mirrors the opportunity. Each is a single event that has never happened to the hero before. While the opportunity *begins* the forward movement of the story—begins the hero's visible journey by taking him to a new situation—the climax *ends* that journey by resolving the hero's outer motivation. And though the climax doesn't necessarily occur at the 90-percent mark (in the way the opportunity occurs at 10 percent), it will always take place in the last half of act three.

The climax is the sequence in which the hero faces his greatest visible obstacle—the zenith of his outer conflict. This is where he will win or lose, once and for all. The climax is that visible finish line he has been desperate to cross since the beginning of act two, and the resolution of this outer motivation must be the peak emotional moment in the movie.

While there are exceptions, the climax will almost always involve the final confrontation between hero and nemesis, as in everything from *Michael Clayton* to *The Illusionist* to *Kung Fu Panda* to *L.A. Confidential*.

If the hero of your screenplay is pursuing two visible goals, as in most romantic comedies, then you must include a second climax, resolving that second outer motivation as well. The first climax of *The Proposal* involves the final confrontation with the nemesis—the immigration agent who wants to deport Margaret and possibly arrest Andrew; the second is the moment that follows almost immediately, when Margaret and Andrew reunite and resolve the love story.

In dual or multiple-hero stories like *The Holiday*, *He's Just Not That into You*, or *Love, Actually*, every story line must be resolved through a series of successive climax scenes.

There can be no ambiguity to the climax of your screenplay. Your hero achieves her outer motivation or she doesn't, but you can't leave that issue unresolved. The reader and the audience have been waiting at least an hour and a half to find that out; you can't leave them up in the air.

The end of your screenplay may still contain some ambiguous elements or unresolved plot lines. But these must never leave the hero's outer motivation unresolved. *The Graduate, Manhattan, Memento, The Ring, No Country for Old Men, Doubt, Up in the Air, Inception*, and many other superb films do just that. But in each case, the audience knows by the end of the movie whether the hero achieved his or her overall outer motivation.

After the peak emotion of the climax, the aftermath is the scene or sequence that carries the story to the fade-out. It not only gives us a glimpse of the new life your hero will now live, the aftermath allows the audience time to experience the emotional impact of your ending. If your hero dies at the end of the film, the aftermath will usually give us a glimpse of a world that the hero has transformed, and which now must go on in his absence. The climax of *Gladiator* is the final showdown between Maximus and his nemesis, Commodus. The aftermath shows us Maximus's body being carried out of the arena by the Romans who (thanks to Maximus's sacrifice) will now live in a more democratic empire, as well as Maximus being reunited with his family in the afterlife.

Sometimes, when there is little left to show of the hero's new life, or when the writer wants to leave the audience reeling from a peak emotional moment, the aftermath will be very short, with the end of the film occurring just seconds after the climax. *Thelma and Louise, The Karate Kid*, and *The Departed* all employ such abbreviated endings.

Finally, the ending of your screenplay must be the one the reader and audience accept as the most emotionally satisfying resolution of your story. This doesn't mean that you have to give your screenplay a happy ending; such a rule would eliminate decades of successful tearjerkers, all classic tragedy, and all film noir. But avoid *defeated* endings. In some way, the conclusion of your film should preserve and convey the dignity of the human spirit and a sense of hope or growth or enlightenment about the human condition. *One Flew Over the Cuckoo's Nest* is a superb example of a sad ending that retains an uplifting sense of redemption, with the dignity and beauty of the human spirit preserved.

All I'm really saying here is that an audience is willing to hear that life is hard, that life is sad, or even that life is tragic. But they don't want to hear that life is shit. They probably already suspect that it is, and they certainly won't pay ten bucks to have that feeling reinforced.

Finally, given a choice, give your movie a happy ending, because, by and large, *happy endings sell*. This isn't just an arbitrary Hollywood choice. Audiences go to movies and watch television to see problems solved, and to identify with characters that overcome the seemingly in-surmountable obstacles they face. Movies and TV series can give the audience a sense of hope and fulfillment, even if their own lives are in the crapper. Providing an audience with that emotional satisfaction, particularly if you are trying to launch your screenwriting career, in-creases your chances of getting work.

USING THE THREE-ACT STRUCTURE

At this stage of development, you have a clear idea of your basic story concept, your hero, your hero's outer motivation, the other primary characters, and their outer motivations. Possibly you have even created some secondary characters and begun to explore inner motivation and inner conflict.

Your next step is to divide the overall outer motivation for your hero into its three acts, then further divide acts one and three by determin-ing the setup and the aftermath. This will give you a basic, broad-strokes structure on which to build your plot, characters, action sequences, and individual scenes.

Everything begins with your hero's outer motivation. Once you can state your hero's objective in a way that creates a clear, consistent image in the mind of anyone who hears it, you immediately know what two of the key events of your screenplay will be: the beginning of act two and the climax. Because whatever your hero's outer motivation, he must begin actively pursuing it at the 25-percent mark, and he must achieve it (or fail to, once and for all) at the climax.

Assume, for example, that you're writing a story about a woman who commits a bank robbery. Robbing the bank is her outer motivation. As soon as you read those words, you can easily imagine what accomplishing it would look like on the screen. So the outer motivation is visible, and has a clearly defined end point.

We know that your hero must begin taking action toward robbing the bank at the beginning of act two. So, at the 25-percent mark, she might begin digging a tunnel under the bank, or she might hire an experienced bank robber to help her, or she might try to seduce the bank president in order to steal the combination to the vault. But whatever she does, it must represent her first step toward the robbery. If she takes that step earlier, the reader's emotion will not last to the end of the story; if she starts after the 25-percent mark, the reader will lose interest and move on to another script.

We also know that if robbing the bank is her outer motivation, the climax must be the big moment where she gets away with the money once and for all—or where she is caught or killed by the cops before she can. Either choice resolves the story with no ambiguity. You just can't end the film in the middle of the getaway, leaving us wondering whether she succeeded or not.

Having defined these two essential moments in the script, you can address the other key events of act one. Ask yourself, "What would lead my hero to the point where she begins robbing a bank?"

Suppose the bank unfairly fired your hero, and now she wants to get her revenge. This event gives us her inner motivation, as well as our 10 percent–mark opportunity: losing her job. This is something that has never happened to her before, and it will move her into a new situation: unemployed, angry, and desperate, and looking for a way to get rich—and get even.

Now one more key turning point to determine: the event at 75 percent that marks the end of act two and the beginning of act three. This must be some major loss or setback for your hero—a moment where the plan she's been implementing goes out the window, a whole new obstacle appears, and it seems to the reader and audience as though all is lost.

So we'll say that this is where she thinks she's gotten away with the money, but then discovers her partner conned her and took all the money for himself. Now she has to find him, get the money back, and still avoid the cops who are now on her trail because the robbery has been discovered. Overcoming all of these new obstacles and still achieving her outer motivation seems impossible.

It may very well be that this idea sucks, and that by the time you get to the end of act two as you write the screenplay—or even as you develop an outline of the story—you'll toss it out the window and come up with something better. If so, that's great—that's the way writing a story always works. You follow one idea or plot line to see where it leads, and if it doesn't work, you backtrack and come up with a new one. But because you have the basic foundation of your story, you still have something solid to build on, so these changes aren't overwhelming.

It's possible you might decide to change even the broad strokes of this story. Right now, act one is about a woman who gets fired and wants to plan a robbery, act two about a woman who wants to execute the robbery, and act three about a woman who wants to get away with the money she has stolen. But act one could as easily be about a woman who wants to keep her job at a bank, act two about a woman who wants to plot a robbery of the bank that fired her, and act three about a woman who wants to carry out the robbery.

And what about a love story? What if she falls in love with the professional bank robber she teams up with, who plans to betray her? Or with the cop who is increasingly suspicious of what she's planning? Try them all until one combination clearly emerges as the most emotionally involving, both for you and for the mass audience.

However you define each act, you now have a pretty good foundation for your screenplay. Around page 10, a woman loses her job at a bank. This takes her to a new situation, where she has to come up with a way to make money, and to get back at the bank that fired her. So around page 30 (25 percent) she begins taking steps to rob the bank. Act two will comprise the robbery, which is successful until, at the 75-percent mark, her partner steals the money and the cops start coming after her. Now she must find the partner who betrayed her, get the money away from him, elude the police, and escape with the money once and for all at the climax of the movie.

Now you can start to fill in the big blanks between these key moments, beginning with the setup. Who is this woman? What's her job? How do you introduce her? You have countless options, but you know you must accomplish certain things in the setup. We must empathize with her. So is she a victim in some way even before she's fired, to create sympathy? Perhaps she's repeatedly passed over for a promotion, and then her boss promises it to her if she'll go to bed with him. She refuses, and that's why she's fired. This makes her sympathetic (undeserved misfortune) and puts her in jeopardy of losing her job.

This might also give us a glimpse of her inner conflict—she's been passed over before because she refuses to stand up for herself, even though she's a highly skilled teller, or low-level bank executive, or whatever. A story about a rather meek bank teller who finds the courage to rob a bank sounds kind of fun.

Now move to the new situation. What's her initial reaction to getting fired? What kind of emotional tailspin does she exhibit? Does she look for a new job in the traditional way, with no success? When does she first get the idea for robbing the bank? What's her initial plan? Does she talk to anyone about it? Does she already have a skill set she can exploit in committing the robbery? And what's the first step that will show she is now taking direct action toward the robbery itself, signifying that we've moved into act two?

Using the principles of character and structure we've already covered, you continue developing your story in just this way. Brainstorm ideas for filling in the gaps between the turning points you've already defined, modifying or replacing them with better alternatives whenever they present themselves.

But as you can see, you've now reached the point where you are defining the individual scenes of your screenplay. The broad strokes are becoming more sharply defined, and your story is coming into focus much more clearly. So it's time to apply some additional structural principles—powerful tools for maximizing the emotional potential of each successive scene.

THE STRUCTURE CHECKLIST

The following checklist contains the more specific structural principles and devices available to you, scene by scene, after you have established the overall three acts and key turning points to your story. Apply these as you begin writing in scene format, and return to this checklist with each successive draft to continually sharpen your plot structure.

1. **Every scene, event, and character in the screenplay must contribute to the hero's outer motivation.** The outer motivation determines the three acts of the screenplay and must relate to *every single scene*. You can write a hilarious mother-in-law encounter or a thrilling car chase or any other provocative, moving, or side-splitting scene, but if it doesn't relate to the central thrust of your story, you've got to lose it, change it, or save it for another screenplay. This can be excruciating, because sometimes these scenes are the ones you love the most or are even those that you envisioned first when you began developing the script. But no single scene can take priority over your hero's outer motivation.

2. **Show the audience where the story is headed.** Early in your screenplay, you want to create a question in the mind of your reader so he'll keep turning pages to find out the answer. Specifically, that question pertains to the resolution of the hero's outer motivation. Even though your hero will not take *action* to achieve the goal until the quarter-mark of the script, you should let the audience know earlier in act one what that goal is likely to be.

   Viewers know very quickly that by the time the movie is over, they will have learned whether Jane has an affair with Jake in *It's Complicated*, whether Giselle will win the love of Robert in *Enchanted*, and whether Sheriff Bell will have stopped psychopath Anton Chigurh in *No Country for Old Men*. None of these heroes begin pursuing those specific characters until the 25-percent mark of those movies (in fact, Jane and Giselle would both vehemently deny that they had any romantic interest in those two men). But the audience pretty much knows where these stories are headed as soon as all the characters are introduced.

It is sometimes possible to replace one question in the reader's mind with another, as long as the new question logically evolves from the first, and is more serious and provocative. In *Inglourious Basterds*, the initial question in the audience's mind is whether the basterds will be able to kill Nazis without being caught. But eventually a more specific issue replaces this question: will they succeed at killing the Nazi high command during the movie premiere? This question logically grows out of the initial one, and is much more specific—and provocative.

In a biography, the question may simply be, "How will this hero's life play itself out?" But in the more effective biographies, the hero's life is linked to a specific issue. In *Walk the Line*, for example, the question is not simply, "What's that Johnny Cash guy gonna do next?" The more focused, more effective question that drives the story is, "Will Johnny Cash win the love of June Carter?"

3. **Build the conflict.** Make each successive hurdle and obstacle for your hero greater and more provocative than the previous one. In *Ghostbusters*, it would be ludicrous to imagine Peter Venkman and his crew confronting all the demons in New York City in act one, and then facing only the single ghost in the library in act three. Each element of the hero's outer conflict must be more formidable and seemingly more insurmountable than its predecessor.

4. **Accelerate the pace of the story.** The momentum should steadily build as you drive the story to its climax. This applies not only to action films but also to comedies and straight dramas. Even in films like *Ratatouille*, *The Pursuit of Happyness*, and *Superbad*, the obstacles confronting the heroes occur with increasing frequency as the films move toward their climaxes.

This structural principle requires that the *exposition*—the factual information the audience must have to understand what is going on—must be provided as soon as possible.

In *Men in Black*, James Edwards (and the audience) needs to learn all about the presence of aliens on earth, who Kay is, the MiB organization, how it functions, where it's located, who the boss is, and what they might be up against. But all of that information is presented in act one—specifically between the 10 percent–mark opportunity and the beginning of act two, when Edwards (now Jay) and Kay begin pursuing the specific bug who threatens the planet.

If the screenplay for *Men in Black* had been structured differently, so that all this exposition had been given in the latter half of the movie, the accelerating pace would grind to a halt, the emotion would dissipate, and the audience would drift away.

5. **Create peaks and valleys to the action and the humor.** High emotional moments in your screenplay must be followed by scenes with less impact, so the audience can catch its breath or so you can build up to the next, even higher peak. There is no such thing as an effective thirty-minute action sequence or joke or car chase. Such a scene would ultimately dissipate emotional involvement, because the reader would eventually become bored with, and distanced from, the high emotional level.

There is a classic scene in *Jaws* that occurs on the boat, when the three men are comparing their scars, and Quint talks about the USS *Indianapolis*. The audience has just about reached the point where the shark encounters could become routine. So screenwriters Peter Benchley and Carl Gottlieb give the audience a moment to catch its breath, while humor, sadness, and character revelation are added to the film. Then, just as the viewer is lulled into a false sense of security, the shark arrives and we're off to the races.

Humor follows the same principle. No matter how broad or hilarious the comedy, you can't have a ninety-minute joke. Humorous action and dialogue must be interspersed with more serious scenes that serve other purposes and maximize the reader's emotional involvement. *The Birdcage* may have a hilarious dinner party scene with Albert pretending to be Val's mother, but it also has a soft, touching scene of Armand declaring his love and trying to get Albert's forgiveness.

6. **Give the story both humor and seriousness.** This simply means that even if you are writing a tragedy, give it some moments of humor, lightness, and comic relief. In real life, even the darkest and saddest of situations will contain some elements of humor, often as a necessary emotional release for those involved. The same principle applies to film, as exemplified by such emotionally heavy movies as *The Reader*, *Seven Pounds*, and *Precious*, which contain moments of levity despite their serious tone.

   The reverse is true as well: if you are writing a comedy, no matter how broad, take your story and characters seriously. Even in such seemingly off-the-wall movies as *Borat: Cultural Learnings of America for Make Benefit Glorious Nation of Kazakhstan*, *The Hangover*, and *Airplane!* the characters are presented as real, sympathetic people in the midst of all the broad, slapstick, or satirical goings-on. The films may be winking at the audience, but they're not copping out with an attitude of "this is just comedy so it doesn't matter what we do." We are meant to be involved in and believe in the story and characters, and the humor grows out of that emotional connection.

   The finest examples of this principle are those films that are almost impossible to classify as comedy *or* drama. *Sleepless in Seattle*, *Up in the Air*, *Juno*, *Lars and the Real Girl*, and *Julie and Julia* combine hilarity with very serious moments and never get their laughs at the expense of their own characters, or of the audience's emotional involvement.

7. **Create anticipation in the reader.** When a reader reads a screenplay or when an audience sees a movie, they try to guess what's going

to happen next. It's the *anticipation* of where the story is going that keeps a reader or audience engrossed.

Jaws again serves as an excellent example. If you asked anyone to summarize that film in a single word, he would probably say, "Shark." But the fact is, the shark is only on screen a total of about fifteen minutes in the two-hour movie, and for much of that time, only the dorsal fin is seen. It isn't *seeing* the shark that keeps the audience riveted to the screen, it's the *anticipation* of the horrible, frightening, unknown things that will happen when the shark attacks.

It is the anticipation of the showdown with the night seekers in *I Am Legend*, the big race against War Admiral in *Seabiscuit*, the battle of the bands in *School of Rock*, and the revelation of the secrets in *What Lies Beneath* that sustains our emotional involvement in each film.

It is because of this principle that the mass audience usually prefers suspense thrillers to films of nonstop violence. Any time you set up anticipation, you have to pay it off, so there will eventually be some degree of violence in any thriller. But a few hatchets in the skull go a long way.

8. **Give the audience superior position.** *Superior position*, or audience omniscience, occurs when the audience is given information that some of the characters in the film don't have. *We* know what drug lord Frank Lucas is up to in *American Gangster*, but cop Richie Roberts does not. We're aware that the thieves are executing a bank robbery in *The Bank Job*, that there is a plot to kill the Nazi high command in *Inglourious Basterds*, and that Bruce has been given God's job in *Bruce Almighty*, long before the other characters in those movies realize what's going on.

This device, when used in combination with anticipation, becomes extremely effective at eliciting emotion. Superior position *creates* anticipation. The audience anticipates what will happen when the characters learn or encounter what the audience already knows.

In many interviews, Alfred Hitchcock cited an example of a movie scene where two people are sitting at a desk, discussing some banal subject. All at once, out of the blue, a bomb that was hidden in the desk goes off, and the two people are blown to bits.

Now, such a scene *would* create high emotional involvement, but only for a short time. After about sixty seconds of shock and surprise, the audience would start wondering, "Okay, what now?"

Imagine the same scene, however, if the camera cuts from the two people's conversation to a shot of the bomb ticking away in the drawer. You could milk that scene for a good five minutes, even more if you cut away to the bomb squad rushing to save the people at the desk. Because *we* know the bomb is there even if the characters don't (superior position), we imagine how horrible it will be if the bomb goes off (anticipation).

For a more recent example of this very situation, watch the tense opening sequence of *The Hurt Locker* to see just how long anticipation of a bomb exploding can be sustained.

The same principle can be equally effective in comedy. In *Hitch*, we know that Hitch is secretly the date doctor, and that he is helping Albert win the love of Allegra Cole, but Hitch's new love, Sara, does not. The humor comes from the anticipation of this secret being discovered.

9. **Surprise the audience and reverse the anticipation.** Even though anticipation is one of the strongest structural devices you can use, you don't *always* want your reader to anticipate what might be coming. Occasionally, to create fear, humor, shock, and to avoid predictability, you must surprise the audience and jolt them out of their sense of security. Keeping the audience slightly off balance by reversing the anticipated action with something totally unexpected will further increase emotional involvement.

Look again at *The Hurt Locker*. After several scenes where bombs must be defused, we see a situation where a bomb goes off unexpectedly, with no anticipation at all. This shocking event is made more powerful because the audience has come to expect that every explosion can be anticipated. We're thrown off balance, and the emotional impact is even stronger. We're also given a much deeper sense of the horrific situation these men are in, where death can strike quickly, randomly, and with no warning.

Reversing audience anticipation can also heighten comic possibilities. *Raiders of the Lost Ark* offers a well-known example when Indiana Jones, after fighting off scores of bad guys with his whip, is confronted by a giant henchman wearing a black turban and whirling a huge scimitar. Everyone now expects to see a duel between the sword and the whip, so when Indy merely shrugs, pulls a gun, and shoots him, it is a memorable comedic moment.

A double reversal for humor is employed in *Tootsie*, when Michael, posing as Dorothy, is given a scene in which he is supposed to kiss the actor that the other actresses refer to as "the tongue." When Michael gets out of it by hitting him with the folders instead, we laugh, because it wasn't what was anticipated. Then, when he gets kissed after all, it is doubly funny.

Remember, the audience wants to *try* to guess and anticipate what's coming next; they just don't want to be right all the time.

10. **Create curiosity in the reader.** When a character, event, or situation is not explained fully at the outset or when the hero must find the answer to some question or mystery in the course of the story, the reader will "stick around" to learn the solution and satisfy his own curiosity.

Grant Nieporte's script for *Seven Pounds* provides lots of examples of creating curiosity in an audience: What is the meaning of the mysterious 911 call Ben makes in the opening scene? Who are all the people listed in those computer printouts? Why would he make a call to an 800 number and then cruelly start harassing the blind salesperson? What does the cryptic phone call to his brother mean? And why is the title *Seven Pounds*?

By gradually revealing the answers to these questions, rather than providing all of Ben's backstory and motives right away, the screenplay increases the audience's emotional involvement.

Obviously, curiosity is the *key* structural device in a whodunit; the entire film hinges on finding the solution to a murder. But feature-length murder mysteries are usually less successful commercially, and produced less frequently, than suspense thrillers, because curiosity does not carry the emotional impact of superior position and anticipation. Curiosity is always most effective when used in combination with the other structural devices on the list.

This raises another key issue: the longer you withhold a secret from the audience, the more important it becomes, and the more satisfying it must be when it's revealed. A good example is Zach Helm's screenplay *Stranger than Fiction*. In the early scenes of the movie, IRS auditor Harold Crick hears a mysterious voice describing his every action. Immediately the audience is curious—where is this voice coming from, and why is it "commentating" Harold's life?

By the beginning of act two, we learn Harold is actually a fictional character created by a novelist, one who plans to have Harold die at the end of her novel. Now he must find and stop this author from killing him off before she finishes writing the book. This establishes his outer motivation, and the audience's curiosity is satisfied. The device has been effective, because it increased emotional involvement until additional, more exciting events in the screenplay could occur. If the entire film had rested on the meaning of "Where's that voice coming from?" the revelation would not have been sufficiently satisfying to sustain emotional involvement in the film. Instead, the structural device is very effectively used to *increase* emotional involvement until the other structural devices can raise it to an even higher level.

11. Make the story credible. I recently advised a screenwriter who complained when I told him that his screenplay lacked credibility.

"Movies aren't ever real," he argued. "Is it believable that a pig could talk in *Babe*, or that a guy could travel back in time in *12 Monkeys*? Is it even believable that Bruce Willis could stop all those bad guys in the *Die Hard* movies?"

My answer to him was, "Yes it is."

All movies are fantasies that arise from that powerful question, "What if . . . ?"

"What if the two dumbest guys on the continent try to return a suitcase full of money to a beautiful woman while being chased by gangsters?" (*Dumb and Dumber*)

Even movies that are grounded in reality, or actually based on true stories, are told as fantasies, where an everyday person is thrust into an out-of-the-ordinary, bigger-than-life situation:

"What if a good-hearted, politically liberal nun became involved with a gruesome killer on death row, and in fighting for his sentence to be commuted, had to resolve her own conflict over his hateful nature, and over her sympathy with his victims' families?" (*Dead Man Walking*)

"What if a lawyer from a small California town worked his way up from poverty to become the president of the United States, only to end up the only chief executive ever to resign from office?" (*Nixon*)

It is the fantasy element of each of these stories that draws the audience into the theater. No one really wants to see a movie that is truly realistic, unless that movie makes us realize that everyday life can be as extraordinary as fiction.

So the fact that movies are fantasies is not a problem. The problem arises when writers fail to make their stories logical and believable *within their own set of rules.*

To understand movie credibility, you must realize that movies are false on the surface but true underneath. Real life, on the other hand, is believable on the surface but unbelievable underneath. Here's what I mean:

If I said it had taken me a long time to write this book because I had been abducted by aliens and was trapped in their spaceship for a year, you'd probably be looking up Amazon.com's return policy. But if I told you I just saw a *movie* about a guy who claimed he was abducted by aliens and had to convince the world that an attack was imminent, you'd simply wonder when it opened at your local megaplex. In other words, you would readily accept that a movie story would be unbelievable in real life.

On the other hand, if I said I was delayed because I was involved in a horrible incident where a stranger, for no apparent reason, came into a supermarket, pulled out an automatic weapon, and began shooting at everyone before finally killing himself, you might think it horrible, but you wouldn't find it impossible to believe. But if I said I had a screenplay where the hero opens fire and then commits suicide, and in the end we still don't know what his motive was, you'd rightly tell me that I'd never be able to sell it.

In movies, we need to know the inner truths for the characters. Their actions in response to whatever incredible situation you've created must be reasonable, justified, and believable.

Lots of unusual things happen in real life, and people often behave in strange ways. But in your screenplay, even if you're adapting a true story, the characters' actions must seem logical, and the events believable, *within the context of the story*. And you must never confuse credibility with documented reality. One of the weakest arguments you can make in support of your characters' actions is, "But that really happened."

Here is the key to creating make-believe situations: it isn't the fantasy element of a story that is interesting, exciting, romantic, or funny. It's the *reaction* of the everyday world to that fantastic situation. You are only allowed to introduce that single incredible element into your story; everything else must be logical and believable.

Big, for example, is a fantasy about a twelve-year-old boy who makes a wish and wakes up with the body of a thirty-year-old man. I hope I'm not spoiling anything by telling you this couldn't happen in real life.

But think about everything that happens to Josh after he's transformed. He runs away from home, finds a job and a place to stay, falls in love with a woman who thinks he really is thirty years old, and must eventually decide whether to go back to his old life. In other words, every single conflict he faces is logical, believable, and grounded in reality. Gary Ross and Annie Spielberg's screenplay explores what might really happen *after* the fantasy situation occurred.

Now imagine the same movie if, when he got big, Josh entered a world where his best friend had the power to disappear, his girlfriend could travel through time, and everyone could read minds as they battled the dinosaurs that roamed the earth. Such a movie would hold little interest (except for some dazzling special effects) because the story would lack any reality or believability at all.

One of the reasons such a broadly fantastic scenario would fail to capture the emotion of the audience is that the conflict for Josh would become meaningless. When the powers of the hero or the other characters become limitless, there's nothing difficult to overcome, and the audience feels no real tension, worry, or fear. They simply observe the action, rather than becoming a part of it.

Anything you choose can become possible in your screenplay; people can fly; disappear; travel through time and space; and defy death, gravity, and the Internal Revenue Service. But if you are going to alter the rules of real life in any way, the parameters and limitations of your fictional characters and universe must be clearly stated for the audience.

This is why fantasy movies are so tough to pull off. It is very difficult to clearly explain the rules of your make-believe universe and the limits to your hero's powers and still keep the story from becoming confusing. But if the limits to your hero's powers and abilities aren't clear, there will be no tension or conflict, since it will seem that your hero can come up with whatever superhuman skill is necessary to overcome the obstacles of the plot.

Introducing more than one unbelievable situation or action into your screenplay also eliminates the possibility of any real depth to the characters, or to the theme of your script. Movies allow us to look at ourselves by putting our desires, beliefs, and feelings within bigger-than-life situations, in order to reveal the deeper aspects of our human nature. If the characters you portray do not behave in any recognizable way, the audience feels no emotional connection to them, and has no opportunity for self-examination, enlightenment, or catharsis.

Regardless of the level of fantasy you want to create, logic and believability are still crucial to your screenplay. Your characters must talk and act the way we are accustomed to seeing characters talk and act, and their actions must be consistent with the background and situations you have given them.

The two greatest violations of this principle are: (1) Why don't they get out of the house? and (2) Why don't they call the cops?

Anyone who's ever seen a run-of-the-mill haunted-house or splatter movie understands the first consideration. Most people, when presented with danger, will try to get away. Yet, repeatedly, movies show characters who ignore killings, ghosts, blood seeping from the plumbing, and ominous warnings in order to stay put in an obviously unfriendly house/basement/campground/amusement park/youth hostel/foreign country/back-road farmhouse.

The solution to this dilemma is fairly easy: give the characters some compelling reason why they *cannot* leave. Perhaps they are trapped, as in the *Saw* movies, or the survival of a loved one depends on confronting the evil force, as in *The Ring*. If it's impossible for your hero to flee the danger, then your story will become far more believable.

The second consideration is similar; most people who can't escape from a threat will try to get help. Rather than defying believability by ignoring the issue, make help inaccessible for your character. Communication is cut off (*Panic Room*), the authorities *are* the opponents (*District 9*), the nemesis has threatened the hero's loved one if she tries to get help (*Eagle Eye*), the authorities are powerless (*The Terminator*), or the hero can't go to the authorities because they (perhaps correctly) suspect *him* of being a criminal or killer (*The Da Vinci Code*).

Regardless of the genre of your film, when developing your story, ask yourself repeatedly, "Does this situation clearly fit the limits of the universe I have created?" and, "Given my characters' backgrounds and situations, is it logical and believable that they would behave this way?"

When the answer is no, you must either change the behavior or *make it believable*. And the most effective ways to make incredible behavior believable is to . . .

12. **Foreshadow the major events of the screenplay.** I define foreshadowing as giving greater credibility to a character's actions and abilities by laying the groundwork for them earlier in the screenplay. Foreshadowing is used to make the characters' actions believable, and to prevent contrived solutions to the major obstacles the characters face.

When you create your story, you are giving your hero an objective and then placing in the hero's path obstacles that will make it seemingly impossible to achieve that objective. Obviously, this puts you in a dilemma: if the obstacles are too easy to overcome, there is no dramatic tension or emotion; if the obstacles are too hard, then you must make it believable that your hero can somehow overcome them. Foreshadowing is one solution to this dilemma. By laying in, early in the story, scenes that show the audience how the hero will finally achieve his objective, you give the necessary credibility to the climactic moments of the film.

In Luc Besson and Robert Mark Kamen's script for *Taken*, Bryan Mills must somehow get to Paris, figure out who kidnapped his daughter, penetrate their organization, stop every hired killer who gets in his way, overcome a police cover-up, and rescue her before she is taken out of the country as a sex slave. This seemingly insurmountable series of obstacles makes it seem impossible for their hero to succeed—as it should, so this thriller will sustain the highest possible level of emotional involvement.

The problem for the writers was that doing all these things truly would be impossible for any ordinary person. So they made their hero anything but ordinary—he's a former government agent with, in his words, a very special set of skills. These brilliant and deadly abilities are revealed at the beginning of the film, both through the dialogue with his friends and former coworkers, and through action—when he protects the rock star from a homicidal fan. By the time he gets to Paris and we see him figure out the truth and wipe out an army of bad guys, we believe it, because of what we saw and heard in act one.

If none of this information had been given to the audience until Bryan Mills was in Paris, as soon as he started tracking down his daughter or surviving gun battles with twenty henchmen at a time, the audience would hoot in disgust at how contrived that was. The fact is, it *is* contrived. It's just skillfully contrived, because his skills were foreshadowed well before they became important to the hero achieving his outer motivation.

Foreshadowing can also be subtler, and simply add credibility to a small part of the overall story. In *Seven Pounds*, Ben has to be able to insert himself into people's lives, and know confidential things about them. So screenwriter Grant Nieporte presents him as an IRS agent, which we see almost as soon as Ben is introduced. The entire story isn't built on this premise—he might have obtained the information some other way and the story would still work—but learning about his job early in the film does prevent this hero's abilities from seeming contrived or incredible.

Matt's knowledge of computers in *Live Free or Die Hard*, Robert Langdon's ability to figure out *The Da Vinci Code* because of his knowledge of art history, and Will Turner's swordsmanship in *Pirates of the Caribbean: The Curse of the Black Pearl* are all examples of foreshadowing.

Foreshadowing enables you to avoid *deus ex machina* endings in which the hand of God comes down to save your hero because you couldn't come up with any believable solution. If you sufficiently foreshadow your big resolutions, they will be much more credible and acceptable to the audience.

13. **Echo particular situations, objects, and lines of dialogue to illustrate character growth and change.** Did you ever return to your old high school years after you'd graduated to be reminded of the old days and see how much the place had changed? What you were actually doing was measuring your own growth. High school buildings never change; you're the one who had changed. And comparing yourself to the person you were the last time you saw the high school enabled you to see how far you had come, how much you had lost, or what a different person you were. This basic principle has kept reunion committees busy for decades.

The principle works the same way in movies. You can repeat an object or situation or line of dialogue in your screenplay at regular intervals through the course of the story, and it will illustrate the changes your characters have experienced.

For example, we see the cuckoo clock at least three times in *Out of Africa*; it never changes. But each time it appears, it indicates some new, changed facet of the hero. When Karen unpacks the clock, it symbolizes the home and past she is clinging to in order to withstand the loneliness and isolation of Kenya. When the natives wait for it to cuckoo and then run in fear and surprise, it shows how foreign she seems to them, but also their growing acceptance of her. When she is finally forced to sell it, the clock illustrates how much she is having to give up and the inner strength that she has acquired to replace the outer trappings she clung to in the beginning of the film.

Echoing can also involve recurring situations, as with the "What's in Your Backpack?" lectures in *Up in the Air*, or Lars allowing himself to be touched in *Lars and the Real Girl.* Or a screenplay can echo dialogue, as with the "pickup" encounters between Ray and Claire in *Duplicity*, or the word "magic" in *Sleepless in Seattle*. In each case, the repeated words or images indicate growth or change for the characters.

14. **Teach the audience how to do something, vicariously.** Often a story will be more emotionally involving if the hero must learn some particular skill, which the audience can then "learn" through that character. In *The Karate Kid*, we learn the skills and philosophy of kung fu (or of karate, in the earlier version) just as Dre (or Daniel) does. Similarly, the samurai training in *The Last Samurai*, the romantic coaching in *The Ugly Truth*, and the martial arts instruction in *The Matrix* all serve to involve the audience in those stories.

    Notice that this structural device is closely related to superior position, anticipation, and foreshadowing in that the instruction points to the later events when the knowledge will be used. The reader anticipates the critical attempts to use the skills, and the scenes in which the new skills are used are given greater credibility.

15. **Pose a threat to one of the characters.** Putting any significant character of your film in jeopardy will increase emotional involvement in the story. As long as there is impending danger for one of the characters, the reader will hang in there to see if she gets out okay. This applies not just to suspense thrillers, where the threat is to a character's life, but also to comedies and dramas, where it might be the threat of exposure (*The Proposal*), loss (*Milk*), or failure (*Little Miss Sunshine*).

    This device can work even if the threat is not to the hero. In *2012*, we are emotionally involved in the threat to the two aging musicians on the cruise ship, although they are only secondary characters in the screenplay.

16. Maximize the use of time. There are three key ways to use the time span of the story to elicit the greatest emotion:

▶ *Condense the time span of the story.* Most Hollywood movies take place over very short periods of time—weeks, days, or even hours, rarely years or decades. *Shutter Island, The Hangover, Four Christmases, Live Free or Die Hard, Air Force One*, and *Collateral* all occur over a period of less than two days. This kind of focused, intense storytelling keeps the outer motivation clearly in sight, and keeps the audience deeply involved.

▶ *Announce the time span.* In *My Best Friend's Wedding*, Jules announces, "I've got four days to break up a wedding and steal the bride's fella." In *The Hurt Locker*, we know (thanks to a title card on the screen) that there are thirty-eight days left in Bravo company's rotation. And *(500) Days of Summer* is going to last . . . let's see . . . I'm gonna guess five hundred days. These screenplays all tell the audience, "Don't worry, we're not going to grow old together. This will all be resolved in *this* amount of time."

▶ *Create a ticking clock.* One of the best ways to add conflict for your hero, and emotion to your story, is to give your hero an *impossible time limit*. And if they take a second longer, all will be lost. So in *Panic Room*, Meg Altman doesn't just have to escape from the panic room and the thieves who will kill her, she has to do so in time to get her diabetic daughter her needed glucagon injection. In *Stranger than Fiction*, Harold has to find the author who's created him before she finishes her novel. And in numerous thrillers, such as *The Rock, The Peacemaker*, and almost every James Bond movie ever made, the villain must be stopped or a good portion of the world will be blown to bits.

SUMMARY

1. Structure consists of the events in the plot of a screenplay and their position relative to one another. Proper structure occurs when the right thing happens at the right time to elicit maximum emotion.

2. A properly structured film story has three acts, determined by:

► The screenwriter's goals:

Act 1—establishing setting, character, situation, and the hero's outer motivation

Act 2—building up the hurdles and obstacles to that motivation

Act 3—resolving the hero's outer motivation

► The three distinct segments or stages to the hero's outer motivation

► The necessary quarter-half-quarter proportion for the three acts

3. Two additional elements must be present in Act 1 and Act 3:

► The Setup

The "before" picture of the hero

We see the hero living his everyday life before anything new happens to get the story moving forward

If there is an arc for the hero, we see him emotionally stuck, mired within his inner conflict

► The Aftermath

The "after" picture of the hero

Shows the new life the hero will now live after having resolved the outer motivation

If there is an arc for the hero, we see him rewarded for having overcome his inner conflict (or stuck once again, if he's a tragic figure who failed to overcome it)

4. The opening of your screenplay must seduce the reader in the first ten pages by:

► Transporting readers from the world they occupy into the world you've created, usually employing one of four opening sequences:

Broad to narrow

Narrow to broad

Black screen

Narration

► Using title cards when necessary to establish time and/or location

► Avoiding any mention of the opening credits

► Introducing the hero

► Creating empathy with the hero

► Showing the hero living her everyday life

► Giving a glimpse of the hero's inner conflict

► Presenting the hero with some opportunity by the 10-percent mark

► Taking the hero into some new situation with this opportunity

5. There are at least seven types of setups you can employ, alone or in combination, to open your screenplay:

- ► The action hero introduction
- ► The everyday hero introduction
- ► The new arrival
- ► Outside action
- ► The prologue
- ► The flashback
- ► Bookends

6. An effective ending to your screenplay will include:

- ► A satisfying climax that clearly resolves the hero's outer motivation
- ► An aftermath revealing the new life the hero will now live

7. As you define the three acts to the screenplay, including the setup, opportunity, climax, and aftermath, you will begin employing the more specific structural principles and devices for maximizing emotion:

- ► Ensure that every scene, event, and character in the screenplay contributes to the hero's outer motivation
- ► Early in your screenplay, show the audience where the story is headed
- ► Build the conflict by making each successive hurdle and obstacle for your hero greater and more provocative than the previous one
- ► Accelerate the pace of the story by providing the exposition early in the screenplay, then having the obstacles come up more frequently as the story moves forward

► Create peaks and valleys to the action and the humor, so that high emotional moments in your screenplay are followed by scenes with less impact

► Give the story both humor and seriousness

► Create anticipation in the reader

► Give the audience superior position

► Surprise the audience and occasionally reverse the anticipation

► Create curiosity in the reader

► Make the story credible by:

> Limiting yourself to a single fantasy element

> Making the story internally logical

> Clearly defining the limits to the characters' abilities

► Foreshadow the major events of the screenplay

► Echo particular situations, objects, and lines of dialogue to illustrate character growth and change

► Teach the audience how to do something, vicariously

► Pose a threat to one of the characters

► Maximize the use of time by:

> Condensing the time span of the story

> Announcing the time span

> Creating a ticking clock

PART TWO

WRITING THE
SCREENPLAY

SIX

SCENE WRITING

AT THIS STAGE IN THE DEVELOPMENT OF YOUR SCREENPLAY, YOU ARE ready to write the individual scenes in proper screenplay format. The way you put the words on the page is as essential to eliciting emotion as are concept, character, and structure. And just as those three previous tasks involved specific methods for seducing and holding the reader and the audience, so are there underlying principles for writing action, description, and dialogue in a way that ensures the reader's emotional involvement.

THE BASIC PRINCIPLES OF WRITING SCENES

These are the overall rules and guidelines for putting the words on the page and eliciting maximum emotion with your screenwriting style:

1. **You must create a movie in the mind of the reader.** If you have ever become so engrossed in a novel that you lost all sense of time and place in the real world, you know exactly the emotional experience you hope to create for the person reading your screenplay. Anything that slows the reader down or calls attention to the words themselves, such as awkward and confusing style, incorrect spelling and grammar, typographical errors, or a script that is twenty pages too long, works against you.

Conversely, whatever you can do to make reading your screenplay *fast*, *easy*, and *enjoyable* is to your benefit. If there is a single quality that distinguishes screenplays that sell from those that don't, it's this: *the people with the power to make movies choose the scripts that they enjoy reading.* When you crystallize your movie in the mind of the reader, that enjoyment is far more likely.

2. **Nothing goes on the page that doesn't go on the screen.** Screenplays are made up of action, description, and dialogue. That's all. Nothing can be included that can't be conveyed to an audience. There can be no author's asides, illustrations, interior thoughts of the characters (unless they are verbalized on the screen), or background information that isn't dramatized.

With each scene, ask yourself, "How will the *audience* know what I've just told the reader?"

3. **There are three uses for any screenplay.** A screenplay can serve as a *proposal* for a movie you hope to get made (what we will call your submission script), a *blueprint* of a movie that is being made (in other words, the shooting script), and a *record* of a film that has already been shot (for postproduction use by editors, composers, and the like). The only one of these three functions that concerns you is the submission script.

At this stage in the writing process, your only objectives are selling your script and using it as a writing sample. Some of the conventions of a shooting script are therefore unnecessary for your submission script and actually slow down the reading process, thus violating principle #1 above. Numbered scenes, capitalized sound effects, and the word *continued* at the bottom of most pages are all shooting script devices that should be eliminated from your submission script.

Don't worry that your screenplay might sell and then you'll have to know how to write a shooting script; any good formatting program will transform your submission script into a shooting script with a single menu selection.

4. **There must be nothing in the script that you know can be improved.** When you finally begin submitting your screenplay, you are submitting it as a professional to other professionals. It must be as close to perfection as you can get it.

It's not the job of a potential producer or agent to tell you how to fix your submitted script. If you haven't done everything you possibly can to make your screenplay the best it can be, then it isn't ready to show.

Once I got a call from a screenwriter in Columbus who was a friend of a friend of a friend of my brother and who wanted to submit a screenplay to the production company where I was head of development. This writer obviously understood the value of networking, and I was ready to take a look at his script until I asked him how long it was. "It's 145 pages," he replied. "I wanted to get your input before editing it any further." So I told him not to send it. I knew the producer I worked for could never get a deal to produce a screenplay that long, so there was no point in even considering it until the writer had done all he possibly could to make it commercial.

Of course, if he had approached me as a *consultant*, it would be a different story; I often work with writers to help them get their screenplays down to a marketable 115 pages. But agents and producers and executives won't do your work for you. And since you often will have only one shot at a potential buyer, make sure your screenplay is as good as you can get it.

Similarly, don't leave anything undone because you figure someone's going to change your script eventually anyway. Leaving out dialogue for the actors to improvise or letting the art directors and special effects artists determine how the film will look is a huge mistake. You must write your screenplay as if every single moment of the film is your responsibility.

5. **Improper format reduces the reader's emotional involvement.** Readers in Hollywood do a great deal of inductive reasoning that goes something like this: "I just read ninety-nine screenplays, they were all horrible, and they were all written in improper format. Therefore, if screenplay number one hundred is also in improper format, it must be horrible too."

This conclusion isn't necessarily true; a great screenplay could conceivably be handwritten on a roll of paper towels. But it's tough enough to get an agent or producer emotionally involved in your script. Why start out with that extra strike against you? Put the screenplay in current acceptable format. With the superb formatting programs available to you, there's simply no excuse for an unprofessional presentation.

The rest of this chapter will show you exactly *how* to write description, action, and dialogue in a style and format that adheres to the five principles listed above and which elicits maximum emotion in your reader.

SCREENPLAY FORMAT

When I originally wrote this book, the only way to properly format a script was by setting the tabs on your word processing program, or even on your typewriter (!) and remembering to indent and shift into ALL CAPS when it was appropriate. So in that first edition, I thoroughly presented all the rules for formatting action and description and dialogue and scene headings and character introductions and parenthetical descriptions and voice-over narration and so on and so on.

Now I have reduced all that information to a single, essential rule: *buy a formatting program.*

Several outstanding programs that will take care of all your margins and spacing and capitalization and a whole lot more are available for less than $200. Consider it a necessary investment in your screenwriting career.

Final Draft and *Movie Magic Screenwriter* set the industry standard, and are by far the most widely used in Hollywood at the time I'm writing this. Both are terrific—thorough, easy to use, and loaded with extras. Recent editions of *Movie Magic Screenwriter* include a template I created just for that program, designed to guide you through the principles of structure and character development as you write your screenplay. But deciding which program will serve you best is ultimately a matter of personal preference. Each one offers a free trial, so I advise playing with both and picking the one that's the best fit for you.

If you're on a budget, or just starting out and not yet certain if you're going to make screenwriting a career, Open Office (OpenOffice.org) offers Screenwright®, a free formatting program created by Anikó J. Bartos & Alan C. Baird.

For any formatting questions not addressed by your formatting program, I highly recommend David Trottier's books *The Screenwriter's Bible* and *Dr. Format Answers Your Questions.*

DESCRIPTION

Original, clever, funny, provocative, vivid, and colorful descriptions add to the reader's emotional involvement by bringing the images into sharper focus and making your script more fun to read.

Some writers and script consultants proclaim that description slows readers down, and that a script should essentially be limited to action, dialogue, and simply naming a location or character. Certainly clear, concise writing is the goal, not long passages of endless prose. But I still contend that two or three words or phrases that crystallize the image of the character or setting increase a reader's involvement in, and understanding of, your story.

The element common to all good descriptive writing is *detail*. The particulars of appearance, attire, decor, attitude, and manner that convey the essence and the uniqueness of a character or setting are the ones to employ. For example, "an aging, dusty Underwood" is a lot more vivid than simply "a typewriter," and "his sleek, newly polished Porsche" creates a more involving image than just "his car."

When introducing characters into your screenplay, instead of resorting to mere physical description, describe such things as clothing, hairstyle, movement, surroundings, or physical details (scars, deformities, body language, or facial expressions instead of overall physical appearance).

Effective description need not be lengthy. In *Body Heat*, Lawrence Kasdan gives the following description of the man who provides Ned Racine with a bomb:

    TEDDY LAURSEN, rock-and-roll arsonist ...

Those four descriptive words are a provocative, clever description of the character that creates a sufficiently vivid image for the movie in the reader's mind. It's fun to read, and it conveys the essence of the character without limiting casting possibilities.

Occasionally, of course, you will *have to* provide a detailed physical description of a character, because the character's appearance is essential to the plot. *District 9, Borat: Cultural Learnings of America for Make Benefit Glorious Nation of Kazakhstan*, and *The Curious Case of Benjamin Button* all portray characters whose physical appearance affects the plot, and in these circumstances detailed physical descriptions are appropriate.

In writing character description, you can cheat a bit on the rule that nothing can go on the page that doesn't go on the screen. It is okay to make *limited* reference to a character's background as part of the description. For example, you might say:

    Earl's every movement projects the ten years he's
    spent pumping iron.

It's impossible to put "ten years" of "pumping iron" on the screen, but the vivid image created might be worth the gamble in your script.

Just don't go overboard and replace character description with a biography.

ACTION

Your primary goal in writing action is *clarity*. You must convey to the reader exactly what is happening on the screen, so that there is no confusion, misunderstanding, or need for the reader to reread the passage.

1. **Use everyday, straightforward language.** Your script should be comprehensible at a high school reading level. This will make it easy to read your script and will steer you away from convoluted words and phrases, excessive technical jargon, and an impressive but tedious vocabulary.

2. **Use action words.** Don't let your writing become static. There are at least twenty-five ways to say "go" in the English language. A character can walk, run, crawl, fly, leap, hurtle, dart, skip, or shuffle down the street. Bring the action to life by letting the specific words convey the movement.

3. **Give your action scenes to someone to read.** It's the only way to verify whether you've achieved the necessary degree of clarity. Ask the reader to tell you what happened in the scene. If the reader misses or confuses any important detail, go back to the computer.

Certain sequences must be omitted entirely from your screenplay. As stated in chapter 5, avoid writing when and how the title or credit sequences will occur. Even though some films employ emotionally gripping opening credits, *reading* about them dissipates the emotion at the very moment you're trying to seduce your reader. Skip the credits altogether and go right into the action of your story.

The words *special effects* should also be eliminated from the script. Your job is to describe exactly what happens on the screen. Let the filmmakers figure out when to call Industrial Light & Magic. If your script contains a thrilling space battle, a hallucination, or a terrifying creature from another dimension, then simply describe it in detail, creating as vivid a mental image as you can. It will be someone else's job to create the image on film.

The same principle holds true for action sequences such as car chases or lovemaking scenes. You must describe the action on the screen in specific detail. Don't simply say,

```
They jump into their cars and there's a terrific
chase.
```

That sentence creates almost no clear image or emotion. Rather, describe exactly what is going on in the scene:

```
As the black limousine comes racing toward Jimmie,
he leaps onto the sideboard of a passing ice cream
wagon. Opening the door of the moving truck, he
pushes the startled driver off the seat and guns
the accelerator.

The limousine fishtails toward Jimmie and the
truck, sideswiping a light pole and narrowly
missing a young girl on her tricycle.

Soon the limo is bearing down on Jimmie's truck at
close to 90 miles an hour as he thunders toward an
irrigation ditch ...
```

Remember the rule about one page equaling one minute of screen time. That means that a car chase that you anticipate lasting five minutes on the screen will be close to four or five pages long. That would be a very lengthy scene, requiring some terrific writing. (If this rule prevents you from putting long car chases into your screenplay, then I've done my part to improve civilization.)

Similarly, when writing lovemaking scenes, you can't just say:

```
They look longingly into each other's eyes, and then
they DO IT.
```

You must say exactly what's going on in detail. You don't have to get pornographic (although that would certainly brighten the days of lots of readers in Hollywood), but you do need to create clear images in the reader's mind.

An excellent example of this kind of detail is Lawrence Kasdan's screenplay for *Body Heat*. Consider the following scene, where Ned Racine breaks through the window and makes love with Matty Walker for the first time:

```
INT. HALL

Racine crosses the dark living room fast. As he
reaches Matty, she lifts her arms to match his
embrace. They come together hard and tight. They
kiss. And kiss again. Her hands travel over his body,
as though she's wanted them there for a long time.

They turn once slowly along the wall, into the
dimness of the central hall. Then he rotates her body
away from him, holding her close. For an instant he
looks down her body from over her shoulder, then he
puts his hands where only his eyes have gone—slowly,
gently, then more desperately—first barely touching,
then firmly palming her.
```

```
                    MATTY
        Yes, yes ...
```

```
Then she is just nodding. Racine puts his face deep
into her hair, closing his eyes as the smell of her
washes over him.
```

Matty turns in his arms and kisses him hard. She moves back a step and her hands are tearing at his shirt, fumbling with the buttons. Their hands are shaking badly. She parts his shirt and kisses his chest as her hands move down to work at his belt.

Racine's hands are moving up the backs of her thighs, pushing her skirt up ahead of them, lifting it out of the way ...

Matty is moaning, whimpering into his neck. Her hands down below, working on him. Sweat covers her forehead. She drops down to the floor and pulls him down with her. He is on his knees before her as she lifts her hips and bunches her skirt up around her waist.

> RACINE
> That's right ... that's right!

Close on Matty's face, a look that might be anguish. She bites her lip in impatience, expectation, heat. Racine's face, shiny with sweat. His eyes move down her.

Racine's hand appears in the light and Matty's silken panties slide off his fingers, into the corner. Racine moves over her.

> MATTY
> Do it ... Please, please ... Yes! Do it.

She pulls him tightly to her, clinging like a drowning woman.

Bet you didn't expect to read that in some old textbook, did you? Lawrence Kasdan was once quoted as saying that he wanted people *reading* the script of *Body Heat* to get turned on. If nothing else, that exhibits a great understanding of the principle of eliciting emotion in the reader.

Notice how much detail he gives to the action, while using simple, clear language and never resorting to four-letter words. The passage creates a vivid mental image but leaves much to the reader's imagination, never lapsing into vulgarity or repetition.

Of course, if you're going for a PG-13 rating, you'll dissolve away before the heavy stuff anyway. The point is that with any kind of action, thoroughly describe exactly what the audience will see, in a way that is as emotionally provocative and enjoyable as possible.

MUSIC

Music can occur in a variety of ways in a movie, each requiring slightly different handling within your screenplay:

1. **The score.** This is the background music that the audience hears, but not the characters in the film. *Omit the score from your screenplay entirely.* No matter how much emotion is created and enhanced by the score of a movie, *reading* about music is a drag. The rule is: if the characters in your film can't hear the music, make no mention of it in your script.

2. **Music played or sung by a character in the movie.** If someone puts on a record, sits down at the piano, or plays some familiar song on the jukebox, that is part of your story, and it is therefore your job to include it. For example, in a key scene from *(500) Days of Summer*, the two lovers sing at a karaoke bar. That scene, with the particular songs identified, would have to be written into the script.

   There are several pitfalls to watch out for when you name an existing piece of music. The first is that the reader won't recognize it. Don't assume a reader will recognize *any* tune besides "Happy

Birthday to You" and "The Star-Spangled Banner." Precede or follow the name of any song with a phrase describing it:

```
The lilting strains of Beethoven's "Moonlight
Sonata" drift up to her balcony.
```

Another danger of using existing music within the story is that the rights to use a particular song may be costly. You don't want the reader to assume the music rights will double the budget of the film.

3. **Original music written by one of your characters.** Occasionally your screenplay will involve a character who writes original music. In this case, since it is part of the plot and will be heard by the other characters, you must describe it.

It is best to simply describe the kind of song being sung or played by the character, along with the reactions of the characters who are listening to it. Do not include the lyrics to these songs! Reading lyrics in a screenplay is like reading poetry; the language is read in a different way and at a different pace, and the adjustment can be jarring. As a result, readers will just skip over your lyrics anyway and go on with the story. But by then, they have already left the mental movie you are creating.

The one time you might want to include some lyrics is when the meaning of the song advances the plot of your film. For example, of all the songs in *Crazy Heart*, the crucial one is "The Weary Kind" by Ryan Bingham and T-Bone Burnett, in the scene where Bad Blake begins composing it on Jean's bed, and later when Tommy Sweet sings it in front of a big audience while Bad watches from backstage. Included in the lyrics are the lines:

Your body aches . . .
Playing your guitar and sweating out the hate

The days and the nights all feel the same
Whiskey has been a thorn in your side
and it doesn't forget
the highway that calls for your heart inside
And this ain't no place for the weary kind

Since the lyrics themselves move the plot forward by showing that for the first time Bad is opening up to Jean about his own life, writer/director Scott Cooper includes them in his screenplay. Here's how that part of the scene actually reads in the screenplay:

```
For a bit, Bad just plays. He moves from harmonic
to melodic and back, responding to signals he's not
conscious of. It's as though his fingers have taken
charge and all he needs to do, must do, is listen to
what they are doing.

                    BAD
          Your heart's on the loose
          You rolled them sevens with
          nothing to lose ...
          This ain't the place ... for the
          weary kind ...

Jean peeks her head in.
```

Of course, this is the shooting script, so the song lyrics were probably added to the script after they began production. But it's still a great example of how just a few lyrics will convey the emotion of a song without turning into some long passage of poetry.

After including just a few lines of your original song, say in your script that the character continues singing, and describe the reactions of whoever is listening. And whatever you do, don't enclose a CD of you singing these original songs.

PLAYING DIRECTOR

I know some of you reading this intend to direct some day. And even if you don't, the temptation to insert every cut and camera movement into your screenplay can be overwhelming. Trying to convey your artistic vision for every aspect of your film in this way is a huge mistake. But there are a couple methods you can use to get the reader to envision specific shots and edits without your having to resort to camera directions or a tiresome (and unprofessional) stream of close-ups, camera angles, and cuts.

Our minds only imagine what we're being told to imagine at that moment. So to create a close-up in the mind of the reader, *simply describe in detail the object the camera would move in on.*

Suppose you want to keep a killer's identity unrevealed. Instead of writing

```
CLOSE-UP on a gloved hand as it picks up the letter
opener and plunges it into the politician's back.
```

Simply omit the words *CLOSE-UP on*:

```
A gloved hand picks up the letter opener and
plunges it into the politician's back.
```

I bet that as you read that last sentence, you pictured a "close-up" of the hand and the dagger, didn't you?

As for "editing" the film of your screenplay, I got this next idea from Björn Carlström, a producer, writer, and director in Stockholm, Sweden. It's a great trick for pacing your scenes, and for avoiding the temptation to fill your script with a lot of cuts and directorial techniques that have no place in your screenplay.

When you're writing an action sequence that has no dialogue—a silent meal, a lovemaking scene, a search, a fight, a car chase—write the first draft of the scene in one single, unbroken paragraph.

Then, when you rewrite the sequence, imagine where, if you were directing or editing the film, you'd put the cuts. In other words, where would you change camera shots within the overall scene?

Every place you'd cut the film, begin a new paragraph. If you do this, the pace of your scene will match that of the movie. So a car chase made up of lots of cuts will consist of a lot of very short paragraphs—sometimes only one or two words long—and the reader will get through the page very quickly. A romantic scene will have fewer cuts, the paragraphs will be longer, and the pace will be slower.

Using this device throughout the entire script also ensures that your screenplay conforms to the one page = one minute formula.

If you don't believe me, check it out. Read a script for an exciting, fast-paced action film, another for a comedy, and another for a drama or love story. Notice the lengths of the paragraphs, and how the differences in style affect the pace and tone of the screenplays.

DIALOGUE

When it's time to write dialogue, you will usually find yourself in one of two situations:

In the first, you begin by writing the scene heading, and open the scene with description and action. Then you figure out who should speak first, write that character's name, and give that first character a line of dialogue. Another character will respond to the first, the first character will answer back or provide another statement or question, the conversation will begin to flow, and soon the characters will seem to be writing their own dialogue.

When this effortless creativity arises, nurture it. *Don't edit as you go.* In other words, when dialogue (or any other aspect of your writing) starts to flow, you are tapping directly into your creative source. You want to facilitate that process as much as possible, so don't stop to decide whether the dialogue is good or not. If you start to engage your critical, judgmental faculties, you will stifle the creativity you've been striving for.

Instead, let the words come, even if they seem awful or irrelevant and even if your three-minute scene gets to be twenty pages long. You can always go back and edit it to meet the overall needs of the script. But when you're in touch with your characters to this extent, they may reveal ideas to you that will take the scene, or the story, in a new and even better direction.

On the other hand, don't *wait* for that glorious burst of creativity to happen. As you probably know, you will far more often find yourself in the second situation:

You write the scene heading, you follow it with some description and action, then you write a character's name, stare at the blank page, and say to yourself, "What in the hell are these people going to say?"

When you simply can't come up with any dialogue, the greatest danger you face is writer's block. For some reason, dialogue can be more frightening than any other aspect of your screenplay. It's easy to allow your anxiety to crush your creativity, and to start sneaking to the refrigerator rather than writing your screenplay.

To prevent writer's block while writing dialogue, you first must realize that what your characters say is *not* the most important part of your script. Dialogue is far less important than character development or plot structure, and any skilled filmmaker knows that dialogue is the easiest thing to change in a screenplay.

This doesn't mean that good dialogue can't help sell your screenplay and even cover up a weakly structured story. You certainly don't want your speeches to be boring or idiotic. But all dialogue doesn't need to sound as if Aaron Sorkin or Quentin Tarantino wrote it, and sometimes "clever" dialogue isn't even appropriate. Your primary goal is for the dialogue to contribute to the overall thrust of the story and to the desired character development.

So if you're close to getting blocked, let go of your fear and go through the following steps. These should enable you to create effective dialogue for any scene in your screenplay.

Begin by asking the following questions about the scene, before attempting any dialogue at all:

1. **What is my objective within this scene?** This is the most important consideration, because this will link the scene to the spine of your story and ensure that the scene contributes to the outer motivation for your hero. You must know the purpose the scene serves within the context of the story. No matter how funny, dramatic, or original your dialogue may be, if the scene doesn't contribute to your hero's outer motivation, you've got to change the scene or get rid of it altogether.

2. **How will the scene end? After deciding on your objective as described in question #1, decide on the outcome of the scene.** Almost all scenes should end with the individual issue in the scene resolved but with some element left unresolved that will compel the reader to turn the page (and the audience to stay tuned). In the scene in *Hitch* where Hitch first meets Albert Brennaman, the issue to be resolved is whether Hitch will take Albert on as a client. That issue is resolved at the end of the scene. But now we want to see how Hitch can possibly help this poor schlub win the heart of the rich, beautiful, and impossible-to-get Allegra Cole.

3. **What is each character's objective within the scene?** Every character in every scene in your screenplay must *want* something. This desire will determine the character's actions and dialogue. In the scene from *Hitch* described above, Albert's goal is to get Hitch to help him, and Hitch's is to find out about Albert and decide whether to do so. Other than some physical comedy involving Albert's lunch, and then a quick flashback to him giving Allegra Cole a pen, the scene is essentially all dialogue—and all of it moves those two characters closer to achieving their goals.

   If possible, put the characters' objectives in the scene in opposition. Emotion grows out of conflict, so whenever a scene involves two characters at cross-purposes, the emotion rises. The *Hitch* scene is written so that it seems like Hitch won't be willing to take Albert on as a client. That's certainly what Albert thinks. This adds an element of conflict to a scene that is already funny, touching, and moves the story forward.

4. **What is each character's attitude within the scene?** How does each character feel about what is going on? Often a character's attitude will remain hidden from the reader, but as the screenwriter, you must know your characters' true feelings at all times.

In the dinner sequence early in *Little Miss Sunshine*, each character has a very pointed attitude about the others. Richard is superior and patronizing, Grandpa is loud and critical, Olive is curious, Dwayne is so angry he doesn't speak at all, Sheryl is frustrated as she tries to keep the peace, and suicidal Frank hears everyone with some astonishment as he becomes increasingly resentful of Richard. As the story progresses, we will learn what is at the root of all these attitudes, but each character's feelings are clear from the hilarious dialogue.

5. **How will the scene begin?** How are you going to get your characters into the situation you're creating? In *L.A. Confidential*, the overall objective of the dialogue-heavy scene where Bud White first questions Lynn is to provide more information for the murder mystery, and more important, to begin their romantic relationship.

Writers Brian Helgeland and Curtis Hanson could have simply opened the scene with Bud White beginning his interrogation. But instead they wisely began before his arrival, as Lynn is saying good-bye to one of her johns. Officer White knocks on the door, has a brief confrontation with the john before putting him in his place, then enters and begins his questions.

The action and dialogue of this opening offer a lot of subtle exposition without any "announcing" speeches. Lynn is obviously a hooker (the man is only half-dressed); Bud White has no fear of wealth or position (he tells the john, "LAPD, shitbird. Get out of here or I'll call your wife to come get you."); the city is corrupt (as the john leaves, he says, "Officer," and White responds, "Councilman.”); and Lynn's silent but amused reaction to this encounter shows she's immediately taken with this cop. And all of this occurs before the crux of the scene—the interrogation—even begins.

How do the above questions work when applied to an original scene?

Let's say we want to create dialogue for a romantic comedy involving a two-character job interview. Frank, an advertising executive, is interviewing Janice, our hero, for the job of secretary. This provides a typical two-character situation that will rely heavily on dialogue.

Let's say that Janice wants this job because her sister Bonnie got fired from the same position after Frank made a pass at her and she wouldn't play along. Now Janice wants to get revenge on this sexist pig by nailing Frank when he tries the same thing with her.

Given that story line, how would we answer each of the above questions before attempting to write any dialogue?

1. **What is my objective within this scene?** To get Janice working for Frank. This will contribute to the hero's overall outer motivation of getting Frank fired or humiliated.

2. **How will the scene end?** To accomplish the above objective, the scene will have to end with Frank offering the job to Janice and Janice accepting.

3. **What is each character's objective within the scene?** Janice wants to get the job. Frank wants to decide whether to hire her.

4. **What is each character's attitude within the scene?** A person can have any number of feelings in a job interview: fear; trepidation; confidence; curiosity; resentment. But from the story we've outlined, Janice's attitude and feelings must include anger, determination, and duplicity.

   Frank's attitude, given what we know about his past behavior, will probably include curiosity, lust, and anticipation.

5. **How will the scene begin?** A logical opening might show Frank dismissing the previous applicant, whose age, sex, and appearance are obviously not to his liking, and then calling for the next secretarial candidate, Janice.

Now that you have the answers to all of the questions, you give your characters what is known as *on-the-nose* dialogue, where they say exactly what they think, feel, and mean. In other words, bad dialogue. *Nobody* says exactly what she thinks or feels or means. We all hide our true intentions, feelings, and desires, gradually tap-dancing our way up to what we really want. If you don't believe me, think back to the last time you were angry with a friend, bought a car, or asked someone out on a date.

But I am saying you *should* give your characters this bad, on-the-nose dialogue. Because when the process started, you had no idea what the characters would say and you were in danger of getting blocked. At least with on-the-nose dialogue you'll have a scene. From then on, you can tell yourself it's all editing, which is psychologically much easier than creating dialogue on a blank page.

So in this example, the on-the-nose dialogue would be as follows:

> JANICE
> I really want this job, Frank, be-
> cause I'm angry about what you did to
> my sister, and I want to get revenge
> for her.

> FRANK
> Since I'm attracted to you, I'm going
> to give you the job, and hope you'll
> be more cooperative than my previous
> secretary was.

Awful, isn't it? But now we at least have something to fall back on. From now on, we're simply rewriting.

Now we return to the original list of questions and develop the scene from the opening we chose in question #5 above, this time allowing the characters to lead up to the on-the-nose dialogue, which will serve as the turning point of the scene. We'll assume that in the previous scene, Janice outlined her plan to Bonnie, so the reader already knows these characters and their true desires.

```
INT. FRANK'S OFFICE—DAY

Frank is sitting at his desk, interviewing an
unattractive woman.

                    FRANK
          Well thank you, Miss Klunk. We'll
          call you when we've made our final
          decision. Just leave your résumé with
          the receptionist.

Miss Klunk leaves, and Frank speaks into his
intercom.
                    FRANK
          Gladys, could you send in the next
          applicant, please?

Janice walks into Frank's office, looking beautiful.
Frank looks excited. He looks at her résumé.

                    FRANK
          Please have a seat, Miss Johnston. Could
          you tell me a little about yourself?

                    JANICE
          Well, I've had eleven years of office
          experience, I was previously an
          executive secretary for the CEO of
          Moclips, Incorporated, and I type 80
          words per minute.
```

```
                    FRANK
        That's quite impressive. How soon
        would you be able to start?


                    JANICE
        I'm available immediately.


                    FRANK
        Wonderful. Be here Monday at 9:00.
        You've got the job.
```

It's still pretty bad, with stilted dialogue, awkward wording, and no emotion at all. But we've accomplished our primary objective (getting Janice the job), each character's individual objective is clear, and the dialogue is consistent with the attitudes of each character, even though the characters keep their feelings from each other.

Notice that we have thrown out that on-the-nose dialogue. It was only to get us rolling and to pinpoint the moment where the hero's primary desire could be revealed.

Our goal now is to go back and accomplish some more refined goals for the scene:

► Create more interesting, vivid description and action.

► Add humor to the scene (if the scene is supposed to be funny, as in the example).

► Reveal more of the inner motivations and attitudes of the characters.

► Create a few more obstacles for the hero (Janice).

► Make the dialogue more consistent with the speech patterns of the characters. If Janice and Frank are from the Fortune 500 crowd, they will exhibit distinctly different vocabulary and syntax than if they are junior high school students, soldiers, or art history professors.

Given these considerations, the next rewrite might look like this:

INT. FRANK'S OFFICE—DAY

Frank is sitting at his desk, interviewing a middle-aged WOMAN. It is clear from the glazed-over look in Frank's eyes and the forced smile sewn onto his face that this isn't his first interview of the day. And since this applicant has the face of Mrs. Potato Head, it's pretty clear she's not going to get the nod from Frank either.

> FRANK
> Well, thank you for coming in. We'll call you when we've made our final decision.

The woman leaves, and Frank speaks into his intercom.

> FRANK
> Any more out there? An earthling this time, maybe?

Janice walks into Frank's office, and Frank almost slides out of his chair. If *Maxim* did an issue on secretaries, she'd be in it.

> FRANK
> Well, let's see here, Ms. ...

> JANICE
> Johnston. But you can call me Janice.

Her voice has gotten breathy, and her eyelashes
lower seductively as she leans toward Frank's desk.

> FRANK
> Well, Janice, I see that for the last
> four years you've been director of
> marketing at Moclips, Incorporated.

> JANICE
> I'm sure anyone there will vouch for me.

A trace of suspicion enters Frank's voice. Maybe
this woman is too good to be true.

> FRANK
> You know, you'd just be my personal
> secretary. Don't you think maybe
> you're a bit overqualified?

A slight look of panic flashes over Janice's face,
but she catches it in time.

> JANICE
> Well, Frank ... can I call you Frank?
> That position was fine, but I find I
> am really happiest working under a
> powerful man.

She's laying it on thick now, and we can tell it's
grating on her, but she's determined to reel this
guy in. Frank, who seems just short of panting out
loud, decides to test the waters.

> FRANK
> Well, I can certainly understand your
> feeling that way. But this job isn't
> easy. For instance, there could be a

> lot of late hours. You know, the two
> of us, working closely together ... at
> night.
>
> JANICE
> That would be fine. I'm usually at my
> best at night.
>
> Frank stands, and barely resists leaping over the
> desk.
>
> FRANK
> It's settled then. You can start Monday.
>
> Janice rises and gives him a lingering handshake.
>
> JANICE
> I can hardly wait.

Not exactly Woody Allen, but it's reading a lot better than it was.

At this point, if you're going full steam ahead and *want* to do a re-write of the scene, go ahead. Otherwise, leave the scene and go on with the rest of your script.

By the time you complete this first draft, you will be much more familiar with your plot and characters. So when you return to this scene on your second draft, you'll be able to make it more consistent with whatever new directions your plot and characters might be taking.

With each successive draft, concentrate on accomplishing more with the scene, making it more consistent with your plot and characters, and improving the writing style. If there is an opportunity to employ some added structural devices, then do so: reveal more about inner motivation, conflict, character background, or theme; strengthen character identification; or add the appropriate humor, action, and conflict.

Then, after sharpening all of those qualities, start cutting. Lose any unnecessary, wordy, or repetitive dialogue you can, without losing the emotional power of the scene. The most important considerations for your dialogue are that it contribute to the overall thrust of your story, that it be true to your characters, and that it sound "real." The above process should accomplish all of that.

A SCENE-BY-SCENE CHECKLIST

The following checklist can now be applied to each scene in your screenplay to ensure that the scene is as effective as possible.

Use this list *after* you have completed your first draft. Although you will have these principles in mind as soon as you begin the writing process, it is helpful to have new tools to employ with successive rewrites. The longer you have been working on a screenplay, the more likely you are to lose your critical objectivity, to feel frustrated, foggy, or burned out, and to begin settling for scenes that aren't eliciting maximum emotion. Approaching your screenplay in new ways can help you figure out additional improvements.

1. **How does the scene contribute to the hero's outer motivation?** Even when a scene doesn't involve the hero, it can contribute to the spine of the story. In *The Illusionist*, the scenes between Inspector Uhl and the Crown Prince don't include Eisenheim, the hero. But they contribute to Eisenheim's outer motivation and determine his later actions nonetheless, because each creates additional conflict he will have to overcome as he pursues his goal of rescuing, and then avenging, Sophie.

2. **Does the scene have its own beginning, middle, and end?** Each scene in your screenplay is like a mini-movie: it must establish, build, and resolve a situation. The scene doesn't necessarily follow the quarter-half-quarter layout of the full script, but it must employ that same basic emotional arc.

    In Scott Neustadter and Michael H. Weber's screenplay *(500) Days of Summer*, a key scene is established when Tom and Summer walk their drunken coworker McKenzie to the cab. The scene then builds when McKenzie tells Summer that Tom likes her, and she asks Tom if that's true. It resolves when Tom tells her yes, but as a friend, and they go their opposite ways home.

Occasionally you may purposely break this beginning-middle-end rule in order to keep an audience curious and emotionally involved. Let's say you have a scene in which a babysitter goes into the house where a killer is lurking. We follow the babysitter into one room after another, until she hears a sound coming from behind a closet door. We see her open the door and let out a scream, a look of terror on her face.

The screenplay then cuts away to another scene and *later* reveals the babysitter's dead body. By cutting away, we end that first scene in the middle, with no resolution. The resolution (her murder) is then revealed in the later scene, and in the meantime, the audience's emotion has been heightened through curiosity and anticipation.

Even though this can be an effective approach, don't overdo it; once or twice in a script is plenty.

3. **Does the scene thrust the reader into the following scenes?** At the end of each scene, you must compel the reader to turn the page; any time a reader doesn't care about what happens next, your screenplay has failed. So each scene must have the reader wanting more.

4. **What is each character's objective in the scene?** *Every* character in every scene wants something. It may be as simple as observing what's going on or spending time with another person, but whatever it is, that visible objective must be clear in each scene.

5. **What is each character's attitude in the scene?** Every character in every scene *feels* a certain way about what's going on. Whether happy, sad, angry, bored, scared, uninterested, or turned on, everybody has an attitude about the action.

While the characters' visible objectives will always be revealed (or at least one of them will, even if they are hiding others), their attitudes may not be apparent to the audience or reader. But as the writer, *you* must know how your characters feel.

6. **Does the scene contain action, and not just dialogue?** When you create a scene that revolves around what the characters say, rather than what they do, it should serve as a danger signal to you as the writer. Obviously, some scenes in any film will be primarily dialogue. But if the majority of scenes fall into that category, you're in trouble.

Here's an effective trick: imagine the movie of your screenplay with the soundtrack turned off. Ask yourself if an audience would still understand the characters' motivations, the conflict, the resolutions, and the relationships among the characters. If the honest answer is no, your screenplay is talk-heavy, and you have to focus on more action or find a more action-oriented story concept.

Even in movies that contain a great deal of dialogue, such as *Notting Hill*, *A Few Good Men*, or *Up in the Air*, watching only the action will clearly reveal who the primary characters are, their desires and conflicts, and how the stories are resolved. The films might no longer be particularly entertaining, but the thrust of the story will be clear for each.

7. **Does the scene serve multiple functions?** Does the scene do as much as possible to keep the audience emotionally involved? The following could all be included in a single scene: character background, inner motivation, inner conflict and identification; theme; humor; exposition; and any number of structural devices (superior position, anticipation, surprise, foreshadowing, echoing, and so on).

Some scenes should contain nothing but action. When Sam Baldwin is racing to New York to find Jonah in Jeff Arch and Nora Ephron's *Sleepless in Seattle* script, it would be detrimental to the emotion, and ludicrous as well, to have Sam stop the cab to begin telling the driver about his inner conflict. When the emotion is high from the action alone, don't burden the scene with added objectives.

It is in those scenes eliciting a *lower* level of emotion—where the visible conflict is not as great—that these other objectives are usually accomplished. Consider the earlier scene in *Sleepless in Seattle*, when Sam is talking to the radio psychologist, alternating with shots of Annie Reed listening to him on the radio. The sequence contains little action, and the adrenaline is not particularly high. But these intercut scenes contribute an enormous amount to the story in terms of character background, empathy, inner motivation, inner conflict, echoing, anticipation, curiosity, credibility, and theme.

Refer to this checklist after each draft of your screenplay and especially when you feel you are so close to your story and have done so many rewrites that you have lost your objectivity. These principles can then serve as a tool to help you identify which scenes work most effectively, which need rewriting, which need to be combined with other scenes, and which should be eliminated altogether.

SCRIPT READINGS

Eventually you will reach a point where you don't think you can make your script any better. That's when you need a recorder, a friend or two to serve as impartial observers, and as many actors as there are major characters in your script, another to play all the minor roles, and one more to read the action and description. If you can't find any willing actors or acting students, just use other friends, or contact one of the audio script reading services listed in chapter 9.

Give the performers copies of your screenplay (don't give scripts to your audience; you want them to *listen* to the dialogue, not read it). Turn on the recorder, and have the actors do a reading of the scene. From then on you have to keep your mouth shut. *You can't play director in this exercise.* You want to see if the writing will stand on its own, since you won't have the opportunity in the real world to talk to the readers of your screenplay and "explain" what they missed.

When they finish, first ask your audience what they thought. Was the story involving? Was the dialogue clear, interesting, real, true to the characters? Was it funny? (A good clue to the success of a comedy is this: if your friends laughed during the reading, it was funny. If your friends didn't laugh but they *tell* you it was funny, they're just being nice.)

Next ask the actors their opinions of the script and get any suggestions they have for improving it.

Finally, if the actors are trained and willing, ask them to put the pages away and, knowing what they now know about the story and characters, improvise any scene that worries you.

When you have all the performances and everyone's comments and suggestions recorded, thank everyone, go home, and in light of all that you heard, do another rewrite and polish of the script.

CHARTING THE SCREENPLAY

For a truly left-brained exercise, chart your screenplay scene by scene. Wait until you've done at least a couple drafts of your script before employing this device, because if you get this organized too soon in the process, you run the risk of eliminating all spontaneity from your screenplay. Charting is more effective when you've exhausted the brainstorming possibilities of your story and feel too close to your writing to come up with anything new. The chart can then give you a new perspective to stimulate creativity.

First, number the scenes in your screenplay. (This is for your own use; don't number the scenes in the final draft for submission.) Then, using index cards, sheets of paper, your computer, or large sheets of newsprint, make the following chart, creating a column for each scene in your script.

Begin filling out the chart by putting the appropriate page number after each scene number at the top of the page. For example, if scene 19 begins on page 54 of your script, the top of that column should read: 19 (54).

SCENE:	1(1)	2(1)	3(2)
Summary			
Setting			
Hero			
Romance			
Nemesis			
Reflection			
Major Secondary			
Major Secondary			
Other Secondary			
Empathy			
Structural Devices			
Character Arc and Theme			
Color code			

Next put the name of the appropriate character at the beginning of each of the character rows. If your hero is Jerry and your romance is Charlotte, the first two character rows should be labeled accordingly: Hero JERRY and Romance CHARLOTTE. The romance character is listed second on the chart because, if there is such a character, she is probably the second most important character in the movie.

Of course, if you have more than one primary character in any of the categories, you must add a row for each of them.

After the scene numbers and primary character names are added to the row and column headings, go through each scene and fill in the appropriate blanks for each row, as follows:

In the Summary and Setting rows, write a brief description of the scene—enough so you will be able to identify which scene you're outlining—and then the setting where it occurs.

In the primary character rows, describe exactly what each of the characters does in each scene, in the appropriate column.

If a character doesn't fit into any of the primary character categories but is significant enough that it seems logical to outline that character specifically, devote one of the Major Secondary rows to that person. Add as many of these rows to your chart as you feel is helpful and put those characters' actions into each of the appropriate columns, just as you did with your primary characters.

In the Other Secondary row, put only the names of the secondary characters who appear in each particular scene. You don't have to outline what they do; giving their names is sufficient.

Let's say you were charting Simon Beaufoy's multi-award winning screenplay for *Slumdog Millionaire*, which is published by Newmarket Press and is available (along with countless other invaluable books, programs, and tools for writers) at my absolutely favorite resource center, the Writers Store (thewritersstore.com).

As you will see, you want to take whatever liberties you like with this chart, and mold it into a tool that will be most helpful to you, and most suitable to your screenplay.

Because the script rapidly intercuts among the opening scenes, we're up to scene #10 by the time the opening title appears. But for the purposes of our chart, I don't want to regard each separate scene heading as a new scene. Instead I'll list them as only three scenes, to correspond to the three locations in the pre-title sequence. (I recommend you do the same when charting intercut scenes in your own script.)

Here is how the chart would look initially:

SCENE:	1(1)	2(1)	3(2)
Summary	Jamal is introduced on *Who Wants to Be a Millionaire?*	Money in a bathtub and a gun being loaded	Jamal tortured and threatened by the cops
Setting	TV studio	Javed's safe house	Police station
Hero JAMAL	Interviewed by Prem		Tortured and interrogated
Romance LATIKA			
Reflection SALIM		Unseen hand loading a gun	
Nemesis PREM	Interviews Jamal; makes jokes at his expense		
Nemesis POLICE INSPECTOR			Interrogates and threatens Jamal
Nemesis MAMAN			
Nemesis JAVED			
Major Secondary CONSTABLE SRINIVAS			Tortures Jamal

SCENE:	1(1)	2(1)	3(2)
Other Secondary	TV Audience	Voice (O.S.) hollering at Salim	
Empathy			
Structural Devices			
Character Arc and Theme			
Color Code			

Jamal is the hero of the film, Latika is his romance character, and Salim is his reflection—those are easy. But *Slumdog Millionaire* has a fairly complex structure; it is told as three separate, intertwined stories, taking place at three different times, each with a separate outer motivation for the hero. In the first, Jamal is a contestant on *Who Wants to Be a Millionaire?*, and his outer motivation (we assume) is to win 20 million rupees. The second story line has Jamal being interrogated by a police inspector, and his goal is to prove he hasn't been cheating on the quiz show. The third is Jamal's life story, where his outer motivation—and the thread that unites all the biographical events, and all three story lines—is to win the love of Latika.

In each of these stories, Jamal faces a different nemesis. Prem the quiz show host tries to keep him from winning the top prize. The police inspector has him tortured, and won't believe Jamal's claims of innocence. And in the biographical flashbacks, first Maman, and then Javed, tries to keep him from being with Latika. So the chart shows four separate nemesis rows.

Finally, I've listed Constable Srinivas as a major secondary character. He's not prominent enough, nor a big enough obstacle, to serve as a nemesis. But he reappears several times through the course of the screenplay, so I listed him separately. All the other characters, such as Jamal's mother, or Arvind, the blinded singer, appear only once or twice, so they will be listed as secondary characters only in the appropriate scenes.

The intercut action sequences occur in the studio of the quiz show, the police station, and (very briefly) in a bathroom at Javed's. Jamal is in two of these, so his action is listed in those spaces, but not in the scene at Javed's, so his space is blank there. The actions of the other primary characters are included as well, in the appropriate spaces. Because Latika won't be introduced until page 22, her spaces are all blank (as one would expect; in most love stories, the hero doesn't meet the romance character until after the 10-percent opportunity).

Continuing with these first three scenes, you would now fill out the Empathy and Structural devices rows by listing all of those techniques (see chapters 3 and 5) you employ within each scene. For example, the opening scenes repeatedly use sympathy and jeopardy to create empathy for Jamal: he's tortured; he's threatened by the inspector; he's insulted by the TV host; and he's only a "chai-wallah" nervously trying to answer increasingly difficult questions, so he's in great danger of losing.

Structurally, the screenplay creates immediate curiosity (How will he do on this quiz show? Why is a game show contestant being tortured? How *did* he answer the questions if he didn't cheat? And where does this gun fit in, and who is loading it?). We're also given superior position (we know he'll be accused of cheating and tortured, but the characters in the quiz-show flashback do not), and this creates anticipation of the conflict this hero is obviously about to face. The abrupt switch from quiz show to torture is surprising. Jamal is in great jeopardy. And there are peaks and valleys to the emotion (the torture and quiz show are very intense, but when Jamal is placed in a chair and allowed to begin telling his story, the tone becomes quieter, with less conflict, as he begins the "once upon a time" story of his life).

The row for character arc and theme reminds you to look for ways within each scene to reveal more of your hero's inner conflict and character arc, which will ultimately define the theme of the movie. *Slumdog Millionaire* is one of those rare films where the hero has no arc but still contributes to the theme. Jamal (like the characters of Olive in *Little Miss Sunshine* and Eli in *The Book of Eli*) is fully evolved emotionally. He lives his truth and his essence from the very beginning of the film, and does not allow his fear to keep him from standing up for who he truly is, and doing what is right. Ultimately, the transformation in the screenplay is Latika's; Jamal gives her the courage to let go of her cynicism about life and humanity and to stand up to Javed in order to live her own life.

But it is still valuable to use this section of the chart to see how Jamal's courage and his influence on Latika and Salim reveal the themes of the movie. At this deeper level, *Slumdog Millionaire* is about choosing the moral path. When you ask how Jamal is like his nemesis, you see that at the level of inner motivation and conflict, he is not. But when you say, "How is Jamal unlike his reflection Salim?" the answer is pretty clear. Jamal believes in love, honesty, and integrity, while Salim chooses the same path as those four nemesis characters, the path toward wealth, power, and fame, which leads to dishonesty, corruption, bigotry, and ultimately failure. The screenplay delivers a familiar but powerful moral statement: love and honesty are the path to redemption and fulfillment, anything else leads ultimately to tragedy. Salim will realize this too late to save himself, and hopes only for final redemption in God's eyes as he sacrifices his life for his brother and Latika.

Charting the screenplay for *Slumdog Millionaire* shows how skillfully this theme is developed, and how instances of characters choosing one path over the other echo through the entire story. In the column for scene #1 we see how Prem, the host of a quiz show that is all about money, immediately exhibits his prejudice toward Jamal. A chart of the entire script would show how again and again he tries to tempt Jamal with wealth, and how each time Jamal refuses, choosing instead to continue the game until it leads him to Latika. We would also see that Prem was a slumdog, too, but one whose desire for the fame and wealth that the show represents has made him dishonest and corrupt.

Similarly, the gun, and later the money that fills the bathtub, will symbolize the path of wealth and violence that Salim has chosen. And the police station scenes show a different form of corruption—that of an institution that wields power for its own sake rather than for truth or justice. (We will later see mobs of Hindus attacking the Muslims of Mumbai, and policemen doing nothing to protect them. Religious institutions are no more honest or righteous than the police.)

But Jamal refuses to lie. "Funny," the inspector will tell him at one point, "you don't seem that interested in money." And he's not. He doesn't want to be a millionaire. He only wants his real destiny: Latika.

Again, these thematic elements are laid into the script, and appear on the chart, immediately, even though none of this would yet be clear to the audience.

The color code row gives you an opportunity to "graph out" such elements as action, humor, and exposition in your screenplay by assigning a different color or symbol to each of those elements as they occur within each scene.

Since we're not about to add color to this book just for this one chart, we'll do it the cheap way and say that the symbol for action is !!!!!!!!!!, the symbol for exposition is XXXXXXXX, and the symbol for humor is HAHAHAHA. We can then draw a line for each scene to indicate how much of each of these components is present in that particular scene. A scene with a lot of action would have a long line of !!!!!!!!!!, little action would mean few exclamation points.

This is obviously subjective, relative to the amount of action occurring in the screenplay overall. And you can add other symbols for any other qualities in your script you wish to measure, such as inner conflict, romantic encounters, or echoed images and dialogue.

The completed chart for the first three scenes of *Slumdog Millionaire* would now look like this:

SCENE:	1(1)	2(1)	3(2)
Summary	Jamal is introduced on *Who Wants to Be a Millionaire?*	Money in a bathtub and a gun being loaded	Jamal tortured and threatened by the cops
Setting	TV studio	Javed's safe house	Police station
Hero JAMAL	Interviewed by Prem		Tortured and interrogated
Romance LATIKA			
Reflection SALIM		Unseen hand loading a gun	
Nemesis PREM	Interviews Jamal; makes jokes at his expense		
Nemesis POLICE INSPECTOR			Interrogates and threatens Jamal
Nemesis MAMAN			
Nemesis JAVED			
Major Secondary CONSTABLE SRINIVAS			Tortures Jamal

SCENE:	1(1)	2(1)	3(2)
Other Secondary	TV Audience	Voice (O.S.) hollering at Salim	
Empathy	Nervous; danger of losing; insulted		Tortured; threatened
Structural Devices	Curiosity; anticipation; echoing; jeopardy	Curiosity; anticipation	Curiosity; anticipation; surprise; jeopardy
Character Arc and Theme	Money; fame; bigotry; given the first of many choices	Violence	Violence; corruption; telling the truth; bigotry
Color Code	!XXX	!	!!!X

In the color code row, scene #1 provides a little action (the excitement of the quiz show) and a lot of exposition, as Prem's introduction of Jamal tells us much about his background—in a very credible way, since any new contestant on a quiz show would be asked this. The second scene contains only action (the shouting and the appearance of the gun), but nothing is explained, so there is no exposition. But then scene #3 adds a lot more action with the torture sequence, and a little more exposition about Jamal, and why he is being questioned. None of these scenes has any humor, so there are no HAHAHA symbols at all.

As the chart progresses, the colors or symbols will indicate that some scenes have lots of action (the shootings and the many chase sequences), and some are more humorous (diving into the outhouse; becoming "tour guides" at the Taj Mahal). Again, the amount of color you use isn't important; you just want an overall picture of how much action, exposition, and humor each scene has relative to the others.

So what is the point of all of this? What good does this huge chart do you?

The interesting thing about charting your screenplay is that such a detailed, left-brained exercise results in a very right-brained tool. The chart allows you to step back from your screenplay and get an overall look at the development of your story. It is an excellent device for noting problems with your screenplay that may have escaped you. And if you're writing a multiple-hero story like *Crash* or *Valentine's Day*, a dual time, parallel story script like *Titanic* or *The Usual Suspects*, or a script with a more complex structure, like *Memento*, *(500) Days of Summer*, or *Slumdog Millionaire*, charting is invaluable.

After charting every scene or sequence in your screenplay, look first at the entries for your hero. He must appear in almost every column, because by definition the hero must be on screen most of the time. This usually won't be a problem, because you will tend to focus on the hero of your story as you are writing. It is in analyzing the development of the *other* primary characters that the chart can be particularly useful in revealing unnoticed weaknesses.

Before leaving the Hero row of entries, look below on your chart and make sure that you are making full use of the methods for creating empathy. These must be employed within the first few scenes, before you begin revealing major flaws in your hero.

Now move on to the entries for the other primary characters, and make sure the following needs are met:

1. Are your Romance, Nemesis, and Reflection defined in terms of the Hero's outer motivation?

2. Are all of your primary characters introduced by the beginning of act two?

3. Once a primary character is introduced, are there any long gaps on the chart where the character doesn't appear? This is a danger signal. A primary character should always appear regularly throughout a screenplay, unless she dies or is purposely removed for a long stretch for the sake of a dramatic return, as with Joanna Kramer, the wife and mother in *Kramer vs. Kramer* who abandons Ted and Billy, then returns at the end of act two to fight for custody.

4. Do your Nemesis, Reflection, and Romance all possess clear outer motivations, and are those desires built up and resolved by the end of the screenplay?

5. Do the primary characters other than the hero interact? This won't always occur, but as a general rule, your screenplay will be stronger if your reflection, nemesis, and/or romance confront each other.

Think of the wonderful—and very revealing—coffee shop scene in Paul Haggis's screenplay *Million Dollar Baby*, when Scrap and Maggie (Frankie's two reflection characters) talk about why Frankie doesn't want to risk putting Maggie in the ring. Such scenes provide opportunities for added conflict, humor, and character revelation and help prevent a narrower story line involving only your hero.

6. Does each of your primary characters have at least one "big moment"? It's nice if you can create a particularly dramatic, funny, or revealing scene or two for characters besides your hero.

Such scenes are critical when it's time to cast the movie. In selecting which movies they want to make, actors look for opportunities to shine, scenes where they can react to real obstacles, reveal inner conflicts, and convey multiple layers of emotion. These moments don't just give your characters added depth, texture, and emotional involvement: they help sell your screenplay.

In the row or rows for secondary characters, make sure that each provides the desired logic, humor, conflict, and so on, but that you haven't overloaded your screenplay with more minor characters than is necessary. And don't leave any of those characters dangling; the reader should never finish your script wondering what became of one of your secondary characters.

In the row for character empathy, have you established sympathy to some degree for your reflection? Is the romance someone we can fall in love with as the hero does? Why? Even the nemesis must be given qualities that will make him unique, interesting, and perhaps sympathetic. This row on the chart will help ensure the necessary emotional connection between your reader and your primary characters.

The structural device row will help you focus on the events you have chosen for your story and the order in which you have arranged them. Begin by marking the key turning points in the story: the opportunity at the 10-percent mark, the pursuit of the outer motivation that begins at the end of act one (25 percent), the major setback at the end of act two, and the climax of the film somewhere in the final 10 percent.

When you have identified the three acts of the story on your chart, check the page numbers of the scenes where they occur. If the changes don't occur a quarter and three-quarters of the way through the screenplay, your act breaks are misplaced. For the story to effectively elicit emotion, it *must* follow the quarter-half-quarter pattern.

Now go to the checklist of structural devices in chapter 5 and make sure that you have employed as many of those principles as possible throughout your screenplay. Is the screenplay repeatedly creating anticipation? Do you reverse expectations occasionally to surprise the reader? Is there frequent use of superior position? Curiosity? Jeopardy? Echoing? And most important of all, *does each scene relate to the hero's outer motivation?*

Use this row to ensure that the characters behave logically and believably within each scene. If you feel any scene might be hard to believe, the solution might be to go to an earlier scene to provide the necessary background or foreshadowing to *make* the action believable. Similarly, look at the color coding to see which scenes contain the most action. These are usually the scenes involving the biggest hurdles the characters face. Then use the structural device row to ensure that the characters' abilities to overcome those obstacles have been effectively foreshadowed.

The row for character arc and theme should show that the hero's inner motivation and inner conflict are affecting his behavior from the time he is introduced, even though the reasons for his desire and emotional fear have not been identified for the reader. As you move forward in the chart, you should see that these invisible qualities are gradually revealed in the dialogue-heavy scenes, and that your hero is showing increasing emotional courage as he moves toward the finish line.

The color coding can reveal several other qualities of the screenplay:

1. The action lines should generally become longer as the story progresses, with the longest and most frequent lines occurring in act three. This indicates the necessary accelerated pace.

2. Similarly, the exposition lines should all but disappear about halfway through the script, because giving the audience information slows down the pace. The exception might be an aftermath where the solution to a crime or the explanation of the story resolution occurs after the climax, as in a murder mystery.

3. Make sure there is occasional humor in your screenplay, no matter how serious or dramatic the subject. If you're writing a comedy, the humor symbol, or color, should occur in at least half of the scenes.

4. Both the action and the humor lines should be alternately long and short: one to three scenes of heavy action or humor, followed by a few quieter or more serious scenes. This indicates the necessary peaks and valleys to the emotional level of your story.

You can add as many other colors or symbols or rows to this chart as you feel are helpful in rewriting your screenplay. But if you look at this device and declare, "I didn't get into screenwriting to become a CPA!" then simply don't use it. All of the principles employed in the chart are also contained in the checklists and methods outlined earlier in this book. If you truly believe that turning your screenplay into a spreadsheet will rob you of your creativity and fun, then use the other methods to evaluate and rewrite your script.

Most of my past consulting clients who initially resisted this process, however, tried it anyway and were surprised at how helpful it was. The chart can provide you with a fresh look at your screenplay just when you're starting to believe your creative well is dry.

The rule is always this: *If a particular approach doesn't work, or if it blocks you, don't do it; if it works, keep doing it until you discover a method that's even more effective.*

SUMMARY

1. The overall rules and guidelines for putting the words on the page and eliciting maximum emotion with your screenwriting style are:

   ► You must create a movie in the mind of the reader

   ► Scripts are action, description, and dialogue only— nothing goes on the page that doesn't go on the screen

   ► There are three uses for any screenplay

   A proposal for a movie you hope to get made (the submission script—and the only one that concerns you)

   A blueprint of a movie that is being made (the shooting script)

   A record of a film that has already been shot (for postproduction)

   ► Before submitting any script, be certain there's nothing that you know can be improved

➤ Improper format reduces the reader's emotional involvement

2. To ensure proper format, obtain a good formatting program

3. Write character and setting description that is concise, clever, provocative, and detailed, and that conveys the essence of a character or setting rather than mere physical description, which might limit casting

4. Clarity is your primary goal when writing action

➤ Use everyday, straightforward language

➤ Use action words

➤ Ask others to read the scene to verify that it's clear

➤ Omit any mention of the credit sequences or musical score

➤ Make no reference to special effects—simply describe what the audience will see and hear

➤ Use detail to create vivid images

5. Ask the following questions about any scene before writing dialogue:

➤ What is my objective within the scene?

➤ How will the scene end?

➤ What is each character's objective within the scene?

➤ What is each character's attitude within the scene?

➤ How will the scene begin?

6. With each successive rewrite, polish the dialogue so that it:

➤ Contributes to the scene's objective and the overall outer motivation for your hero

➤ Is consistent with the characters

- ► Reveals character background, inner motivation, conflict, or theme, when appropriate

- ► Is as clever, funny, original, provocative, interesting, and enjoyable to read as is appropriate

7. Conduct a reading of your screenplay to elevate the story and style

8. After each new draft, apply the following checklist to each scene in your script:

   - ► How does the scene contribute to the hero's outer motivation?

   - ► Does the scene have its own beginning, middle, and end?

   - ► Does the scene thrust the reader into the following scenes?

   - ► What is each character's objective within the scene?

   - ► What is each character's attitude within the scene?

   - ► Does the scene contain action, not just dialogue?

   - ► Does the scene serve multiple functions?

9. When the second or third draft of the screenplay is complete, chart the script using the method outlined in the final section of this chapter

SEVEN

EXCEPTIONS TO THE RULE

IF YOU'VE READ THIS FAR, AND CERTAINLY IF YOU EVER HEARD ME lecture or worked with me as a client, you know that the foundation of my approach to story is built on this simple idea: *mainstream movies are about heroes pursuing clear, visible objectives.* But what about the ones that aren't?

What about movies where the hero has no clearly defined finish line—who are simply put in a tough situation, or who pursue a series of goals, or whose desires aren't visible?

I'm not talking about experimental films or foreign-language films or documentaries or porn—those movies are outside the scope of this book and have their own criteria and methods for eliciting emotion. I'm referring to Hollywood movies that appear in your local neighborhood multiplex, and which appeal to the same mass audience that goes to see *Avatar*, *Twilight*, *Toy Story*, and *The Hangover*.

Almost all of these exceptions-to-the-rule screenplays fall into three basic categories: biographies, arena movies, and feminine-mode movies.

BIOGRAPHIES

Biographies are simply life stories. We follow real or fictional heroes for long spans of time, usually from youth (and sometimes birth) to their final years (and sometimes death). *Citizen Kane*, *Ray*, and *The Curious Case of Benjamin Button* are all biographies.

A movie is not a biography simply because it is based on a true story about a real person. *Thirteen Days* is not a biography. It's the story of John F. Kennedy trying to stop the Russians from bringing missiles into Cuba. The story is true, and the characters are based on real people, but it doesn't follow JFK from childhood to his assassination. It's just about his pursuit of this one visible goal. (And by the way, *JFK* isn't a biography either—Kennedy isn't even the hero of that one.)

For the same reason, *Milk*, *Frida*, and *Forrest Gump* are all biographies; *The Queen*, *The Pursuit of Happyness*, and *Invictus* are not.

Biographies usually depart from the rule of a single outer motivation, because over the course of a lifetime, a character will have a series of goals in succession. In *Walk the Line*, Johnny Cash wants to play with his brother, deal with his brother's death, serve in the army, sing, get married, cut a record, drink, take drugs, sing some more, win the love of June Carter, hang with Elvis, perform at Folsom Prison, stop drinking and taking drugs, deal with his father's rejection, and win June Carter back. The screenplay gives us an avalanche of things to root for, rather than just one or two goals.

The big pitfall of biographies is that with so many successive outer motivations, the audience has no clear finish line in sight. At that all-important 25 percent turning point, no single, visible objective emerges that tells the reader when the story will end, or how we will know whether the hero has won.

If you doubt that this is a problem, just look at how few biographies Hollywood releases each year, and how few of *those* become blockbusters. For every *Forrest Gump* or *Braveheart*, there's a *Chaplin*, *Hoffa*, or *Amelia*.

If, in spite of the limited market for this genre, you want to write a biographical screenplay, you must somehow overcome the inherent lack of a single outer motivation for your hero. The key is to find a desire that will run through the character's entire life—or at least from the 25-percent point forward. In almost all successful biographies, this is the *love story*.

Forrest Gump experiences a multitude of adventures and conflicts through his life, including polio, Vietnam, shrimping, ping-pong, and the death of his mother. But the thread that unites them all is his love for Jenny. Though he isn't always actively pursuing her, audiences stay deeply involved in the story because of their desire to see Forrest and Jenny end up together.

The desire to win—or retain—the love of the romance character is also at the heart of *Walk the Line*, *Frida*, *A Beautiful Mind*, and *The Curious Case of Benjamin Button*. We root for these heroes and romance characters to overcome their obstacles and end up together, just as we do with love stories that aren't biographical, and which don't cover long spans of time.

In some biographies, the goal that defines the hero's life is not a romantic one, but is still so compelling and enduring that it unites all the action. In both *Braveheart* and *Gandhi*, the heroes' entire lives are committed to winning independence and freedom from English rule.

Citizen Kane shrewdly addresses this issue by giving a minor character a goal that unites the episodes in the hero's life. Charles Foster Kane pursues lots of desires through his life. But it is the reporter's search for the meaning of "Rosebud" that propels us to the end of the film. *Amelia* tries to do the same, building the biography around the story of Amelia Earhart's final flight. But, perhaps because most of the audience knew the tragic outcome of that pursuit going in, the film was less than successful.

ARENA STORIES

In what I term "arena stories," a hero is dropped into a situation filled with conflict, where his only goal is physical or emotional survival. He has to figure out how to cope with and overcome all of the obstacles thrown at him in this new environment. If he survives long enough, the movie is over and he has won, even though there was never a single, visible finish line to cross, even at the climax.

The Hurt Locker is an excellent example. After a tension-filled prologue opening, the hero, Sergeant James, reports for duty as the new team leader of an Explosive Ordnance Disposal unit in Iraq. From that point forward we experience a whole string of obstacles Sergeant James must overcome as he and his team try to defuse a series of bombs, survive a sniper attack, and find those responsible for the death of an Iraqi boy. The film is undeniably emotional—exciting, suspenseful, thoughtful, funny, and tragic—but it lacks any single, overriding finish line. The hero's ultimate goal is just to keep doing his job until his tour of duty is over.

Sergeant James, or Queen Elizabeth in *The Queen*, or Frances in *Under the Tuscan Sun*, or Andrea in *The Devil Wears Prada* are like gladiators in an arena. Each enters a new situation, either by choice or by circumstance. Each has a desire (to defuse bombs, to weather the controversy surrounding the death of a princess, to start a new life after a divorce, or to move up in the world of journalism by working for a top fashion magazine), and each faces overwhelming obstacles. But none pursues a specific outer motivation with a clearly defined endpoint. These heroes just have to keep going, hoping to be better off, or at least alive, when their situation is resolved.

While there may be a romantic relationship in an arena story, the romantic pursuit has either already occurred (as with the married or romantically involved heroes of *The Hurt Locker*, *The Queen*, and *The Devil Wears Prada*), or it comprises only a small part of the entire story (as in *Under the Tuscan Sun*). If the hero's pursuit of a romance lasts from the beginning of act two to the climax of a film, it's a traditional love story, and not an exception to the rule requiring an outer motivation.

In arena stories, just as in biographies, you want to give the reader something to root for, and some anticipation of closure, even in the absence of a visible finish line. So in *The Hurt Locker*, as soon as James arrives, the audience sees a title card announcing the number of days remaining in the company's rotation. As a result, they subconsciously start rooting for him to survive until he gets to go home. It's not an outer motivation, but it is a finish line of sorts.

Similar parameters are added to the situations in *The Queen* (from Princess Diana's death until her funeral) and *Under the Tuscan Sun* (the remodeling of the villa over the course of a year).

Don't confuse arena stories with sports movies that actually *involve* arenas, like *Million Dollar Baby*, *Remember the Titans*, or the roller derby film *Whip It*. "Arena" is just the best term I could come up with to describe screenplays where the hero's circumstance, not his desire, sets up the conflict and emotion. And as you can see, examples of mainstream arena movies are no more plentiful than for biographies—a sign that marketing a script in this category won't be easy.

FEMININE-MODE STORIES

Consider the movie *Steel Magnolias*. While this ensemble piece focuses on six different Southern women, the hero of the screenplay is M'Lynn, who is on screen more than the others, is the one with whom we most empathize, and, most of all, is the one whose desire to support and protect her daughter Shelby provides the spine around which the others' stories are revealed.

But what, exactly, is M'Lynn's outer motivation? Certainly she always wants to be there for her daughter and her friends from the beauty parlor, but "being there" has no visible finish line. M'Lynn also wants to put on a wedding for her daughter, help her daughter through her pregnancy, and even fight her daughter's illness by donating a kidney. But none of these desires lasts the entire screenplay. In fact, the movie is divided, like the play it was based on, into three segments, separated by gaps of time.

Okay, so no outer motivation. This is an exception to the rule. But it is neither a biography nor an arena story. It's what I term a *feminine-mode movie*.

Now before I explain anything at all about feminine-mode movies, let me make it clear that I'm not talking about "chick flicks." Feminine-mode movies don't even have to have women heroes. Again, it's just a term I created to describe a third category of story that lacks a clear outer motivation.

Let's start by defining what a "masculine-mode" story would be. Imagine a knight in shining armor, getting ready to ride off to slay a dragon, rescue a maiden, find the Holy Grail, or conquer the heathens in the Crusades (the Big Four, as far as knights in shining armor are concerned). These are all missions with clear, visible finish lines—hardly different from the win/stop/escape/deliver/retrieve goals of most Hollywood movies.

Now imagine the princess who doesn't go off on some quest but remains back in the castle. Perhaps a curse has been placed upon the kingdom, or a magic spell has turned things dark in some way. The people of the kingdom are suffering. Things are out of whack. So now the princess must perform some act of courage to stop the curse, end these dark days, and make things right again.

In other words, the story is not really about conquest or accomplishment—it's not about venturing off to win anything or cross any finish line. It's about staying put and making things right in order to bring things back into equilibrium.

This is what I mean by "feminine mode." *In a feminine-mode story, the goal of the hero is to resolve a non-romantic relationship.*

In *Steel Magnolias*, M'Lynn's primary goal, through all three segments of the story, is to bring her relationship with Shelby into balance. Shelby tells M'Lynn, "I never worry 'cause I always know you're worried enough for both of us." Their relationship is lopsided rather than truly equal.

Though they love each other, M'Lynn's insistence on protecting Shelby repeatedly threatens to limit Shelby's life and hurt their relationship. As Shelby tells her mother, "I'd rather have thirty minutes of wonderful than a lifetime of nothing special."

As with the princess in the castle, something has gotten out of whack in this kingdom, and it's up to M'Lynn to make it right.

When I say M'Lynn's goal is to bring their relationship into balance, I don't mean that this is entirely conscious on her part. As in a love story, the audience knows what the hero will ultimately want and need, even though the hero may not acknowledge it until well past the beginning of act two.

The reason the relationship must be non-romantic is because in a story about a romantic relationship, the hero is trying to win, or win back, the love of the romance character. This gives the hero's motivation a clear, visible end point, so it's not an exception to the rule. Love stories are, by definition, masculine-mode.

Feminine-mode movies can be about resolving relationships with a parent, a child, a sibling, a best friend, or a group of friends. But most share these qualities:

► Feminine-mode movies are almost always location-bound. Daughters go back home to stay with their mothers in both *One True Thing* and *Hope Floats*, a son returns to his father's home in *A River Runs Through It*, a brother goes to his sister's in *You Can Count on Me*, and a mother spends Thanksgiving with her daughter in *Pieces of April*. In *The Big Chill*, *Enchanted April*, and *The Family Stone*, a group of friends, strangers, or family members come together for a weekend, a vacation, or a holiday.

► If there is a romantic relationship in a feminine-mode movie, it is always secondary to the non-romantic one. Heroes of *Hope Floats*, *You Can Count on Me*, and *The Big Chill* all have affairs with other characters, but these plot lines never extend from the end of act one to the climax.

► Feminine-mode movies almost always use time in one of two ways. Either they consist of three stages covering long spans of time (*Driving Miss Daisy*, *Steel Magnolias*, *When Harry Met Sally*), or they occur over a short span of time with a predetermined end point, such as a terminal illness or a holiday visit (*A River Runs Through It*, *One True Thing*, *Pieces of April*).

Unfortunately, one of the other things most feminine-mode movies share is a lack of strong commercial appeal. The examples above contain only five movies that qualify as genuine blockbusters: *The Big Chill*, *Driving Miss Daisy*, *Steel Magnolias*, *The Devil Wears Prada*, and *When Harry Met Sally*. Of those, three were based on hugely successful books or plays, leaving *The Big Chill* and *When Harry Met Sally* as the only original feminine-mode screenplays on this fairly exhaustive list to become huge hits. And *The Big Chill* was initially rejected by every studio in Hollywood. So before you rush to begin your original feminine-mode script, realize that it will be a very, very difficult screenplay to sell.

You may be wondering why a romantic comedy like *When Harry Met Sally* is even on the list, since it's a love story, and therefore a masculine-mode movie. I include it because, unlike almost every other Hollywood romantic comedy, the story is told in three stages and extends over a long span of time. And after a feeble attempt at seduction by Harry early in the film, the romantic pursuit and conflict don't occur until the last third of the screenplay.

To me, *When Harry Met Sally* is more about two people who must bring their *friendship* into balance in spite of the fact that they sleep together, and ultimately fall in love. So yes, it's funny, and yes, it's romantic. It's also one of my favorite movies of all time. But, oddly, it fits the definition of feminine-mode movie as closely as it does that of romantic comedy. If you disagree, just ignore it and focus on the other examples.

RECOGNIZING THE EXCEPTIONS TO THE RULE

Don't be too quick to label a movie an exception. When you watch a film or read a screenplay, here's how you decide where it belongs:

- ► If the script is about a hero pursuing a clearly defined, visible finish line, it's a masculine-mode movie. End of discussion.

- ► If it's not, and the hero's story extends through a long span of her life and a whole series of goals, then it's a biography.

- ► If it's neither masculine mode nor biographical, ask if the screenplay puts a hero in a confined or well-defined situation filled with conflict, just to see if the hero can survive physically and/or emotionally. If so, it's an arena story.

► If it's none of the above, *then* (and only then) ask if the hero's primary goal is the resolution of a relationship with a family member, friend, or a group of relatives or friends. If so, it's a feminine-mode story.

Never begin by asking if a movie you see or a script you're writing is about the resolution of a relationship. Every movie ever made is about the resolution of a relationship. It's only when you've eliminated every other possibility that you want to consider the feminine-mode category.

And if you encounter a movie that doesn't seem to fit into *any* of the categories, don't worry about it. Just remember that the vast majority of Hollywood movies have heroes pursuing visible, clearly defined outer motivations, and keep that fact in mind when choosing your next story concept.

SUMMARY

I. Three types of screenplays use a story approach other than the hero/outer motivation model:

► *Biographies* tell a character's full life story—not simply a single incident or two from the character's life

Successful biographies usually have some desire that unites all of the episodes in the hero's life

This thread is most often a love story

► *Arena stories* put their heroes in some new, conflict-filled situation, where their desire is simply to survive physically or emotionally

The hero's situation should be given some clear or predictable endpoint

Love stories are secondary, and either don't involve pursuit or the pursuit consumes only a portion of the story

► *Feminine-mode movies* portray a hero whose primary goal is the resolution of a non-romantic relationship

The relationship will be with a parent, child, best friend, or group of friends or relatives

The stories are almost always location-bound—the hero goes to visit or stay with the person with whom he is out of balance

Any romantic relationship is secondary to the non-romantic one

Two frequently used time spans in feminine-mode movies are:

–Three stages in the characters' lives, covering a long span of time

–An abbreviated span of time defined by some external situation, like a terminal illness or holiday visit

2. Screenplays in all three of the categories presented are extremely difficult to sell, due primarily to their typically weak box-office performance when compared to traditional story modes.

3. To determine if a film is an exception to the rule, ask the following questions *in this order*:

► Is it about a hero pursuing a clearly defined outer motivation? If yes, then it's not an exception. If no, then ask:

► Does it follow a hero for nearly all of his life, through a series of visible goals? If yes, it's a biography. If no, then ask:

► Does the screenplay put a hero in a situation filled with conflict, just to see if she can survive physically and/or emotionally? If yes, it's an arena story. If no, then ask:

► Is the hero's primary goal the resolution of a non-romantic relationship? If yes, it's a feminine-mode movie.

► If the answer to all of these questions is no, it's a rarity that doesn't fit into any of the above categories.

EIGHT

AN ANALYSIS OF *AVATAR*

NOW LET'S SEE IF IT'S POSSIBLE TO TAKE A SINGLE SUCCESSFUL SCREEN-play and use it to illustrate all of the principles I've presented. To do this, I decided to use *Avatar*, the highest-grossing film of all time (as of the time I'm writing this). Beyond just its financial success, *Avatar* is also a wonderful example of story concept, the four categories of primary character, plot structure, character arc, theme, and scene writing. More than anything, I want this exercise to reinforce these principles and increase your ability to apply them to your own writing. And perhaps help us understand just why this screenplay was so successful.

Before you begin reading this chapter, please see the movie and read the screenplay. It's essential that you have whatever emotional experience *Avatar* provides before you read what I have to say about it. Plus I don't want to spoil the ending or any part of the story by giving it away.

The movie is available on DVD, and the screenplay is available in a variety of print or digital forms. Just do a Web search of "avatar screenplay" to find ways to acquire a copy. This chapter is based on a free PDF version that was posted by Twentieth Century Fox upon the film's initial release. I'll avoid using page numbers as much as possible so if you refer to a slightly different version, you won't be confused.

Personal opinions of *Avatar* aren't really that pertinent to this discussion. I hope you liked the movie, but even if you think it's dreadful, this will still be useful, as long as you figure out *why* you think it's dreadful. Ask yourself specifically which principles and methods for eliciting emotion were not met when you read the screenplay or saw the movie. Then be certain you employ those principles more effectively when writing your own screenplay.

STORY CONCEPT

The story concept for *Avatar* can be expressed in this way:

Avatar is a story about a marine sent to the moon of a faraway planet, who wants to stop mercenaries from destroying the moon's indigenous Na'vi civilization, and who wants to win the love of a Na'vi woman.

Saving the Na'vi and winning Neytiri's love fulfill all of the criteria for a proper outer motivation: both have clearly defined endpoints; Jake the hero desperately wants to accomplish both; he'll actively pursue both goals until the climax of the screenplay; it's within his power to achieve them; and he'll risk everything, including his life, to succeed.

Notice that I've condensed these desires for the sake of expressing them succinctly in a single sentence. But both of these outer motivations actually evolve through the course of the script. As with any good love story, the hero doesn't start pursuing the love interest immediately. First he just wants her not to kill him, then he wants to learn from her, then he falls in love with her, and eventually he'll lose her and have to win her back.

Similarly, though his goal is to keep the Na'vi from being slaughtered by the mining company's mercenaries, at first he just wants to observe them, then to infiltrate their civilization to get information on them, then persuade them to leave peaceably so the company can have the unobtanium, then finally lead them and protect them. But through all these stages, his goal is to prevent them from being destroyed in open warfare.

I point this out so you'll see that even though an outer motivation can be expressed as a single, visible goal, that goal will evolve and change in the course of a well-told story.

This concept is clearly built on at least one *"What if . . . ?"* question: "What if it were possible for a person to occupy the body of an alien creature, and in doing so to begin preferring the alien culture to his own?" This may not be the exact way the writer/director thought of it, but it certainly seems to be one of the unique elements of the story.

James Cameron combined this provocative idea with many other, more familiar ones to develop the story concept. What if a small band of warriors came up against a much more powerful army (as in *The Seven Samurai*, *The Wild Bunch*, and *Star Wars: A New Beginning*)? What if a hero from one culture fell in love with someone from another (*Dances with Wolves*, *The Last Samurai*)?

Apparently, James Cameron had been sitting on this idea for decades before finally having the technology to execute it, so who knows exactly where his concept came from. But you can see how combining these different *"What if . . . ?"* situations could lead to a story like this.

In evaluating the potential of this story concept, first look for the five essential elements of any film story. *Avatar* has all five: a hero, empathy with the hero, desire, conflict, and risk.

With regard to commercial potential, this can certainly be regarded as a high concept. The idea of a battle between alien warriors led by a human and a powerful, well-armed band of mercenaries promises a lot of action, and the love story promises romance. In other words, the concept alone promises an emotional experience, regardless of casting, theme, etc.

The story also fits into two of the commercial categories for a Hollywood concept: *to stop* and *to win*.

It's pretty hard to verify the commercial potential of the story concept alone, since the majority of the people who lined up to see it did so because of James Cameron's reputation, and the buzz about the astonishing art direction, special effects, and 3D. But even if this had been an original screenplay by an unknown writer, readers would still have recognized the potential for conflict, emotion, and commercial appeal.

CHARACTER

The hero of *Avatar* is clearly Jake: he's the main character; he's on screen (and on the page) more than any other; he's the character we're rooting for, and with whom we most empathize; his outer motivation drives the story forward; and his arc defines the theme of the movie.

Avatar employs a number of methods for creating empathy with Jake. Here is how he is introduced on the first page:

```
JAKE SULLY, a scarred and scruffy combat vet,
sitting in a beat up carbon-fiber wheelchair. At 22,
his eyes are hardened by the wisdom and wariness of
one who has endured pain beyond his years.
```

His narration then reads:

```
                JAKE (V.O.)
        They can fix a spinal, if you've got
        the money. But not on vet benefits,
        not in this economy.
```

So immediately we feel sympathy for Jake because of his undeserved misfortune. And three pages later (sooner in the finished film), we learn that his brother was killed. "A guy with a knife took all Tommy would ever be, for the paper in his wallet."

Jake describes himself as " . . . just another dumb grunt getting sent someplace I was gonna regret." This not only increases sympathy, it hints at the jeopardy Jake will soon encounter. The jeopardy is made much more obvious when Jake reaches Pandora, and we hear warnings of how the atmosphere will kill a person in four minutes, and how "every living thing that crawls, flies, or squats in the mud wants to kill you and eat your eyes for jujubes."

In the opening of the script, though not in the film, we also see Jake tear into a guy in a bar who slaps a woman and is threatening to beat her. Jake the narrator says, "All I ever wanted in my sorry-ass life was a single thing worth fighting for." This all serves to make Jake likable—a defender of the helpless who longs for something that will give his life meaning. Something he will find in the course of the screenplay.

Supplementing these methods for establishing empathy are several other devices: Jake doesn't seem to care what people think; he serves as the eyes of the audience (we see and are introduced to everything on Pandora as Jake sees it, with no superior position for the audience until the last half of the script); and the dialogue with Quaritch reveals that Jake was a skilled marine serving a tough tour of duty in Venezuela (this also foreshadows Jake's later ability to survive the attacks, become a Na'vi warrior and lead the Na'vi against the mercenary army).

I will discuss the inner motivation and conflict for Jake later, in the section on his character arc. For now, let's look at the other categories of primary character.

—

THE NEMESIS IS THE CHARACTER WHO MOST STANDS IN THE WAY OF the hero achieving his outer motivation. If Jake's goal is to stop the Na'vi from being wiped out, the character who creates the greatest conflict is Colonel Miles Quaritch. Quaritch's outer motivation is to destroy the Na'vi "terrorists" so that the mining company can get the unobtanium. So Quaritch and Jake are at cross-purposes.

The nemesis, like all primary characters, is defined by his relationship to the hero's outer motivation at the beginning of act two. So even though, when he's introduced, Quaritch seems to be supporting Jake, as soon as he asks Jake to secretly give him recon information to help him go against the Na'vi, we know that eventually they will be in opposition. "This is my war here," he tells Jake, making no attempt to disguise his disdain for the Na'vi (he refers to them as "hostiles"), the avatar program ("a bunch of limp-dick scientists"), or his desire to do battle.

When defining primary characters, what the audience knows and anticipates is more important than what the hero realizes. Sometimes the villain is clear to everyone at the outset. But sometimes, as with *Avatar*, it will take longer for the hero to realize whose side he's on, and who his real allies are.

The stronger and more formidable the nemesis is, the greater the conflict for the hero will be, and the greater the emotional involvement of the reader and audience. Quaritch is a tough, ruthless, fearless commander backed by a huge army of mercenaries and tons of equipment and firepower. Jake is none of these—he's just "another dumb grunt" who can't even walk, and who is completely out of his element.

The first meeting between Jake and Quaritch emphasizes how much more powerful he is than Jake. Quaritch climbs into a giant, two-ton amp suit—the antithesis of Jake's wheelchair—and begins making powerful wushu moves. Everything we see and hear is designed to make Quaritch seem invincible.

Quaritch is not the only character standing between Jake and his outer motivation. Selfridge, who heads the entire mining expedition, will ultimately be the one to order the attack on the Na'vi. And Tsu'tey, the Na'vi warrior betrothed to Neytiri, wants to kill Jake, or at least keep him away from the clan and from Neytiri. But neither Selfridge nor Tsu'tey are as great an obstacle as Quaritch, so he is the nemesis and they are secondary characters.

——◆——

THE REFLECTION IS THE CHARACTER MOST CLOSELY ALIGNED WITH the hero, who most supports the hero and helps him achieve his outer motivation. Lots of characters are on Jake's side, especially Neytiri, who rescues him, teaches him, trains him, and joins him in battle. But she is the romantic object of part of his outer motivation, so we have to save her for the next category.

The character most suited to this category is Dr. Grace Augustine, the head of the avatar program, whose own outer motivation is the same as Jake's: to infiltrate, learn from, and connect with the Na'vi, and ultimately to defend them. She helps Jake do those same things—they aren't in competition for the hero's goal—so she is his reflection. Again, primary characters are not defined by how they *initially* react to the hero. When they first meet, Grace pretty much despises Jake's very presence in her program.

—

THE ROMANCE IS THE OBJECT OF AT LEAST PART OF THE HERO'S OUTER motivation, sexually or romantically. Neytiri is the character Jake falls in love with, and the audience roots for him to be with her at the end of the movie. As with any effective romance character, Neytiri is at times at cross-purposes with Jake (she threatens him, tells him to go away, objects to teaching him, insults him repeatedly, and turns her back on him when she learns of his deception), and at other times is supportive (teaching him, falling in love with him, joining him against the mercenaries).

James Cameron creates a romance that the audience will fall in love with as well. She is smart, courageous, a skilled fighter, and a great teacher. Were she not appealing, the audience couldn't root for the love story, and would ultimately lose sympathy for the hero.

Were we to create a character chart for the *Avatar* screenplay, at this point it would look like this:

	OUTER MOTIVATION	OUTER CONFLICT	INNER MOTIVATION	INNER CONFLICT
Hero **JAKE SULLY**	Stop the mercenaries from destroying the Na'vi; win the love of Neytiri	The Na'vi don't trust him; Quaritch and the mercenaries are immensely powerful		
Nemesis **QUARITCH**	Destroy the Na'vi	Jake leads the Na'vi against the mercenary army		

	OUTER MOTIVATION	OUTER CONFLICT	INNER MOTIVATION	INNER CONFLICT
Reflection GRACE	Help Jake connect with, and protect, the Na'vi	The Na'vi don't trust her or any humans; the mercenaries are powerful		
Romance NEYTIRI	Teach Jake; stop the mercenaries; win Jake's love	The mercenaries are powerful; Tsu'tey and Neytiri's family are opposed to her relationship with Jake; Jake deceives her		

To complete the right side of the chart, we need to move to the next component of *Avatar* . . .

CHARACTER ARC AND THEME

The first step in determining the arc for the hero—and the theme of the movie—is to look for the character's inner motivation and inner conflict.

Inner motivation is the path the character thinks will lead to self-worth. It's the reason the character is pursuing his outer motivation.

Figuring out Jake's inner motivation is a little tricky, because his reasons for replacing his dead brother in the avatar program, and for joining the Na'vi, change over the course of the script. And the screenplay doesn't spell out Jake's initial motives. The implication is that he looked up to his brother, and probably thought his brother was a better person than he was, so he may be going to Pandora to honor Tommy's memory.

But we also see that Jake feels lost. He's a paraplegic, so he's a warrior who can no longer fight. Quaritch persuades Jake to spy on the Na'vi by promising he'll get him his legs back. But it seems that Jake wants his whole *life* back. To be a marine again, to have "a single thing worth fighting for."

So Jake's inner motivation is finding that thing worth fighting for. This is fine—he isn't a character who has chosen the wrong path. But at first he tries to get there in a way that's familiar, by simply following orders that will recapture what he lost. This is why his outer motivation seems to shift—he wants to help and protect the Na'vi to get meaning in his life, but he thinks he can protect them by listening to and trusting Quaritch. He'll keep the same inner and outer motivations, but in the second half of the movie, he achieves it by listening to his heart and rejecting Quaritch.

Jake's other outer motivation is to win the love of Neytiri, and his inner motivation for that, as in all love stories, is love. Again, he thinks he'll feel better about himself if he wins the love and desire of the person he loves and desires.

—◆—

INNER CONFLICT IS WHATEVER QUALITY WITHIN THE CHARACTER prevents him from achieving real self-worth. So what is it that keeps Jake from finding real meaning in his life, and real love?

When we first meet Jake, he's a cynical loner ("You want a fair deal, you're on the wrong planet.") who is cut off from others ("I don't want your pity. I know the world's a cold-ass bitch."). He gets drunk, gets into fights, does none of the prep work he's supposed to do before joining the avatar program, and pays no attention to the commands. He's a loose cannon (as we see when he runs off in his new avatar body, not caring that he's knocking stuff down and scaring everyone) who thinks little of himself and less of others. Jake the narrator says of his past, "I told myself I could pass any test a man can pass." But then he had " . . . a big hole blown through the middle of my life."

This is Jake's inner conflict. As long as he dwells on the past, on what he lost, and sees himself as a loser who failed the test he was given, he'll never find real self-worth or meaning.

The inner motivation of the nemesis, Quaritch, is power. He doesn't even seem that interested in the great wealth that the unobtanium can bring (as Selfridge is). Quaritch tells us that he could have gone back home after the injury that scarred his face, but he didn't. "I kind of like it," he says of the scar. "Besides, I can't leave. This is my war, here." His path to self-worth is through the battlefield.

Quaritch's inner conflict, the thing that keeps him from achieving real self-worth, is that he feels nothing other than vengeance and blood-lust. He'll sacrifice honesty, honor, and humanity to be able to kill the Na'vi. "That's how it's done," Jake tells Grace. "When people are sitting on shit you want, you make them your enemy. Then you're justified in taking it." When Quaritch sees the Na'vi, or anyone who's on their side, all he sees is the enemy (he calls them "terrorists" and "roaches").

The inner motivation for Grace is discovery. She's a scientist who longs to understand the power the Na'vi tap into, to learn whatever she can from them—for the benefit of mankind, perhaps, but more for the benefit of science. She wants to "see" them for exactly who they are, clearly and deeply.

Grace exhibits no inner conflict that I can see. At the end of her life, she tells Jake that she always "held back." But we see no real evidence of that. In her final scene, the screenplay reads, "Grace gasps and her eyes snap open. Her expression is amazed, as if seeing something so beautiful it can never be explained." And her final words to Jake are, "I'm with her, Jake—*she's real*—" She has earned, and achieved, her inner motivation of connecting, and of gaining a deep and unimaginable understanding.

Like Jake, Neytiri has two inner motivations. Love (in winning the love of Jake) and serving her people (in teaching and learning from Jake, in fighting for them, and eventually as a spiritual leader, following in her mother's footsteps).

Her inner conflict is less prominent, but clear: she doesn't see humans—the sky people. Because they killed her sister, she's bigoted; she won't trust or get close to them (she's ready to kill Jake until the *atokirina*—those wood sprites from the Great Tree—intervene). As she tells Jake when he returns, "I see you. . . . I was afraid, Jake—for my people. I'm not anymore."

The completed character chart for *Avatar* would therefore look like this:

	OUTER MOTIVATION	OUTER CONFLICT	INNER MOTIVATION	INNER CONFLICT
Hero **JAKE SULLY**	Stop the mercenaries from destroying the Na'vi; win the love of Neytiri	The Na'vi don't trust him; Quaritch and the mercenaries are immensely powerful	Get his old life back; find something worth fighting for; love	Blinded to what's right; disconnected; emotionally shut down
Nemesis **QUARITCH**	Destroy the Na'vi	Jake leads the Na'vi against the mercenary army	Power; experience victory in battle	Blinded to what's right; doesn't care what he's fighting for
Reflection **GRACE**	Help Jake connect with, and protect, the Na'vi	The Na'vi don't trust her or any humans; the mercenaries are powerful	Discover; understand; connect	N/A

	OUTER MOTIVATION	OUTER CONFLICT	INNER MOTIVATION	INNER CONFLICT
Romance NEYTIRI	Teach Jake; stop the mercenaries; win Jake's love	The mercenaries are powerful; Tsu'tey and Neytiri's family are opposed to her relationship with Jake; Jake deceives her	Serve her people; love	Fear; bigotry

——

THE THEME OF *AVATAR* CAN NOW BE DETERMINED BY ASKING HOW the hero is like the nemesis and unlike the reflection.

Obviously Jake and Quaritch are both military men, but more than that, they are both blinded by the past in some way. Both were scarred in battle (Jake lost his legs; Quaritch was wounded on Pandora), and both are reacting to those wounds. Jake wants his legs back, and Quaritch wants vengeance (or if not that, he's so battle-scarred he's simply addicted to killing any possible enemy he can find). So, like Quaritch, Jake initially can't "see" the Na'vi for who they truly are. To him, as to Quaritch, they're "hostiles."

One of the lines of dialogue echoed through the screenplay is the Na'vi greeting "I see you." This clearly means more than simply laying eyes on someone. It's about truly connecting with another, feeling their energy, their deeper selves. It's closer to empathizing than to observing.

This connection is not limited only to humans and the Na'vi but encompasses all other living things (thus the repeated action of linking the braided queue of a Na'vi to the antenna of a banshee or to the tendrils of the tree, and to some deeper spiritual source). Jake says, "It's hard to put in words the deep connection the People have to the forest. They see a network of energy that flows through all living things."

Or after they have made love, Neytiri says to Jake, "Spirit is all that matters."

So if seeing means connecting, and Quaritch and Jake are both unable to see the Na'vi, then the hero is like the nemesis in his inability to connect. And, as stated above, Jake is emotionally isolated and disconnected from the moment he's introduced.

When we first learn about unobtanium, the mineral worth twenty million a kilo, which Selfridge and Quaritch use to justify their attempted genocide, Selfridge is staring at a piece as it hovers over a magnetic base. It touches nothing; it's connected to nothing. A small, symbolic moment in the script, but kind of cool, isn't it?

Jake is unlike Grace in regard to the same issue. Grace is all about connection. She wants to see the Na'vi, understand them, tap into the powerful energy that connects them all to each other, to the rest of their world, and to the Great Mother that is at the source of their existence. So until Jake can find the courage to let go of his isolation and learn to really see and really connect, he will never complete his arc and never find that one thing worth fighting for.

Just consider these lines of dialogue, in the order they appear. Quaritch to Jake: "You got heart, kid, coming out here." Neytiri to Jake: "You have a strong heart. No fear." Jake to Grace: ". . . if [the clan doesn't] cut my heart out and show it to me." Jake to Grace: "Just tell [Selfridge] what you know in your heart." Jake (as narrator): "The Well of Souls. The heart of the forest. I knew the People would go there." Grace (as she's dying) to Jake: "I—always held back. But you gave them your heart. I'm proud of you."

Subtly but clearly, James Cameron is echoing the dialogue to remind us of the figurative transformation Jake needs to experience along with his literal one from human to Na'vi. They truly are going to show him his heart—the deeper truth underneath his inner conflict that will give him his courage and enable him to finally see.

There's another line from the movie, which I love but was unable to find in the shooting script. In the first minutes of the film, Jake as narrator is talking about replacing his brother after his brother was killed. "One life ends, and another begins," he says. Little does Jake know at this point that it is his current life of emotional disconnection that will end and his new life as a brave, loving, and deeply connected Na'vi warrior that will begin.

Putting this all together, the theme of *Avatar* is something like this: *To be fully evolved human beings, we must connect to others, to everything around us, and to our spiritual source.* James Cameron put it more eloquently, but it is certainly a universal prescription for how we should all live our lives.

STRUCTURE

Structurally, the three acts of *Avatar* are as follows:

- *Act one* is about Jake Sully, a marine in the year 2154 who is sent to the distant moon Pandora to join the avatar program, whose mission is to connect with, and learn about, the indigenous Na'vi tribe

- *Act two* is about Jake wanting to protect the Na'vi from destruction by infiltrating their tribe as an avatar and persuading them to leave their home before the mining company's mercenaries drive them out

- *Act three* is about Jake wanting to lead the Na'vi in battle against the mercenaries, in order to save their lives and their home

Each of the three acts is expressed as a visible outer motivation for the hero, and each is a facet of the hero's overall outer motivation in the film.

The three acts of *Avatar* follow the necessary quarter-half-quarter pattern:

▶ *Act two* begins when Neytiri rescues Jake. Even though he has already been ordered by Quaritch to get close to the Na'vi, and told by Grace that that is the goal of the avatar program (though for much different reasons), it is only after Neytiri rescues him from the viper wolves that he makes contact with the Na'vi and begins actively pursuing the goal of becoming one of them in order to protect them from a deadly encounter with the mercenaries. The screenplay is 151 pages long, and Neytiri saves him on page 38—almost exactly the quarter mark.

▶ *Act three* begins on page 113 (exactly the three-quarters mark), when Jake and the others escape from the compound and head to the Well of Souls to find the surviving Na'vi and lead them in battle. "What do you say?" Jake says to Grace. "Time for a revolution?"

───

THE SETUP MUST ESTABLISH THE HERO, SHOW HIM LIVING HIS EVERYday life, create empathy with him, and give us a "before" picture relating to his arc.

When we meet Jake, we not only empathize, we see how he is mired in his inner conflict. He longs for something meaningful but he is shut down emotionally, a cynical loner who is stuck in the past and in what he's lost.

The script combines three of the four possible opening sequences: a *black screen* with the sound of drums in the distance, followed by a *broad to narrow* aerial shot of Pandora from above, followed by the *narration*.

The setup in the script is an *everyday hero* introduction; we meet Jake living his everyday life on Earth before he learns of his brother's death and his enrollment in the avatar program. The movie eliminates this introduction and begins with a *new arrival* setup as Jake awakens right before landing on Pandora.

The screenplay employs almost all of the structural devices discussed in chapter 5. For example:

1. **Every scene, event, and character contributes to the hero's outer motivation.** To illustrate, simply pick any scene in the screenplay and ask if it moves Jake closer to his desire to join and protect the Na'vi, closer to his desire to win the love of Neytiri, or both.

   All of the scenes where Neytiri teaches Jake, where Jake proves himself as a warrior and as one of them, and where Jake does battle with the mercenaries support both of his goals. But so do the scenes with Grace and the rest of the avatar crew (learning about the Na'vi and about living "inside" his avatar).

   The only possible exception might be the earlier scene with Quaritch, where he is supplying information that will help them defeat the Na'vi. But Jake is following orders, and his vacillation between his nemesis and his reflection is indicative of his inner conflict—he hasn't yet decided on the true path to self-worth. So these are also related to his outer motivation, even though they increase the obstacles that will stand in the way of Jake ultimately protecting the Na'vi.

2. **The script shows the audience where the story is headed.** From the moment we see the primitive arrows in the tires of the giant tractor, we begin wondering about, and anticipating, the conflict to come. The audience sticks around to find out whether Jake will survive in this hostile place, become a Na'vi, win the love of Neytiri, and whether he and the Na'vi will ultimately prevail. And these questions are what keep readers turning the pages.

3. **Each hurdle and obstacle is greater than the previous ones.** Obviously, learning to use his avatar is not as difficult as surviving in the jungles of Pandora. And that's not as difficult as becoming a Na'vi warrior, or of leading them in battle again Quaritch's powerful army.

4. **The pace of the story accelerates.** Act one contains a lot of narration and exposition as Jake arrives, learns about Pandora and his

avatar, and talks to Grace and Quaritch. Act two has a *lot* more action, as Jake is taken through Na'vi "boot camp" by Neytiri, must capture and tame a banshee, makes love with Neytiri, and must escape the attack on Hometree. And, of course, act three is pretty much one big battle sequence, with moments of conflict coming at the hero and the Na'vi in rapid succession.

Because of the futuristic, faraway setting, *Avatar* requires a *lot* of exposition: information about the planet Pandora and why both scientists and mercenaries are there and what avatars are and who Jake Sully is and why he has been brought to this dangerous outpost. But the script skillfully presents all this information in the first act of the film, before the pace needs to be accelerated and the conflict shifted into high gear.

Avatar employs the added expositional device of delivering the information through emotion. We meet Jake in a fight. Instead of dry lectures about Pandora and avatars, we hear what a hostile place it is from the nemesis Quaritch, who then secretly recruits Jake as they prepare for battle with the Na'vi. And as Jake is giving his introduction to avatars and to the scientists' mission, Dr. Grace Augustine criticizes him for being a marine, and unprepared, and for knowing nothing about science or what they are doing. Emotion grows out of conflict, and even these expository scenes are delivered in moments of conflict, or in ways that create curiosity and anticipation of the conflict to come.

5. **There are peaks and valleys to the emotional level.** All that action mentioned in #4 above is interspersed with quieter scenes of Jake recording his log, arguing with the others at the base camp, getting language lessons, looking at the totem skull of a great leonopteryx, and hearing the legend of the Toruk Macto.

6. **The screenplay creates anticipation.** Like the arrows in the tires, numerous scenes create anticipation of the ultimate conflict between Jake and the mercenaries. Neytiri's resistance at teaching

Jake creates anticipation of their conflict, and of what he'll have to do to prove himself. And the early dialogue about the need for the breathing mask creates anticipation of the later scene where Jake can't reach his and is suffocating.

7. **The audience is given superior position.** We know that Jake is under orders from Quaritch before Grace does; we know Jake's hidden agenda before the Na'vi do; we know Selfridge has ordered Quaritch to attack before Jake or the Na'vi do; and we know Jake is falling in love with Neytiri before she, her parents, or Tsu'tey do. All these instances create anticipation of the conflict to come when the information is revealed to everyone.

8. **There are surprises and reversals to audience anticipation.** We don't anticipate the encounter with the hammerhead titanothere, followed by the unexpected attack from the much scarier thanator. Nor are we expecting the creatures of Pandora to come to the Na'vi's defense in their battle with the mercenary army.

9. **The screenplay creates curiosity.** Most of all, we're curious about how Jake and the Na'vi will ever defeat Quaritch and his army. But earlier in the script we're curious (among many other things) about what makes Pandora so threatening, who fired those arrows, when and how Jake will find and tame his banshee, and how he will win back the hearts of the Na'vi he betrayed.

10. **The story is credible.** *Avatar* is a great example of a fantasy story that clearly defines the limits of the fantasy and the characters' abilities. This may be almost 150 years in the future, but the humans possess no super powers—we are to believe they function exactly as humans today do. The only real nod to the futuristic existence is the somewhat modern military equipment, and the creation of avatars.

But even with the avatars and the Na'vi, there are limits. The creatures are big, highly skilled, and have a sort of telepathic ability to connect with and hear their deity. But they can't fly, or become invisible, or make objects sail through the air with just their thoughts. So by the time of the big act three battle, there is great conflict, because the limits to their powers seem too great to overcome the attacking army.

11. **The characters' actions and abilities are foreshadowed.** Examples of this abound. Jake is a marine with combat experience. Avatars are big, strong, fast, and nimble. Na'vi warriors (and Neytiri) are big, strong, smart, courageous, skilled flyers, and great hunters. Quaritch's mercenary army is large and well-armed. He's skilled at "driving" an amp suit. Trudy is a skilled pilot. Jake learns that Neytiri's grandfather's grandfather united the clans by taming and riding a leonopteryx. Every single one of these facts is introduced well before it seems important to the story. And every one adds credibility to the characters' actions, including the Na'vi's willingness to let Jake lead them after his earlier deception.

12. **Echoing is used to illustrate character growth and change.** Besides all the dialogue cited earlier involving the word "heart," we also hear "I see you" repeatedly. The attempt to save Grace's life by transferring her "soul" into her avatar body is echoed when Jake attempts the same thing at the end of the film. And each time we see Jake add to his log, or enter the link unit, he has moved a little farther from the person he was at the opening.

13. **The audience learns vicariously.** This may sound silly, but as the audience sees Neytiri teach Jake to hunt, or to capture and ride his banshee, we feel like we are acquiring those skills as well. That's how empathy works.

14. **Characters are in jeopardy.** Everybody's in danger at some point in the script—it's an action film. But as an example, consider how concerned we are about Grace's survival after she's shot.

15. **The use of time is maximized.** Quaritch tells Jake he has three months to get the Na'vi to leave their home, or he will attack. This condenses the time for the story, it announces how long the story will last, and it creates a ticking clock that greatly increases the conflict for the hero. And remember that line at the beginning of the script about the breathing mask? " . . . you lose your mask, you're unconscious in twenty seconds and you're dead in four minutes." This creates a *severe* ticking clock at the climax of the script, when Jake is unable to reach his mask and passes out.

16. **The screenplay has an effective ending.** The climactic battle is the hero's final confrontation with the nemesis, it clearly resolves Jake's outer motivation, and it gives the audience what it's been rooting for. Jake has also won Neytiri's love once and for all when she greets him upon his return. And in the aftermath, we see the new life the hero will now live. All of the earthlings involved in the mining operation are being sent back home, and Jake goes to the Well of Souls to connect with the Mother Tree, enter his avatar body permanently, and begin his life as a Na'vi.

WRITING STYLE

Using passages from James Cameron's screenplay of *Avatar*, I want to illustrate the principles of writing effective description, action, and dialogue.

Description

Here is how we are introduced to Hell's Gate, as Jake wheels himself off the shuttle and toward the OPS center:

```
Jake, pumping his chair, looks around as—

A huge tractor, taller than a house, roars past on
muddy wheels. He notices something sticking in the
```

tires—arrows. The Neolithic weapons are jarring
amid all the advanced technology.

Beyond the tractor, two VTOL vehicles take off.
Armored and heavily armed, they are AT-99
"scorpion" gunships.

Mitsubishi MK-6 AMPSUITS—human-operated walking
machines 4 meters tall—patrol the perimeter. They are
heavily armored, and armed with a huge rotary
cannon called a GAU-90.

Beyond the outer fence stands a black wall of forest
hundreds of feet high. A sentry gun opens fire from
a tower. Tracers light up the twilight. A shadowy
shape shrieks and drops off the fence. *It is an
armed camp in a state of siege.*

Wainfleet and Fike give Jake and his chair the
hairy eyeball as he approaches.

The writer's goal is always to create a movie in the mind of the
reader, but in a way that is fast, easy, and enjoyable to read. Notice first
that the language is simple—no big, esoteric words, no long, convoluted
sentences, no confusing syntax. This is an easy read.

Only those details that create a vivid image quickly and succinctly
are included. The above passage is a bit less than half a page, and would
consume only about half a minute of screen time.

But the elements of the settings are carefully chosen to convey the
threatening nature of Pandora—to give us its essence. Everything
seems big: a tractor taller than a house; walking machines 4 meters tall;
a black wall of forest hundreds of feet high. Nothing is inviting; nothing
even seems human. All we "see" with this description are machines and
weapons. The two people who finally appear give Jake a dirty look—he's
not welcome there.

Notice, too, that the description isn't just visual. The tractor roars past, a shape shrieks, and a gun opens fire. The writer wants you to see, hear, and almost feel the surroundings.

Now read the introduction of Quaritch from the next page of the script:

> On a walkway of the OPS Center, seen from above, a
> UNIFORMED FIGURE grips the railing, watching Jake
> pump his chair through the tunnel below.
>
> The hair is clipped short. The scalp is etched by
> long parallel scars where some Pandoran denizen's
> claws raked across it. The bare arms, below tightly
> rolled sleeves, seem hewn out of some hard tropical
> wood. Criss-crossed by scars.
>
> The MAN raises his masked face to look at the sky.
> His eyes are an icy steel gray.
>
> HIS POV—the mighty POLYPHEMUS seems to fill the sky,
> beyond the clouds.
>
>   MAN (V.O.)
>   You are not in Kansas anymore...
>
> CUT TO:
> INT. COMMISSARY—TWILIGHT
>
> The man from the balcony—COLONEL MILES QUARITCH—is
> the HEAD OF SECURITY for the Hell's Gate colony. A
> hundred new arrivals watch raptly as he paces like
> a panther across the front of the large cafeteria.
> He stops, stance wide.
>
> Without his mask, we see that Quaritch's features
> are rugged and handsome, except for the SCAR, which

```
runs from scalp to jaw down one side of his face. On
one hip he carries a very large PISTOL.
```

Again, the goal in writing description is to convey the *essence* of the setting or character. And everything revealed about Quaritch tells us he's a tough, threatening fighter: the short hair, the scarred scalp, the scarred arms, the icy steel gray eyes, the scarred face, the very large pistol.

The word choice is still simple, but also unique and vivid. He doesn't just have muscular arms; they "seem hewn out of some hard tropical wood." He's not just scarred; his scalp is "etched," his arms are "crisscrossed," his facial scar "runs from scalp to jaw." He doesn't just stand and greet the arrivals; he paces like a panther.

When first introduced, Quaritch is simply a UNIFORMED FIGURE. When a character's name isn't given, then their role has to be written all in capital letters. Then, when we later learn his name, it must also be indicated with all caps. The writer could have given Quaritch's name when first introduced, but delaying it created a bit of anticipation, and made the moment when we fully see him more dramatic. If you like this technique, use it—but probably only once per script so it won't become repetitive.

Action

Now read the following action passage, where Jake chooses his *ikran*—his personal banshee:

```
The banshees. They eye him as he approaches.

Several shriek and take flight. Others flap their
wings and yawn, showing rows of fangs, in a threat
display.

Jake unrolls a weighted leather strap, like a one-
ended bolo.
```

A large male spreads enormous wings, shrieks, and
glares straight at him.

Jake looks directly into its eyes—and strides toward it.

                    JAKE
        Let's dance.

The challenged banshee hisses and leaps at him, jaws
wide as—

Jake times the lunge, swinging the bolo, feinting
and then slipping aside as the banshee's jaws miss
him, snapping shut.

Jake whaps the bolo across its snout. The weighted
thong whips twice around its long jaws, tying them
shut. A muffled scream and it slashes at his stomach
with razor talons but—

Jake is already leaping, over the talons and
tackling the banshee around the neck. It topples
on its side, and he swarms it—arms around its
thrashing head.

Jake grabs its whip-like antenna and brings it
toward his queue but—

The bony head slams sideways, and bam!—clocks him
right in the face, almost knocking him out and—

It writhes, flinging him to the ground. He slides on
the rock and almost goes over the edge as—

Neytiri gasps. Tsu'tey laughs and yells mockingly.

The bolo is coming loose as the creature shakes its
head, way pissed off now, but—

Jake scrambles up and leaps straight at it. Claws
rake his leg but he gets his arms around its head
and clamps down hard. They flop to the ground and he
scrambles on top, pinning it and—

Grabs its whipping antenna, locks it under his arm,
and jams the end of his queue into it. They fuse
together and—

The banshee stops struggling. It lies there panting.
They are locked together, literally eye to eye.

                        JAKE
            That's right! You're mine.

The first thing you might notice reading this passage is how fast it
seems to move. That's because the sentences and the paragraphs are
shorter and more staccato than the examples of description. And the
double spacing between the paragraphs greatly accelerates the pace. It's
easy to imagine a cut in the film every time a new paragraph begins.

This is one of the big action sequences in the screenplay, so it's appropriate to write it this way—so the action moves as fast for the reader
as it does for the audience watching the movie.

Notice the language as well. Again, it's simple and easy to read. But
the writer employs vivid action verbs to create the images and keep us
emotionally involved. Jake doesn't just "go" toward the banshee. He
strides, *lunges*, *whaps*, *leaps*, *tackles*, and *scrambles*. The banshee's jaws *snap*
shut. Its head *clocks* him. The claws *rake* his leg.

Notice, too, how much detail there is to this action. If the writer
merely said, "Jake jumps on the banshee's back, falls off, jumps on again,
and is taken for a wild ride," not only would the image created be fuzzy

and emotionally uninvolving, the entire three or four minute scene (from the arrival at the banshee rookery to Jake's conquest and flight) would only last half a page. In the shooting script, it lasts, as it should, three full pages.

With both the description and the action, the goal of all this carefully chosen language is to keep the reader so emotionally involved that she forgets she's reading words on a page. The effect of these scenes is to make us feel like we are on Pandora, we are meeting Quaritch, and we are taming and flying the banshee.

When James Cameron wrote this, he knew he was going to direct it himself. And after the success of *Titanic*, he was probably pretty certain he'd get it financed. Yet he still made the script as vivid and emotionally involving as he could. So, if he can be that conscientious, shouldn't you show the same care with *your* screenplays?

Dialogue

Finally, here's a dialogue passage from the scene where Grace goes to Selfridge to ask that Jake be replaced:

```
INT. OPS CENTER—DUSK

It looks like an air-traffic control tower, with
lots of screens and bay windows showing the whole
complex.

ADMINISTRATOR PARKER SELFRIDGE takes a ball from a
newly opened case of Titleists and sets it on the
floor. Selfridge is young, charismatic, focused.
Some would say ruthless.

He assumes the stance and lines up his putt, toward
a practice cup across the control room floor. He
glances up as Grace strides toward him.
```

                    GRACE
          Parker, I used to think it was benign
          neglect, but now I see you're inten-
          tionally screwing us.

                  SELFRIDGE
          Grace. You know I enjoy our little
          talks.

                    GRACE
          I need a research assistant, not some
          jarhead dropout.

Selfridge looks down and hits the ball. Grace kicks
the practice cup aside, and the ball rolls past.
Selfridge looks at her with a sigh.

                  SELFRIDGE
          Actually, we got lucky with him.

                    GRACE
          Lucky? How is this in any way lucky?

As Selfridge saunters over to retrieve the ball—

                  SELFRIDGE
          Well—lucky your guy had a twin broth-
          er, and lucky the brother wasn't an
          oral hygienist or something. A marine
          we can use. I'm assigning him to your
          team as security escort.

                    GRACE
          The last thing I need is another
          trigger-happy asshole out there!

                    SELFRIDGE
          Look, you're supposed to be winning
          the hearts and minds of the natives.
          Isn't that the whole point of your
          little puppet show? If you look like
          them, if you talk like them, they'll
          trust you?

Selfridge crosses to his office, behind a glass wall
nearby. Grace follows.

                    SELFRIDGE
          But after—how many years?—relations
          with the indigenous are only getting
          worse.

                    GRACE
          That tends to happen when you use
          machine guns on them.

On Selfridge's desk is a magnetic base, and hovering
in midair, in the invisible field, is a lump of
METALLIC ROCK. Pure UNOBTANIUM.

He grabs it and holds it up between thumb and
forefinger, in front of Grace's eyes.

                    SELFRIDGE
          This is why we're here. Unobtanium.
          Because this little gray rock sells
          for twenty million a kilo. No other
          reason. This is what pays for the
          party. And it's what pays for your
          science. *Comprendo?*

He places it back in the magnetic field.

```
                SELFRIDGE
    Those savages are threatening our
    whole operation. We're on the brink of
    war and you're supposed to be finding
    a diplomatic solution. So use what
    you've got and get me some results.
```

Consider the writer's objective with this scene, which serves several purposes. It's primarily an expository scene—we need to understand why everyone is on Pandora—the mining operation, the mercenaries, and the scientists. But it also serves to introduce Selfridge, to establish the antagonistic relationship he has with Grace, and to set up more of the initial disdain Grace has for Jake. And it lays the groundwork for the hidden agenda Selfridge and Quaritch have—to use Jake to gather information on the Na'vi.

With those goals in mind, the scene begins with Grace simply arriving at Selfridge's command center, and ends with his refusing her request to get rid of Jake. But notice that the scene ends with dialogue—not with Grace saying okay and leaving. By cutting the scene off with Selfridge's line " . . . get me some results," the writer creates more curiosity and anticipation (will she be able to get more results, and how?), and keeps the momentum going more effectively by jumping right into the next scene and back to Jake (seeing his avatar).

Now ask what each character's objective is in the scene. Clearly Grace wants to get rid of Jake, and Selfridge wants him to stay—and to get Grace out of his hair.

Consider the other ways James Cameron could have given us all this information about what's going on: the narrator could have filled us in; an orientation lecture could have been given to all the new arrivals; Max could have told Jake who all the players were as he was showing him around. But none of those options would have what this scene has: *conflict*. Always remember, your goal is to elicit emotion, and emotion grows out of conflict. The scene is far more compelling because Grace's goal and Selfridge's goal are in opposition.

When Grace storms in with her initial accusation, Selfridge responds, "Grace. You know I enjoy our little talks." Selfridge's response is filled with subtext. He's sarcastic and superior—he clearly doesn't like Grace, and he knows he holds the power in their relationship. His sarcasm also implies that her complaining is not a new situation—the two have obviously been at odds for some time.

Their mutual dislike is reinforced with more sarcasm and put-downs as the scene progresses. He refers to the avatar program as a "puppet show" and the Na'vi as "savages." When he says relations have gotten worse, she replies, "That tends to happen when you use machine guns on them."

These lines also illustrate how on-the-nose dialogue can be transformed into more natural, clever, and enjoyable dialogue with slang, jargon, and figures of speech. Grace doesn't call Jake a retired marine but rather a "jarhead dropout" and a "trigger-happy asshole." And Selfridge doesn't say, "The mining operation has provided our funding," he holds up a chip of unobtanium and says, "This is what pays for the party."

Finally, notice how the complete scene meets every item on the dialogue and scene checklists from chapter 6:

1. *It contributes to the hero's overall outer motivation.* Although Jake isn't even in the scene, the scene is still about him, and he will now be able to continue as part of the program

2. *It is consistent with the characters.* Grace represents science and connecting with the Na'vi; Selfridge represents money above all else; and their dialogue is consistent with their education, roles, and attitudes.

3. *It reveals background, inner motivation, conflict, or theme.* Their background (at least with regard to Pandora) is clear; Grace's inner motivation is discovery and Selfridge's is greed; the battle between those two forces is indicative of the bigger theme of the movie,

which values connection over self-interest and emotional isolation.

4. *It is clever, original, and enjoyable to read.*

5. *It has a beginning* (Grace's arrival), *middle* (their argument), *and end* (Selfridge's refusal to remove Jake from the program).

6. *It thrusts us into the following scenes.* We now want to see what will happen when Jake the marine begins working with Grace, and we're curious about exactly what the avatar program is.

7. *The scene contains action.* The business with the golf balls and the unobtanium chip keeps it from being just a talking heads scene.

8. *The scene serves multiple functions*: exposition; character introduction; conflict; anticipation; curiosity; theme.

A FINAL WORD ABOUT *AVATAR*

I know I said at the outset that opinions of *Avatar* weren't really relevant to our discussion. My purpose in choosing this example was simply to show how a very successful screenplay was able to elicit emotion so effectively, and to reinforce the principles I've presented in the book so far.

But I do want to add one editorial comment.

There seems to be a feeling among some that the film was a humongous hit solely because of the dazzling 3-D art direction, cinematography, and special effects. Certainly there's no denying that the breathtaking *look* of the movie, and the way the technological advances immerse the audience in this amazing world, add immensely to the emotional experience. But to think that is the sole reason for its popularity is simply wrong.

Three billion dollars worth of filmgoers don't pay just to watch special effects, no matter how breathtaking they are. If they did, a documentary, a travelogue, or simply a demo reel for the technology could have been this successful. It's the *screenplay* that has made *Avatar* the biggest moneymaker of all time. Not by itself, but in combination with the direction and the performances and all of the other elements that must combine to make a successful movie. Story isn't the only thing, but it's the foundation of everything. Moviemakers are storytellers, and James Cameron's unequalled success as a filmmaker comes first and foremost from his ability to tell a great story.

Avatar is a movie that touches people, and moves people, and excites them and inspires them and makes them think and makes them feel. And it does those things the way great scripts always do, by allowing the audience to get inside a character and go on a journey that connects them with their humanity. And doing all that for millions and millions of people throughout the world has to be worthy of some recognition.

Some critics have admired the experience *Avatar* provides, but call the story "familiar" or "clichéd" or "clunky."

Maybe. Or maybe because it's not dark, or defeated, or esoteric, it's hard to see it as meaningful and artistic.

This is a screenplay that gives us a hero who feels crippled and powerless, who is stuck within his defeat and cynicism in a world suffering from the effects of too much greed and too little humanity. But this hero finds the courage to transform himself, and in doing so finds love and saves what is natural and good. The movie is hopeful. It tells us that the world may seem desolate and overwhelming, but that there are things worth fighting for, that we can be warriors in a battle for what is right, and that by finding our connection to each other, and the planet, and to our spiritual source, we can triumph.

Yes, this is familiar—storytellers have been saying these things since civilization began. But we need to hear it again. And again. And based on the response to *Avatar*, apparently we're all hungry for it.

PART THREE

THE BUSINESS OF SCREENWRITING

NINE

MARKETING YOURSELF AS A SCREENWRITER

THE TITLE OF THIS BOOK IS INCOMPLETE. IT IS NOT THE SALE OF YOUR screenplay but the sale of *yourself* that should be your primary goal in pursuit of a screenwriting career. You ultimately want to make money writing for the movies or television. Selling your completed screenplays is certainly one way to accomplish that. But keep in mind that *you* are the commodity. It is your talent that you are marketing, and your screenplays will exhibit that talent.

The majority of films produced by Hollywood do not originate with completed screenplays. Sequels, remakes, adaptations of novels, comic books, games, and true stories, and movies that originated as ideas—these comprise most of what appears in movie theaters and on television. "Spec" scripts—screenplays written speculatively, which are completed before any deal is negotiated—account for less than a third of the movies seen on the big screen, and essentially none of the episodic series shown on television.

It is far more important that your screenplay indicate your talents and abilities as a screenwriter than that your script is sold outright. The sale of your screenplay is always a goal, and it is wonderful when it happens, but you must also use your screenplay as a calling card and a writing sample that will enable you to get additional work as a screenwriter.

Those of you who have heard me lecture, or who have worked with me as a consultant, know that I believe writers place far too much emphasis on getting an agent, and far too little on writing a script that won't *need* an agent. Talent and commitment rise to the surface quickly in Hollywood, and once you have a well-written, emotionally involving screenplay that has real commercial potential, there are many paths to a deal.

Unfortunately, this doesn't mean you can stick your completed masterpiece under your pillow and wait for the Script Fairy to bring you a three-picture deal. Developing relationships and getting your work read is essential to your success.

I'm talking here about *selling*. Good, old-fashioned, pavement-beating, door-knocking, phone-dialing salesmanship. If your goal is to support yourself as a screenwriter, you can't spend all your time in the closet, writing. You must accept the fact that part of your job entails risking rejection, frustration, and discouragement by putting yourself on the line and selling yourself to the people who can get your movies made.

MAKING SURE YOUR SCRIPT IS READY

Before you begin your marketing campaign, you must be sure you have the *essential* item for pursuing your career: a good screenplay.

In order to market yourself as a screenwriter, you *must* have a completed screenplay. This is absolutely critical. It will not suffice to have book rights, a treatment, a hot idea, interest from a star, or anything else short of a complete screenplay. You can use those other things to pursue producing, but not to become a screenwriter. The exceptions to this are so rare that they are best ignored. Take it as law that until you complete a screenplay, you cannot begin pursuing any of the avenues toward your ultimate goal.

Not only must you have a completed screenplay, it must fall into the category you're pursuing: half-hour situation comedy, one-hour episode, or feature-length film (feature film or TV movie). And two completed screenplays in your area of interest are more than twice as good as one. Each additional screenplay will be better than the previous one, increase your chances of success, and show your contacts that you are committed to your goal.

Don't consider writing a miniseries or a pilot for an episodic series that does not yet exist. These two television forms are almost always written by established screenwriters who have already proven themselves.

And most of all, to market yourself effectively, you must have a *professional caliber* screenplay. So before you start submitting your script, you must be certain it's good enough.

Unfortunately, you can't trust your own judgment in this regard. Of course *you* think it's great; you've been working on your screenplay so long and hard by now that *Plan Nine from Outer Space* would seem great to you if it was your creation. So, to get a more objective sense of the quality of your script, follow this process:

When you finish what you believe is your final rewrite, put your screenplay in a drawer for a week, just to get some emotional distance. Otherwise you'll be so relieved to have completed it that you'll have no objectivity about it at all. Then give it one final polish, making certain, as honestly as you can, that your script meets all the requirements outlined in this book. Go over it carefully for typos and grammatical and spelling errors and put it in the best form you possibly can.

When your screenplay is as good as you can possibly get it, register it for a copyright with the U.S. Copyright office (copyright.gov/register) and with the Writers Guild of America (wgawregistry.org/webrss). This is your best protection against plagiarism, and for proper credit should your script ever be rewritten and then produced.

Then ask five people whose judgment you trust to read the screenplay and give you their suggestions. You trust their judgment because they are intelligent, know something about movies, and work in the film business, or at least have read lots of screenplays.

It won't hurt to give one to your mom, so you can be certain of at least one good response. But the other copies should go to people who you know will be honest, neither overly sensitive to your feelings nor falsely critical.

Script Consultants

Instead of these five friends and contacts, you might want to hire a consultant to either critique your script or coach you on it.

I'm one of those people, and I've been coaching writers and filmmakers for a long, long time. So I'm partial to this choice, provided that: (1) the consultant is knowledgeable about story and screenwriting; (2) the consultant is experienced (both in Hollywood and as a consultant); (3) their fee is fair and within your budget; (4) they are ethical and honorable, and don't promise more than they can deliver; and (5) their personality and approach are a good fit for your own needs, project, and personality.

You can determine all of this by checking out the consultant's background and experience with an Internet search, by hearing the consultant lecture and reading his or her books or articles, by talking to others who have used the consultant's services, and especially by talking to the consultant directly.

The advantage of a good consultant is that working with one should guarantee you both honesty and a high level of expertise. The disadvantage is they cost money—sometimes a lot of money. Fees for script consulting services range anywhere from $50 for simple "coverage," or comments by a relatively inexperienced reader, to thousands of dollars for a top-level consultant.

When I first began coaching writers on their scripts, the term barely existed, and there were just a handful of us offering such services. Now you can throw a stick anywhere in Los Angeles and you're likely to hit someone calling himself a script consultant.

In my experience, and according to a recent poll done by *Creative Screenwriting* magazine, most screenwriters who have used consultants are very happy with the guidance they received. But I have also worked with a lot of screenwriters who came to me after working with consultants and teachers who had never been professional enough (or perhaps knowledgeable enough) to tell them their story had no empathetic hero, no clear story concept, wasn't remotely commercial, wasn't properly structured, or that it wasn't even formatted properly. So do your homework before selecting a consultant and plopping your money down.

Rewriting

When your five contacts or your script consultant have responded to your screenplay, you face one of the toughest stages of the entire process. Because *most of the time* they will tell you that your screenplay isn't ready to show. Nearly all professional-caliber screenplays have to go through lots of drafts, and at least a couple rounds of comments from outsiders, before they can be submitted to anyone in power.

As emotionally wrenching as it will be, often you have to go back to square one (or at least back to square five or six) with your story concept, and do a complete rewrite, using all of the principles you know and all the feedback you got. You might even have to accept that you've done as much as you can with this particular idea, and now your best course of action is to trash it and go on to a new story concept that possesses greater potential.

Either path (a major rewrite or moving on to another story idea) is excruciating for a while. But take courage in knowing that every successful writer has faced this decision many times in his career, that your next script or your next rewrite will *always* be better, and that the process up to this point has been both fulfilling (probably) and educational (certainly).

Never bypass this outside-feedback stage. To submit a weak screenplay to people with the power to get you a deal is worse than submitting nothing.

Let's say, for example, that through your contacts you are able to get your script to Ridley Scott, and in your eagerness to take advantage of this good fortune, you send him a screenplay that isn't ready. So he politely rejects it. Then you write your next screenplay, which *is* terrific.

How eager is Ridley Scott going to be to read another script from the same guy who a few months ago sent him a piece of junk? Now let's assume, more positively, that out of the five contacts who read your script at least two have a strong positive response. If at least two out of the five think your screenplay has strong potential and is ready or nearly ready to submit, then you can move forward. You'll never get all five people to agree on anything, including your script, and two out of five is a positive enough reaction that you should prepare the script for submission.

If you're using a script consultant, they will tell you when they believe it is ready to submit. Or, more likely, they will say, "If you make this and this and this correction, it will be ready to take to producers." When these suggestions have become simple and minimal enough that they are easy to follow on your own, use them as a basis for your final polish.

When you have gone through this entire process and are now confident that your script is as good as it needs to be, register it once again for a copyright and with the WGA. Now you are ready to begin the marketing process.

THE THREE KEYS TO MARKETING YOURSELF

Once your script is ready, and you're willing to put yourself out there with the determination of a Terminator in order to launch your career, there are three principles to keep firmly in mind:

1. **Try everything.** Talk to ten working screenwriters, and you'll hear ten different stories of exactly how they broke into the business and reached that first rung of success. Anything that doesn't hurt anybody should be attempted, even if it stretches the limits of your courage and chutzpah.

2. **Don't listen to statistics.** All of those stories about the number of screenwriters who are out of work, or the thousands of unsold

screenplays the Writers Guild has registered, or the impossibility
of getting an agent, only serve one purpose: to dissuade you from
your goal.

You shouldn't pursue a screenwriting career in blissful ignorance of the realities of the marketplace. But once you decide that
your dream, your path to personal fulfillment, is through screenwriting, then you must focus on those methods and attitudes that
will enable you to realize your goal. *The fact that someone else failed
to achieve the same goal has nothing to do with you.*

But if you're determined to hear some cold, hard statistics, here
are some to consider very carefully:

► *100 percent of the screenwriters who now have agents at one
time didn't have agents*

► *100 percent of the screenwriters who are now working at one
time weren't working*

► *100 percent of the screenwriters who have made money at
screenwriting at one time hadn't made a dime*

And in addition, if you had any notion of the amount of absolute garbage that's floating around Hollywood between script covers, you'd never again wonder if you could compete for talent. In
all my years of meetings and pitches and negotiations and interviews and writers' conferences, I have never *once* heard any producer or agent or star or studio executive say, "We are no longer
looking for good screenwriters."

The difficulty you face has nothing to do with statistics. It's
that wherever there is so much garbage, there has to be a filtering
system. And that's why God made the reader.

That's also why so many of those same producers and agents
and stars and executives *do* say that they won't read "unsolicited"

material. Your goal must be to penetrate that filtering system and get your work read by people (including readers) who can help launch your career.

3. **Knowledge is power.** It is insufficient to assume that somewhere out there somebody is looking for a screenplay and maybe it's yours they will buy. You must know specifically *who* the people are who are getting movies made, *what* they are looking for, and *where* you can reach them.

ACQUIRING INFORMATION

To begin pursuing your career as a screenwriter, you must ignore all negative statistics, find the courage to put yourself and your work out there in the marketplace in any way you can, and start acquiring loads of information. And there are two ways to find out the things you need to know:

Contacts

A contact is anyone you know. It is not just anyone in the film business, not just anyone who has ever written a screenplay, not just anyone who lives in Hollywood. It is anyone you know, period. Your accountant's sister's boyfriend's daughter might be the Hollywood manager who will be willing to read your screenplay or the financier who will want to invest in your movie.

Networking is simply the process of meeting two people and having them each introduce you to two people who in turn each introduce you to two more. By continually pursuing this process, you eventually will have a massive pyramid of names that will lead you to the specific people who will pay you for your work. What you are actually acquiring from each person in that chain, each individual in your network, is information: information about (or introductions to) other people, or about that particular individual's screenwriting needs.

Once you regard everyone you encounter as a contact, you will be-come increasingly effective at expanding your base of operation and at obtaining information. There are numerous situations for meeting people in order to promote your career: attending film classes and writ-ers' conferences, joining writers' groups and professional organizations in the film industry, contacting city or state film commissions, volun-teering on student films or independent productions, even switching your job to one in the movie industry.

This last suggestion does not mean quitting your job as a stockbro-ker to become a grip on the local TV station's farm report. But if you are working as a secretary at a bean cannery, why not see if you can obtain the same position for a film production company? It will give you addi-tional information about the film business and will greatly increase your contacts.

Another well-known source of contacts is the social gathering, which brings us to the myth of the Hollywood Party. Particularly in Los Angeles, there seems to be a notion that unless you're invited to George Clooney's house regularly, you really haven't got much of a chance of being a screenwriter.

Being invited to George Clooney's house would probably be a lot of fun. *I'd* like to be invited to George Clooney's house. But the truth about Hollywood parties is that either (1) people who meet there for the first time are just making contacts, or (2) people who close deals there are just continuing discussions and negotiations that probably began in someone's office or over the telephone earlier that week. It's extremely rare that someone meets a mogul for the first time over cocktails and closes a deal for their screenplay before the party's over. Lots of success-ful screenwriters never even go to parties.

Starting today, make the pursuit of contacts a part of your screen-writing efforts until it becomes second nature. When anyone asks you what you do for a living, say you're a screenwriter. Later on you can mention that you're a neurosurgeon on the side. You must give people an opportunity to connect with your pursuit and give you whatever in-formation they have.

The key to using contacts is this: don't be afraid to ask for a favor, but never depend on one. The film business, like most other businesses, revolves around favors. When you ask for something, assume your contact is enough of a grown-up to say no if he really doesn't want to do it. And you must not be offended if he does say no. This is a key principle of honest, assertive behavior.

But your career will grind to a halt if you ask one person for a favor and then sit back and wait until he delivers as promised. The favor you have asked may be high on your list of priorities, but it won't be high on his. Ask politely for the favor, be very appreciative when it is promised, and then go on to your next contact to get additional information or ask for more help. Then, if the first person delivers as promised, you're in terrific shape, and if he doesn't, you haven't lost ground through laziness or cowardice.

The Media

Books, magazines such as *Creative Screenwriting* and *Scr(i)pt*, the trade papers (*Variety* and the *Hollywood Reporter*), the daily newspaper, television, and even radio are among the sources of information that must supplement your contacts. Given the multitude of articles, interviews, programs, and publicity events that are generated by the film industry, the media offer a wealth of information to aid in the pursuit of your career.

And then there's the Internet. Believe it or not, when I first wrote this book there was no Internet. (Actually, there was, but who knew?) Now it is such a powerful, familiar, and ubiquitous source of information that it often supplants all those others listed above. Directories, listings, newspaper articles, interviews (both filmed and written), panel discussions, video press kits, Web sites, blogs, Twitter, and whatever other information pipelines have been created between the time I wrote this sentence and the time you're reading it—these are all tools you can and must use in the process of marketing yourself and your work.

Let's say you've written a kind of quirky romantic comedy, similar in tone, style, and/or budget to *(500) Days of Summer*. If you go to the

Internet Movie Database (see below), you can get the names of the producers, the director, the stars, and the screenwriters for *(500) Days of Summer*, as well as the names and contact information for the people who represent them. You can also view a video featuring some of these people, to get a better sense of how they made the deal or got involved, or what they look for in projects. You can link to a list of every project each of those people has contributed to, and all the unreleased films they are now involved in. You can even find a link to the PDF version of the shooting script posted by the distributor, Fox Searchlight Pictures (though this is more helpful to your craft than to the marketing process).

You now have the names and locations of a number of people you can approach with your own script. And that's just based on one Web site. If you go to boxofficemojo.com, you can learn what the budget of *(500) Days of Summer* was, and how much it grossed domestically and internationally. If you do a search of screenwriters Scott Neustadter and Michael Weber, you'll find an interview they did for the *Knight News*, where they talk about how they wrote the script. And that site links to an interview with director Marc Webb. And so on.

The Web offers such a huge variety of sites and sources for information on screenwriting that it's impossible to include even a small portion of them here. So instead I want to list just four that I believe are *essential* for screenwriters:

1. **The Internet Movie Database (imdb*pro*.com).** This site has listings for (it seems) just about every U.S. movie ever made, plus lots of foreign films, plus most TV episodic series. Each listing provides log lines and synopses of each film, lots of other goodies such as clips and trivia and quotes and pictures, and, most important, the names of just about everyone involved in that project, with links to lists of all the *other* films they've been involved with. Imdb.com is free. The "pro" at the end refers to their subscription site. For a very modest monthly or annual fee, you can get links to the names and contact information for the producers', directors', and

screenwriters' companies, and/or for the agents, managers, and attorneys who represent them.

2. **Done Deal Pro (donedealpro.com).** This terrific site provides a listing of all the projects in development at the studios and networks cross-referenced by genre, company, the people involved, and their representatives and contact information. It also offers news on the latest script, book, treatment, and pitch deals, interviews with writers and other filmmakers, and a database of screenwriting contests and submission deadlines. The subscription fee is modest, and more than worth the price.

3. **The Writers Store (writersstore.com)** offers every available screenwriting book, CD, DVD, and computer program, plus a wealth of other tools and resources for screenwriters. I've known and worked with the Writers Store since before this book was first released, and can guarantee the people are wonderful, knowledgeable, and will do whatever they can to facilitate your craft and career.

4. **StoryMastery (storymastery.com)** is my Web site. Blatant self-promotion notwithstanding, the site contains an abundance of articles, questions and answers, videos, and other resources for screenwriters and novelists.

Now that you know you must go to contacts and the media to tap into the power of information, what exactly is the information you want, and how will you use it?

THE FOUR PATHS TO A DEAL

Four categories of people will enable you to secure a screenwriting deal: the *representative*, the *producer*, the *element*, and the *financier*. Within each of these categories, you must determine *who* the individuals are with the power to get a movie made, *what* they are looking for in a client or a project, and *where* you can reach them.

Usually you will need at least two of these people attached to you or your project in order to secure a deal. For example, you might sign with a representative (an agent or manager), who in turn will submit your screenplay to a production company, which will attach an element (a star or director) to it and will then set up a production deal for your film with a financier (a studio, distributor, or investor).

You will approach all of these people on your own, *simultaneously*— never just one at a time. Begin by creating a marketing folder, either on your computer or using a three-ring binder. Designate a section of the folder or notebook for each of the four categories of people mentioned above, plus a fifth section for general contacts.

It's actually a great idea to create this folder *as soon as you begin working on your first story and screenplay*. If you've already started work on your script, and you don't have a folder of contacts yet, start it right now. That way, by the time your screenplay is ready to market, you will have a long list of people and companies to approach.

Each time you obtain a new name through your contacts or the media, enter that person's name, address, phone number, and e-mail into the appropriate grouping. If you don't have them all, use the resources above to find them. Enter the date, any additional information you have, and the source of the information or introduction. Whenever you find additional information on this person, add it to their file or listing.

PURSUING THE PEOPLE IN POWER

Understanding what agents, managers, producers, and development executives deal with on a day-to-day basis will help you understand why they sometimes seem inaccessible, and why you must be both tenacious and *considerate* when asking them to read your work. By better understanding how your screenplay affects the agent's goals and workload, you can be far more effective at getting your desired response.

Here's what you should know about agents (and the same holds true for managers, producers, and all the other categories of buyer):

1. An agent is incredibly overworked. Her typical ten- to fourteen-hour day includes a breakfast meeting, a lunch meeting, staff meetings, negotiations, contracts, memos, e-mails, evening screenings, and *at least a hundred phone calls per day*. As soon as you contact the agent, you've added one more item to her endless "to do" list.

2. She is being pulled in several directions at once, with demands from bosses, clients, clients' managers, other agents, producers, development executives, her company's lawyers, the studios' and networks' lawyers, and (if she's foolish enough to try to have a personal life) her own family. As soon as you make contact, you've become one more person who wants to be taken care of.

3. She never has time to read screenplays. Every Friday, her backseat is piled with scripts and novels she must be prepared to discuss at her agency's Monday morning meeting. If she agrees to read your script, her pile will just get bigger.

4. Clients of the agency, bosses' requests, and deals "on the table" will always be given priority over submissions from unknown writers.

5. Her agency only wants clients who can make them money. No matter how nice, or sympathetic, or even talented you are, if the agent doesn't think she can sell your work, she can't take you on.

6. She doesn't want clients who will add to her problems with unreasonable demands or unprofessional behavior.

7. And finally, in Hollywood, there is a single universal principle: *the easiest way to avoid more risk, responsibility, and stress is to simply say NO.*

Sounds hopeless, doesn't it? But it's not. I just want you to approach the people in power, listed below, in an intelligent, professional way by appreciating their point of view.

And before you begin, three final cardinal rules for considering a buyer's needs without thwarting your own screenwriting goals:

1. **Never apologize!** I may have given you the mistaken impression you should feel guilty for taking up an agent's or executive's valuable time. Not at all. You are a professional, giving another professional the opportunity to make money off your work. Be kind and considerate, but also direct and certain of your talent. Courage and assertiveness are always more effective than withdrawal and self-deprecation.

2. **Reject rejection.** You're playing a numbers game here, and if you take rejection personally, you'll get depressed and give up. There are lots of political and commercial reasons scripts get rejected, which have nothing to do with the quality of the writing.

3. **Keep at it.** Sooner or later you'll find others who share your passion for your work. Remember, the one common quality that all successful screenwriters share is neither intelligence, nor talent, nor connections. It's *tenacity*.

THE REPRESENTATIVE

This category includes anyone who represents you as a screenwriter, helps you find work, and negotiates your screenwriting deals. This could be a literary agent, a manager, or an attorney. A literary agent represents you in return for 10 percent of your income as a screenwriter. A manager might take 15 percent but will often do more to oversee your entire screenwriting career (including, on occasion, finding an agent to work with you as well). An attorney will usually be paid an hourly fee for representing you, regardless of the outcome. Established writers often have two or all three: the manager oversees the writer's career; the agent helps them find work and negotiates deals; the attorney represents the writer legally, perhaps gets involved in negotiation, and finalizes the contracts.

If you're a beginning writer, you will certainly want to pursue agents and managers. But keep in mind that you are pursuing the other three categories (producer, element, financier) *simultaneously*. Should you get an offer from a producer or financier, and you have no literary agent, you can hire an attorney to negotiate your deal. Many well-established screenwriters are represented only by lawyers.

Any agent or manager is going to look for three things in a prospective client:

1. **Someone who will make money for her company.** A representative's only income is 10–15 percent of her clients' earnings (unless they receive packaging or producing fees for a client's produced script). If you don't write scripts that sell, she can't afford to represent you.

2. **A writer with career potential.** Any agent or manager knows that the sale of a first or second screenplay will seldom command major monetary figures by Hollywood standards. But they also know that each successive screenplay will earn a greater amount of money, and an established career can be lucrative for all involved.

3. **Someone who won't add to her problems.** Writers' representatives do battle all day long with executives, producers, business affairs departments, attorneys, and other agents and managers. They don't want to do battle with their own clients as well.

This means if you are positive, energetic, and committed to your writing, the agent will maintain a higher level of enthusiasm representing you than if you are constantly bemoaning the sorry state of your career and your life. Grumbling about meetings, refusing to take suggestions about your script, coming to producers' meetings unprepared, and repeatedly blaming your agent, your manager, your producer, or the film industry for making you one of life's victims is a great way not to get your phone calls returned.

You are also looking for three things in a potential representative:

1. **Someone who will look out for your career.** You don't want a manager who is just out to make a fast 15 percent on your script. Such an attitude would be rare among established, credible agents or managers anyway. You want someone who is enthusiastic about you as a writer, not just about your single script, and who will work with you and guide your career toward fulfillment of your own desires, talents, and goals.

2. **Someone powerful.** Power in the film business can take two forms. The first is *clout*: high standing in the Hollywood community; the influence that comes from a stable of major writers; the backing of a big agency; the ability to get anyone in town on the telephone.

   If your agent also represents Shane Black, Nora Ephron, and Ted Elliot & Terry Rossio, then your agent should have no trouble getting through to the people who can give you work. This is the advantage of representation by Hollywood's biggest agencies: their ability to reach the top studio and network executives and to package your project with the major stars and directors they also represent.

   But there can be a negative side to this kind of clout. If your agent also represents Shane, Nora, and Ted and Terry, how much time will be spent on your behalf? Those other writers can make a million dollars per script or more, and you might be struggling to get a $20,000 rewrite deal. This is why clout is not the only form of power to consider.

   The second form of power is *commitment*: energy, enthusiasm, perseverance, and determination expended on your behalf. If your agent or manager is not one of the biggest in Hollywood but is sincerely enthusiastic and devoted to you as a writer and will get out there and dog after the work for you, you may have found your best representative.

Remember, it is an agent who will represent you, not an agency. The backing of a powerful company can be helpful, but your primary relationship is with the individual representative.

3. **Someone who can negotiate.** This is probably the least important of the three qualities, particularly at the early stages of your career. There is a common misunderstanding that agents spend all day negotiating deals, when in fact the majority of their time is spent actively marketing their clients and their clients' work. It is almost impossible to know in the initial encounters with a representative just what their negotiating power is anyway, and the first two qualifications should take much higher priority.

There is often a feeling of discouragement and frustration among unrepresented writers that follows the old Groucho Marx line: "I wouldn't want to belong to any club that would accept me as a member." It sometimes seems that any agent or manager who would be willing to take you on in the early stages of your career must be hard-up for clients and therefore not have much power or clout. Conversely, someone who really has the ability to represent you well is not looking for new clients and will not be a possibility.

Not only is this Catch-22 reasoning unproductive, it isn't even true. Even major agents lose their screenwriter clients from time to time and might be willing to take an unproven but talented writer into the agency. And whatever the agent's standing in the industry, the critical consideration is the relationship you establish with your agent, how he or she feels about you, and how much the agent will actively and aggressively promote your career.

Just as you may be a new, hungry, but talented and hardworking writer, there are always new, hungry, talented, and hardworking agents and managers entering the movie industry as well.

Researching Possible Representatives

To learn the necessary Who, What, and Where regarding representatives, begin, as always, with your contacts. Every time you meet someone who says he has or knows or is an agent or manager, pump the person for information. Who is the agent? Are you happy with him? Who are his other clients? Does he handle both TV and features? And will you introduce me?

Supplement this firsthand information with secondary research by going to one of the first two Web sites listed above, and following the process I outlined there.

The Writers Guild of America and some other Web sites publish lists of agencies willing to accept unsolicited manuscripts. These companies will consider your script even if you haven't been referred by someone they know. So these lists provide you with the names and addresses of at least a dozen agencies to approach on that basis alone.

The agencies (and managers) willing to read your unsolicited screenplay are certainly worth contacting, but you should never limit yourself to only those representatives. Even if an agency has officially stated that it won't read unsolicited material, approach them anyway. I guarantee *someone* within the last six months got his script read without a referral.

Approaching Representatives

As soon as your screenplay is ready to go, you will begin contacting the representatives whose names are now spilling out of your marketing folder. *Do not send these people your screenplay!* Sending hard copies of your script will cost an immense amount of postage, it will usually be returned unopened, and it will at best be placed unnoticed at the bottom of a very large pile. Even an e-mailed script will simply become an instant victim of the DELETE key.

It is cheaper, more professional, and more productive to first establish direct contact with the representative in the hope of persuading someone to take a look at your work. And even though it is free, don't e-mail them your script either. Not until you convince them to read it.

There are several ways this can be done, so I will begin by detailing the query letter and then outline some variations on that method.

THE QUERY LETTER   The goal of a query letter to a potential representative is to stimulate interest in reading your screenplay. It is a brief, professional letter describing you and your screenplay and laying the groundwork for a future conversation. This letter can be a hard copy or an e-mail, but the approach is the same.

A good query letter is never more than one page long and is written clearly and concisely in your own words. Don't make it overly formal or "cutesy." Your letter should be polite, direct, and to the point, neither cocky and full of hype nor groveling and apologetic.

Be professional and positive in your approach and make the following sentence one of your daily affirmations: *I am a good professional screenwriter, and I am giving people the opportunity to make money from my work.* Seeing *Conan the Barbarian* before talking to an agent might also put you in the proper frame of mind.

Your query letter to a potential agent or manager should include the following:

1. **The purpose of the letter.** State clearly and concisely that you have just completed a screenplay for a feature film or series episode and that you are now looking for representation. Don't beat around the bush with lengthy introductions; get right to the point.

   If the screenplay you are writing is your second or third completed screenplay, then say so. This will show that you are not a dilettante and are determined to pursue your screenwriting career.

2. **A personalized comment.** Try, at least, to make your letter more personal than those for the Publishers' Clearinghouse Sweepstakes. And never address it "To Whom It May Concern." If you're

writing to this particular representative because of a friend's rec-ommendation or because he represents a specific writer, then say so. Nobody gets excited about a form letter.

3. Your background. Briefly give the representative any information about your background that will indicate potential as a screen-writer. If you've ever been published; have been paid for your writ-ing in any arena; have received any writing awards or honors; have ever produced, directed, or written a film; or have a degree in film or writing, then say so. If your background gives you particular insight into the subject of your screenplay, mention that as well. But if you're the ambassador to Sweden, don't bother mentioning it, because it doesn't indicate any particular writing talent.

Even if you have extensive writing experience, do not go into lengthy detail about it. Just mention the high points in order to pique the representative's interest and let it go at that. And don't enclose your résumé unless specifically requested.

4. A description of the screenplay. The single most important ele-ment of any query letter is the description of your project. In one or two sentences you must convey your story concept, with enough detail to convey its uniqueness and its emotional and commercial potential.

A well-written story concept should first convey the genre of the film: "I have just completed a feature-length romantic com-edy." Then it should convey who the hero is (by function, not nec-essarily by name), why we will empathize with that character, the hero's outer motivation and the outer conflict. Then add whatever it is that makes your story unique and emotionally involving. This could be the opportunity presented to the hero, or the hero's plan for accomplishing the goal, or the way the story adds an original element to a more familiar situation.

Study at least a hundred script and movie log lines appearing on the Internet Movie Database, at Done Deal Pro, and in the movie listings for Netflix, Blockbuster, and the cable channels. Use the most effective ones—especially for films in the same genre as yours—as models for describing your own story.

Akeelah and the Bee is a wonderful movie written by Doug Atchison. The Netflix listing reads:

With an aptitude for words, 11-year-old Akeelah Anderson is deter-mined to spell her way out of South Los Angeles, entering scores of local contests and eventually landing a chance to win the Scripps National Spelling Bee in Washington, D.C. Despite discouragement from her mother, Akeelah gets support from her bookish tutor, her principal, and proud members of her community.

In two sentences, we know the hero is Akeelah, she has a dis-couraging mother and lives in South Central L.A. (sympathy to create empathy), she wants to win the Scripps National Spelling Bee (her outer motivation) in spite of her background, her mother, and the fact that she has to win scores of local contests and then compete with the best spellers in the nation to take the top prize (conflict). The story combines the familiarity of a "competition" movie with the unique elements of a national spelling bee and a young girl from a tough, low-income neighborhood.

If I were writing a query letter about this script, I'd probably reword it to heighten those elements:

My latest screenplay, Akeelah and the Bee, *tells the story of a deter-mined 11-year-old African-American girl from inner-city Los Angeles, who has an amazing aptitude for words. Despite the reluctance of a with-drawn tutor, and a discouraging mother who has given up on her own dreams, Akeelah wins her way to the finals of the Scripps National Spell-ing Bee in Washington, D.C., where she competes for the top prize.*

Notice I didn't include the genre of the film, because I would have to use the nondescript and not very commercial category "drama." Instead I emphasized the competition element, giving it more conflict and making it sound almost like a sports movie. You must mold your own description to capitalize on the peak emotional elements of your screenplay.

5. **An offer to sign release forms.** A release form is basically a written agreement that if the agency (or production company) is ever involved in a film that is similar to your story, you won't sue them. So many agencies and production companies require these forms that if you are not willing to sign them, your attempts to market your screenplay will be extremely limited.

My personal tendency would be to sign any of the release forms they require, give them my script, and if they really do rip me off, then sue them anyway. But *this is not legal advice*. I would never presume to give legal advice. I could get in big trouble giving legal advice.

6. **Future contact.** Close your letter in such a way that the follow-up contact is left in your own hands. "I will be contacting you in the next few days to discuss this further," will do the job.

Do not say, "If you would like to read my screenplay, please give me a call," because they wouldn't and they won't. The purpose of this letter is only to lay the groundwork for a telephone call.

Close the letter politely, sign it, if it's a printed version rather than an e-mail, and record the date in your marketing folder. And again, *do not send your screenplay to anyone yet.*

THE FOLLOW-UP CALL   It is best if your letter or e-mail arrives on a Tuesday, Wednesday, or Thursday, although this is a small detail. Most people are too busy on Mondays to deal with minor (to them) correspondence and too eager to go home on Fridays to give it their full attention. Allow an extra day or two (but no longer) for the letter to arrive, then call the representative's office and ask to talk to her. Sometimes it is wise to make your call after six thirty p.m., because often a represen-tative's assistant will go home at that time and the agent or manager is answering her own phone. Most often, however, you will deal with the agent's assistant.

This brings up a cardinal rule of marketing your screenplay: *Be nice to assistants!* For at least three reasons:

1. They deserve it. Assistants work unbelievably hard and are given the thankless job of screening out calls like yours.

2. If you don't get the assistant on your side, you'll never persuade the agent to read your screenplay. Piss off an assistant, and you'll be put on hold indefinitely.

3. In many cases, an assistant is trying to work his way up the show business ladder to become an agent, manager, or development ex-ecutive himself. And one of the first extra duties he'll take on is reading unsolicited scripts. In other words, you may be talking to the very person who will end up reading your script anyway.

When you get the assistant on the phone, ask to talk to the agent or manager. When the assistant asks why you are calling, be direct. You can begin by saying that the agent should have received your letter and will be expecting your call. But don't tap-dance around your motives. Tell the assistant that you have completed a screenplay and want to dis-cuss it with his boss.

The stock answer many assistants are instructed to give is simply that the company does not accept unsolicited material. Here is where you must use whatever combination of salesmanship, persuasion, and charm you can muster to try to get through to the representative.

If that proves impossible, ask if there are other agents or managers at the company who might be willing to talk to you. Or ask the assistant if *he* will read your screenplay. If he likes it, you can be sure the agent will hear about it.

Or at least try to come away with another contact: ask if there are any other agencies or individuals the assistant can recommend you approach.

Your objective is not necessarily to get the specific representative you approached to read your screenplay, but to get *anyone* at the company to take a look at it.

As a final objective, leave the door open for future communication. End the conversation with the statement, "Perhaps I'll call back in a month or so to see if the situation there has changed at all." If you're nice and if you keep calling back periodically, eventually you may get enough sympathy from the assistant, or create enough guilt, that someone will take a look at your work.

There will be lots of instances when you won't be able to accomplish any of these things, and your relationship with a particular agency or management company will dead-end right there. But if the process gets your screenplay read even once out of every ten attempts, that means at least thirty out of the more than three hundred literary agents and managers in Hollywood will eventually look at your script. Since you scored at least two out of five positive reactions to your screenplay earlier in the process, you should have a 40 percent chance that these thirty will like it, too. And having twelve agents in Hollywood like your work would be an unbelievably positive result.

The business of pursuing representatives is a numbers game, and it requires perseverance to find the person who is right for you. Never allow yourself to get discouraged to the point of quitting. Remember, you don't *have* to have an agent at all. You're pursuing the other three categories *at the same time*, and you can always hire an attorney to do anything an agent does.

THE SIXTY-SECOND PITCH   When you are able to get an agent or manager on the telephone, be brief. Always ask, "Is this a good time for you, or would you like me to call back when it's more convenient?" A little chitchat is okay to break the ice, but then get to the point.

After introducing yourself, the first question you are likely to hear is, "What is your screenplay about?" It makes less than a great impression when you answer, "Well . . . uh . . . I don't know . . . you see, there's this guy . . . and he . . . well, no . . . first there's this girl . . ." and so on.

It's understandable that you would have a hard time being succinct about your script. You've just spent months or years of your life carefully constructing 110 brilliantly intricate pages. Now someone is asking you to convey your entire story in a couple of sentences. Which brings us to the principle of the sixty-second pitch.

I have actually written an entire book on this very subject. *Selling Your Story in 60 Seconds: The Guaranteed Way to Get Your Screenplay or Novel Read* gives you all the principles for persuading someone to look at your script in just such a situation, along with templates for pitching different genres, and essays by dozens of film and publishing executives on what makes a good pitch. Not surprisingly, I strongly recommend you get a copy when you're ready to begin the marketing process.

Meanwhile, here are the most important elements of describing your story.

When someone asks what your script is about, the worst thing you can do is to try to tell him your entire story. You simply don't have time to meander through all of the plot elements, and you'll get lost in the thicket of your own verbiage.

Instead, tell this person just the key elements of your screenplay: your hero; the situation she is in at the beginning of the story (which includes the reasons we will empathize); the opportunity that is presented to her; the outer motivation that grows out of her new situation; and the obstacles that make achieving her goal seem impossible.

Design a pitch that reveals these components in a way that matches your personality and your particular story. Then practice it. And practice it. And practice it some more, until it sounds natural and conveys your own passion for your project.

Then, when you have the representative on the phone, present these elements in a simple, conversational way—just the way you would recommend a movie to a friend. Finally, end (don't begin) your pitch with the title of your script, and ask if the person has any questions, or if he would like you to send him a copy of the script.

After asking about your story concept, the agent's next question might concern your living outside of southern California (if indeed you do). At this point, you can say that you are prepared to move to Los Angeles if necessary, when there is a definite prospect of work or income by doing so, and reiterate that you can be in L.A. whenever necessary.

It is okay to admit that you can't just move to Los Angeles, giving up your job and your entire support system, unless there is a definite prospect of income to replace your current living situation. There is also nothing wrong with admitting poverty when approaching people in Hollywood. Every agent in town has worked with writers who at one time in their careers were waiting tables or making deliveries.

Some representatives simply won't be willing to discuss your project with you or read your script until you have moved to Los Angeles. But others will look at your material to see what kind of potential you have as a screenwriter, and won't care where you live.

Whatever direction the conversation takes beyond this, your goal is to get the representative, or someone else at the company, to agree to read your screenplay. As soon as someone says he's willing to take a look at it, ask him if he would like you to mail a hard copy or e-mail a digital version. Then politely end the conversation. Immediately mail (or e-mail) a copy of your script to the person you spoke to along with a brief cover letter or e-mail reminding him who you are, thanking him for his time, and expressing your eagerness to get his response to your work. Don't use the cover letter to pitch your script again. You've already won an agreement to read your work; now let the screenplay stand on its own merits.

Be sure to keep copies of all correspondence for your records. If you want to get the screenplay back, enclose a self-addressed, stamped envelope. Usually a script is good for about two or three submissions before it's too dog-eared or coffee-stained to send out. Psychologically, you always want hard copies of your screenplay to look like they're hot off the presses, so each buyer or representative subconsciously believes she's the first person to read it.

After sending the screenplay, wait a few days and call the assistant to make sure it arrived. Then wait a month or so for a response to the screenplay. It's always impossible to say how long it will take to get your material read—turnaround time is sometimes immediate if the company has a staff of readers, but other times a reaction can take endless months. Understand that your unsolicited screenplay always goes to the bottom of a very large stack of scripts, and is always superseded by scripts from the representative's own clients.

Don't be discouraged if it takes a long time to get a response to your script. This often means the agent or producer is reading it himself, rather than passing it on to a reader. Simply call once a month to politely ask the assistant if it's been read yet, just to make sure it hasn't fallen through the cracks at the agency or production company. There is no advantage to getting angry and asking for the script back if it isn't read as quickly as you'd like. Even if it takes the company a year, by then you might have already acquired and dropped one representative, and will again be interested in this first manager or agent's response. Also, since you're pursuing a hundred other people simultaneously, any one person can take as long as they need without you getting frustrated or angry.

If the person pays a reader to read and evaluate your screenplay, the reader will give the agent a *synopsis*, or *coverage*, of your screenplay, plus comments and recommendations. This frees agents, managers, and producers from having to read everything submitted to them.

Don't worry that the agent might not read your script himself. Most readers are very conscientious, and are longing to find a script they can recommend. If your screenplay does a good job of eliciting emotion in a reader, his boss will hear about it.

Synopses are sometimes confused with treatments. A synopsis is written after the completed screenplay. Avoid attempting synopses of your own work unless a potential buyer specifically requires one with your screenplay. Let your script stand on its own merits. Story analysis (the formal term for the job of a reader) requires a different kind of talent and is almost impossible to do well for your own work.

Treatments, which are prose versions of film stories written prior to the screenplay, will be discussed in chapter 9.

Gird yourself for a lot of refusals before you start getting positive responses. Remember that (1) every successful writer had to go through the same thing; (2) it's a numbers game, and there are three hundred-plus representatives in Los Angeles, and dozens more in New York and elsewhere; (3) you are concurrently pursuing other categories of people to get a deal; (4) you can hire an attorney to negotiate for you when the need arises; and (5) the entire time that you're pursuing these people you're also working on your next screenplay. When the new script is completed, you can go back to all of the same people with an even better writing sample.

In addition to the query letter or e-mail, there are at least three other methods of getting representatives to read your work: the cold phone call; dropping in; and recommendations from your contacts.

THE COLD PHONE CALL   Another way to approach representatives is to skip the query letter and go directly to the phone call. Obtain the name of a potential agent or manager, using the methods discussed, and phone the agency with no prior letter. You risk having an agent or assistant hang up on you, but you also stand a chance of being persuasive enough for someone to agree to read your script, if for no other reason than to get you off the telephone.

From that point on, the method is identical to the query letter. The objective is to get someone at the company to read your material. Use whatever tricks seem appropriate to get through to the agent or manager, and then succinctly explain that you have a good commercial screenplay and are looking for representation. Have your sixty-second pitch ready, and be prepared to answer whatever other questions the assistant or representative might have regarding your experience, your project, and your goals.

As you begin pursuing representatives (as well as the other three categories of people), try both the query letter and the cold phone call, until you see which method works better for you.

DROPPING IN   Another method, which requires a lot more chutzpah, is to come to Los Angeles, make twenty or thirty copies of your screenplay, and go directly to the offices of the representatives you're pursuing. When you appear in their offices, you say, "Here I am. I've just written a terrific screenplay. Would someone here be willing to take a look at it?" Most agencies do not hire bouncers to get rid of people who use this method. You may get scowls of disdain or incredulity once in a while, but I've heard more than one beginning screenwriter report a high success rate using this method.

RECOMMENDATIONS   The final approach is by far the best: a personal recommendation from someone the representative knows, especially a producer or one of the agent or manager's own clients. If you meet someone who has a representative, or has a good professional relationship with one, and this contact is willing to at least introduce you, you stand a much better chance that the agent or manager will be willing to read your screenplay. If your contact is willing to read your screenplay and recommend it to the representative, that is the best approach of all.

Combine all of these methods until you find the ones that work best for you. Your goal is always to get as many agencies and management companies as possible to read your screenplay until someone emerges who wants to represent you.

IF AN AGENT OR MANAGER IS INTERESTED IN REPRESENTING YOU

What happens when you finally get a representative to read your screenplay and she loves it—and wants to represent you?

First of all, be pleased, proud, and excited that what you knew all along was a good screenplay has now gotten the approval of someone in the business. At the same time, don't let your relief and excitement allow you to jump into a working relationship just because this person is the first one to come along. You must talk with her at length, preferably in person, to see what kind of potential the relationship holds.

A representative will probably want the same kind of encounter to measure your potential as a client. Remember that you are looking for the three qualities discussed earlier in this chapter (career guidance, power, and the ability to negotiate), and she will be looking for three important qualities in you (the ability to make money, career potential, and a positive attitude).

In this mutual interview, pay close attention to your instincts and gut reaction. The conversation will give each of you a better chance to get acquainted on all levels, and you must trust your feelings about this person as much as you trust the factual information you obtain.

I recommend asking the representative the following two questions in order to focus on the qualities you're looking for:

1. **What did you think of my screenplay?** This will give you some idea of how the representative really feels about you as a writer and how you might work together. Don't assume that negative comments about your screenplay are a bad sign. If this person shares your vision of your screenplay but offers extensive criticism and commercial considerations that hadn't occurred to you, it indicates the potential for a strong, complementary relationship. Constructive criticism is preferable to unending praise.

2. **Who are your other clients?** This question should give you a sense of how established the representative is, how much clout she wields, and whether she represents primarily television or feature writers. And don't be embarrassed if you have to ask what these other clients have written.

Voice your other questions and concerns during this meeting as well, both to satisfy your own curiosity and to establish rapport.

The representative will be weighing your potential as well, and will want to know about your career goals, your other story ideas and screenplays, and so on. Be honest and direct about all of these matters. Don't hide the fact that you're unwilling to write television or that you eventually want to direct features or that your goal is to be a staff writer for *CSI*. Misunderstandings at the outset can lead to major dissatisfaction later on, and if this person won't represent you because of your objectives, the relationship wouldn't have worked even if you had kept your goals a secret.

This meeting is not unlike a job interview, except that you are both acting like potential employers. The representative will technically work for you, but everybody knows that you're the one who *feels* like a job applicant. You are each entering a partnership, and you must approach the relationship with that kind of concern, enthusiasm, and equality.

Remember, the first one who knocks on your door isn't necessarily the best representative for you. As difficult as it might be, sign with an agent or manager only when both your head and your heart tell you it will be a mutually rewarding relationship.

When you finally choose a representative, you will sign a contract that conforms to the Writers Guild of America rules, even if you are not yet a member of the guild yourself. But if, after a predetermined period of time, the representative has not gotten you work, you then have the right to end the relationship and go on to another agency.

It is possible to have both an agent and a manager, or to have one representative for your screenwriting and a separate agent for your fiction. But you may never be represented as a screenwriter by more than one agency at a time.

As soon as you sign with an agency or management company, that entity takes over the marketing of your talent, and you concentrate on writing. It's important to continue making contacts and gathering information on the film business, but you don't want to make end runs around your own agent by pursuing deals on your own.

Finding a representative is much like finding a mate. You search extensively, meet some prospective candidates, go through periods of courtship, and after a few temporary relationships, you finally settle on the person who will be with you for life.

PURSUING OTHER PEOPLE IN POWER

The underlying principles for pursuing the other three categories of people with the power to get you a deal (producers, elements, and financiers) are the same as those previously outlined for the representative category:

1. Using contacts and the media, obtain information on who the people in power are, what they are looking for, and where you can reach them.

2. When your screenplay is good enough to submit, approach these people with letters, e-mails, phone calls, in-person encounters, or introductions from one of your contacts, hoping to persuade the people in each category to read your script.

3. If any of the people in power are interested in attaching themselves to you or your screenplay, meet with that person to decide if the relationship is one you want to establish.

4. Refuse to become discouraged or to accept rejection, and instead play a numbers game by simultaneously pursuing as many people as possible in all four categories.

5. Never let your business activities interfere with your writing. Maintain your writing regimen, adding extra hours for marketing yourself, so that when your next screenplay is completed, you can begin the process again with an additional sample of your writing talent.

Using these principles, I will now outline the process of research and approach as it applies to producers, elements, and financiers.

THE PRODUCER

The key difference between a producer and a representative is that a representative is looking for writers to represent, and a producer is looking for movies to make. While a representative's interest is in your talent and overall career prospects, a producer's is in your completed screenplay or your ability to write a specific project.

I'm referring here to independent producers who *develop* material: their companies are putting up or raising money for projects that can be made into movies. Another function of a producer is to see that the movie actually gets made after it's developed and financed.

Many producers perform both functions, producing the films they themselves have developed. But there are producers who are hired by the studios only to see that a project gets made after the studio decides to finance it. Since they aren't actively developing new projects, they will have no interest in your screenplay, either for production or as a writing sample. Stick to companies and individuals who get involved in projects prior to financing.

It is much easier to obtain information concerning the Who, What, and Where for independent producers than it is for representatives. While there is no source one may use to get a list of an agent or manager's clients, it is easy to acquire information on a producer's credits. This tells you what type of material is apt to interest them.

Simply looking through ads and listings for the movies of the past couple years will provide the names of hundreds of producers. Lists of the top box-office films (available at boxofficemojo.com or in the trade papers—*Variety* and the *Hollywood Reporter*) will provide a more targeted list of the producers who are strong in Hollywood. Producers also do interviews for the media and for the extras on the DVDs of their movies, in order to promote their films.

As described above, the Internet Movie Database and Done Deal Pro are essential sources of credits and contact information for the production companies actively making movies in Hollywood. So is an additional catalog, available in print and online versions: *The Hollywood Creative Directory*.

As the PRODUCER section of your marketing folder begins to grow, you will begin to see which production companies would be most appropriate for your particular screenplay. Let's say you discover that Jerry Bruckheimer was the producer of the *Pirates of the Caribbean* films, the *National Treasure* films, the *Bad Boys* films, *The Rock*, *Con Air*, *Armageddon*, *The Prince of Persia*, and about forty other high-concept, action-driven films. You can probably conclude that he wouldn't be the producer to approach with your small, arty, low-budget, *The Squid and the Whale* type of script.

But don't pigeonhole producers too narrowly with your research; *The Squid and the Whale* might be the very thing that Jerry Bruckheimer would now love to produce. Who knows, maybe he's always dreamed of winning an Independent Spirit Award. Doubtful, but you never know. Most producers grow weary of one particular genre, and if you're the only one bringing a producer something that isn't a clone of his last five films, you might be the writer he notices.

When you are ready to begin approaching any particular producer, check your resources or call that person's production company to determine the name of the head of development. She is the one (though there may be more than one at any company) responsible for acquiring and developing new screenplays and projects. Her title may be vice president of development, director of creative affairs, executive story editor, or something else nondescript. She is the person to approach, not the producer, unless a contact gets you directly to the producer with an introduction or recommendation.

Once you have determined the appropriate individual at the production company, your approach is the same as for a representative. The only important difference is that you are not contacting the producer or head of development for representation—you are calling in hopes that she will read your screenplay for consideration as a project to produce or will consider working with you as a screenwriter on other projects.

Again, the strongest approach to a producer is with the recommendation of another trusted professional. Never underestimate the value of your contacts.

Always be prepared with a very short pitch, and be ready to discuss your story concept and screenplay with everyone you approach in order to persuade them to read your work. And do not let rejection thwart your efforts.

If, after reading your screenplay, a producer is interested in your work, then the result can be either the option of your screenplay or a development deal. Both of these will be discussed in detail in chapter 9.

THE ELEMENT

Elements are components of a package deal: stars or directors with sufficient clout that their willingness to participate in the movie of your screenplay will increase its chances of getting made. The actors and directors whose movies end up at the top of the box-office lists are the strongest elements.

The majority of major directors and stars (both feature-film and television stars) have their own independent production companies to develop projects. They will therefore be approached as producers, through their heads of development, in the manner described above. The difference is that you are approaching the elements with a project that you think would be of interest specifically for them to star in or direct, not simply produce.

If the star or director does not have an independent production company, then you must find another means of getting your screenplay to her. Recommendations or introductions by your contacts are, again, the best method. You can also reach an element through her personal manager, agent, or attorney. This is usually a difficult approach, since the agent will primarily be looking for money offered up front. It's worth a try, even if you have no money committed, but it's a long shot.

You can also try to reach stars and directors by using those bizarre methods you hear about at writers' conferences: hiding your script in a pizza delivery box; taking up tennis to get invited to the star's home court; skydiving onto the set of the star's next film.

The basic rule is that if it makes sense, isn't illegal, and doesn't hurt anybody, it's worth a try. And even if it doesn't seem to make sense, you still might want to give it a whirl.

THE FINANCIER

This category includes anyone who might put up money for the film of your screenplay: studios, networks, private investors, and grant-funding agencies (private foundations or the U.S. government).

Begin by omitting studios and networks from your pursuits entirely, unless you have a direct introduction to someone at the level of story editor or higher. Otherwise your screenplay will at best go to the bottom of a huge hopper and, with no one to champion it, will eventually get rejected. It is far better to approach independent producers, get them involved in your project, and let them approach the studios and networks with which they have deals or relationships.

To research the Who and the Where for other financiers in this category, begin, as always, with your contacts. Anytime you hear about a film project that was independently financed, start asking questions. Or any time you meet someone with dough, get friendly.

Your media research should include information on any independently financed films you hear or read about. Take advantage of city and state film commissions that are eager to support local film activity— they will have information on movies financed and shot within their regions. Numerous film magazines and Web sites offer information on low-budget and independently financed features. A Google search of the term "film financing" lists almost 2 million links.

Besides emotionally involving screenplays, the people in this category are looking for good investments. The lower your proposed budget and the greater the chance of immediate profit, the more attractive the project becomes to most investors. So in addition to evaluating your screenplay, any potential investor will want to know the bottom line: how much an investment in your film will cost, what kind of return on the investment they can reasonably expect, and when the profits will be paid. It is therefore important to have some kind of financial prospectus for your project, including a basic budget breakdown of your screenplay, before approaching investors.

If you don't know how to do this, you can find people with production and investment experience to do it for you. In return, you will probably have to pay the person directly, offer him a flat fee or percentage of the investment contingent on obtaining financing, or attach the person to your project in some way.

This is one avenue where you're at an advantage if you live outside of southern California. Most investors in L.A. are already tapped out or are too shrewd to invest in motion pictures. But there are rich people everywhere, and the glamour of the movies and the possibility of huge profits can often lure potential investors in your own hometown. This is especially true if your screenplay is set in the investors' home state. Knowing their investment will be churned back into their local economy when the movie gets shot is an added incentive to many financiers.

You might also want to research foundations that award grants to filmmakers. Grant-funding agencies look for different qualities in prospective screenplays than do private investors, since, generally speaking, profit cannot be accrued by tax-exempt foundations or U.S. government agencies. While a grant-funding agency will still need to know how much it will cost, their other pertinent question will not be "How much money can this make?" but rather "What information or point of view is being presented by this film?"

These organizations' concerns will either be that the movie of your screenplay advance the state of the art of film (as with the National Endowment for the Arts), that it present information of a general educational or cultural nature (the National Endowment for the Humanities), or that it serve a particular area of need that the foundation supports. For example, if your screenplay concerns a rape-crisis center, foundations awarding grants in support of women's issues will certainly be worth pursuing.

Grants as a source of financing are usually more appropriate if your screenplay is for a short film. But occasionally feature films or TV movies for PBS get foundation or government support for production.

Of course, if you are pursuing financing outside the United States, government funding is not only more prevalent, it is often a necessity. Tax-supported bodies like the Canadian Film Board, Screen Australia, the British Film Council, the Swedish Film Institute, and similar agencies in almost every developed country on the planet are pretty much essential if you're pursuing a deal in one of those places.

Once you have your screenplay, budget breakdown, and prospectus ready to show, begin approaching financiers concurrently with the other three categories, using the same basic methods. Don't let the mystique of high finance deter you from this avenue. Getting even partial financing committed to your film can greatly increase the interest of the people in the other three categories.

MARKETING SERVICES

With the advent of the Internet and the growing interest in everything related to screenwriting, an entire cottage industry has arisen to help you get your work in the hands of the people in power. While the list that follows is by no means exhaustive (and I'm sure as you read this, new shortcuts will have appeared that didn't exist when I wrote it), these are the major categories of services now available to help you market your screenplay.

PITCH FESTS   Once upon a time it was necessary to go through the entire process above in order to speak directly to an agent or executive. Now it is possible to simply pay for the privilege. At a pitch fest, the organizers of the event assemble dozens of potential buyers and representatives in a large room, and anyone who pays the required fee is seated across from them, one by one, and allowed to pitch his screenplay.

Usually the allotted time for each pitch is five minutes, though some pitch fests may provide more time, or allow buyers to continue sessions beyond the stated limits. Some pitch fests also request "leave-behinds"— short synopses of the pitched screenplay that the recipients of the pitch can take back to their bosses.

Fees for pitch fests vary. Some require a single payment for an unlimited number of pitches; others are paid on a per-pitch basis. In all cases, the writers have the choice of the companies they pitch to, provided the buyer has open slots in his or her schedule.

The obvious value of pitch fests is that they shortcut the process of getting access to producers and representatives. Rather than spending a week researching and contacting fifteen people in power, hoping they will respond to your letter or phone call or e-mail, you can speak directly to fifteen in the course of a few hours. The primary impetus for my book *Selling Your Story in 60 Seconds* was the steadily growing popularity of pitch fests.

There are, however, some downsides to pitch fests. The first is the expense; in addition to the fee(s) for the pitching sessions, if you live outside of Los Angeles (or wherever the particular event is offered), you'll incur travel costs. The second drawback is the limited power of many of the people you pitch to. The biggest single complaint I hear about pitch fests is that too many of the people across the table were underlings who were sent just to gather up leave-behinds, and who had no real power to even react to the story one way or the other. This is understandable, since many top executives and agents aren't eager to give up a Saturday or Sunday to hear a stream of often bad (and badly done) pitches.

Nonetheless, if the pitch fest you choose is reputable, and if a sizable number of companies appropriate for your particular script will be in attendance, it's worth serious consideration. If you have diligently followed the process outlined above for making certain your script is professional-caliber before you begin pitching, then it will be among the best at the pitch fest—since most of the people there will *not* have gone through that process. This greatly increases your chances of getting a positive response from at least some of the companies you approach.

Three annual pitch fests stand out as the best-known and most popular in Hollywood: the Golden Pitch Festival, held in conjunction with the Screenwriting EXPO (screenwritingexpo.com), *Creative Screenwriting* magazine's huge conference held every fall in Los Angeles; the Great American Pitch Fest (pitchfest.com) held in L.A. every summer, and the Hollywood Pitch Festival (fadeinonline.com), sponsored by *Fade In* magazine (this was the event that began the whole phenomenon back in the 1990s). Lots of other writers' conferences around the United States and Canada also provide opportunities to pitch to agents and executives (or editors, if you're a novelist) whom they bring in for the event.

Pitch fests are like all the other opportunities outlined below—one more avenue for getting your script read by as many people in power as possible. Whether it's worthwhile for you depends on your project, the likely market for your screenplay, and perhaps, most of all, your budget.

VIRTUAL PITCHING   The popularity and success of pitch fests led to opportunities to pitch your screenplay over the Internet. These take a variety of forms:

► Story Link is an online community created by The Writers Store (see above), with an abundance of articles, blogs, resources, and information. Pitch Perfect at Story Link (storylink.com/pitchperfect) allows you to post a video of yourself actually pitching your project. Your video is then made available to industry professionals who have been screened by Pitch Perfect and are looking for material. If you go to the instructional video on this site (storylink.com/pitchhowto), you'll get to see me offering tips on creating a powerful video pitch. It's worth a visit just for that, don't you think?

► Pitch Q (pitchq.com) also allows you to post video (as well as written) pitches, making them available only to industry pros, or to other members for input and ratings, and offers a variety of other services.

► *Fade In* magazine (see above) currently offers the Online Hollywood Pitch Festival, which allows participants to pitch their projects online to ten participating companies of their choosing over a three-day period. Only written pitches are posted, so this is really more like posting your query letter and directing it to specific producers and representatives, who guarantee a written reply.

► Pitching Clips (pitchingclips.com) offers video clips to help baseball players improve their fastballs, curve balls, and sliders.

I know this has nothing to do with screenwriting, but it's what you get when you Google "video pitching."

LOG LINE LISTINGS AND MASS E-MAILS   In addition to pitches, it is also possible to post your log lines, story concepts, query letters, treatments, opening ten pages, or entire screenplays online. InkTip.com, PitchQ.com, SellAScript.com, ScriptDelivery.net, and ScriptBlaster.com will help you direct your material to selected industry professionals by making them available to the companies who subscribe to their services, by posting them in their monthly magazines, or by sending e-mails to their lists of agents and producers. Many of these sites offer consulting services to help you compose your log lines and query letters as well.

AUDIO SCRIPT READINGS   Operating on the theory that busy executives would rather listen than read, iScript.com and ScreenplayReadings.com will create audio versions of your screenplay using professional actors and narrators. These can then be burned onto CDs, or are available to you and to potential buyers via a unique URL link.

CONTESTS   I'm repeatedly asked if I recommend script competitions, and my answer is the same as for all of these resources: *maybe*. If you finish in first place in just about any competition that has more than fourteen entries, it will be easier to get your screenplay read. Studios, producers, and agencies frequently track down the winners of established contests to get an early look at the winning scripts. Even if you finish in the top three, you can, and should, mention that in your query letters when discussing your background.

Many contests also offer a short critique of your submission as part of the entry fee, which is a nice way to get additional feedback on your work.

But again, it's a question of budget, and maximizing the effectiveness of your time, and what you've got to spend. For example, the Acad-

MARKETING YOURSELF AS A SCREENWRITER   273

emy of Motion Picture Arts and Sciences' Nicholl Fellowship, the best-known of all the script competitions, gets five to seven thousand entries each year. And more often than not, even the winning scripts never get produced, because work that is judged artistic is not necessarily work that is judged commercial by financiers. So even with a wonderful screenplay, the odds that your one-in-five-thousand script will be sold are pretty small.

I would look for contests with fewer entrants, or with parameters that narrow the field. Some contests are open only to residents of their home states, for example. Some guarantee that top production companies and agencies will consider the winning scripts, though the term *consider* is pretty vague, so don't use this as your main criterion.

Get the names of past finalists for any contest you're thinking about entering, then research them on the Internet Movie Database and Done Deal Pro to see if their contest success actually led to any deals. And try to find out what the winning scripts were about. If all the previous winners of a competition were tragic Elizabethan love stories, it might not be the best place for your zombie splatter movie.

Any list of script competitions would be far too lengthy and varied to even attempt including it here. Fortunately, Done Deal Pro has a wonderful, detailed, and free list of hundreds of contests to choose from.

I have one warning, though. Never enter a contest that lays claim to the winning script in any way. If, by entering, you're promising the sponsors the rights to your script if it wins, find another contest.

———

A FINAL WORD ABOUT ALL OF THESE MARKETING SERVICES, AND ABOUT the entire marketing process in general. I have heard success stories for every single one of the approaches discussed in this chapter—screenwriters who got their scripts read and optioned as a result of following some or all of these steps. But I have never heard a success story about someone whose screenplay wasn't emotionally involving and commercially promising.

I know it seems as though the most important thing you can possibly know is how you get an agent, or how you get through that filtering system.

It's not.

Craft is everything—or at least 90 percent of everything. If you have a compelling idea, and a well-structured and well-written screenplay, it will get noticed, and recommended, no matter what avenue you follow and no matter how you get it out there. So follow the marketing process I've outlined, investigate the services listed, and use any that fit your sensibility, your project, and your budget, and which have proved successful for other writers.

Certainly pursuing the people in power is important, but it is meaningless if you don't know how to deliver the goods. The reason that most of this book is about *writing* your screenplay is that a well-written script is the key to getting paid for your talent. You can make contacts till the cows come home, but if you can't prove your ability as a writer, all the connections in the world won't do you a bit of good. And they certainly won't bring you creative satisfaction.

Talent always comes to the surface, so never let the selling process interfere with your writing. When your first screenplay is completed and ready to submit, immediately begin work on your next script. Find other time during the day to research and pursue contacts, agents, producers, elements, and financiers.

SUMMARY

1. You must market *yourself* as a screenwriter, not just your screenplay

2. Before ever submitting your screenplay to someone in power, you must be certain it's ready to show:

   ► Protect your work by registering it with the Copyright Office and with the Writers Guild of America

   ► Give copies of your screenplay to five people whose

judgment you trust, or to a skilled professional script consultant

► Rewrite and polish the script in light of their opinions and recommendations

3. There are three keys to marketing yourself as a screenwriter:

► Try everything

► Don't listen to statistics

► Knowledge is power

4. There are two sources of information regarding who the people in power are, what they are looking for, and where they are (or how you can reach them):

► Contacts—anyone you know

► The media

5. Four essential resources for researching the people in power and designing your marketing plan are:

► The Internet Movie Database (imdbpro.com)

► Done Deal Pro (donedealpro.com)

► The Writers Store (writersstore.com)

► StoryMastery (storymastery.com)

6. Four categories of people in power can lead you to a deal:

► The representative (agent, manager, or attorney)

► The independent producer who develops projects

► The element (major star or director)

► The financiers (studio, network, investor, or grant-funding agency)

7. You must approach all four categories of people simultaneously

8. Representatives look for three things in a potential client:

➤ A writer who will make money

➤ Someone with career potential

➤ Someone who won't add to their problems

9. You want three things in a potential representative:

➤ Someone to guide your career

➤ Someone with power in the film business

➤ Someone who can negotiate

10. Approach representatives with:

➤ A query letter that includes these elements:

The purpose of the letter

A personalized comment

Your background

A description of your screenplay

An offer to sign release forms

A promise to contact the representative

➤ A cold phone call

➤ Dropping in to the office

➤ A recommendation or referral from someone the representative knows and trusts

11. Prior to your follow-up phone call or cold phone call, be prepared to give a succinct, powerful, sixty-second pitch of your screenplay, which includes:

➤ A description of your hero

- ► The situation your hero is in at the beginning of the story

- ► The reasons we will empathize with the hero

- ► The opportunity that is presented to the hero at the 10 percent point

- ► The new situation that opportunity puts the hero in

- ► The hero's outer motivation

- ► The conflict: the obstacles that make achieving that goal seem impossible

12. If the representative wants to read your screenplay, send it to her immediately

- ► Ask if she prefers a hard copy or an e-mailed attachment

- ► In the accompanying cover letter or e-mail, remind the person who you are, but don't try to resell the script

- ► Call the assistant to make sure the script arrived

- ► Wait a month before following up, and continue to follow up once a month until it is read

13. If an agent or manager is interested in representing you, meet with her and ask:

- ► What did you think of my screenplay?

- ► Who are your other clients?

14. Follow the same basic process of researching and approaching the other categories of people in power

15. A variety of events and marketing services can help connect you and your project to potential representatives and buyers:

- ► Pitch fests

- ► Virtual pitching

- ► Log line listings and mass e-mails
- ► Audio script readings
- ► Contests

16. Two final commandments:

- ► Never let the marketing process interfere with your writing regimen
- ► Reject rejection!

TEN

THE SCREENWRITER'S DEAL

NOW THE EXCITING PART. WHAT HAPPENS IF YOU HIT PAY DIRT? WHAT if one of the producers or financiers discussed in the previous chapter has read your screenplay and now wants to make a deal with you?

There are three ways you can earn money as a screenwriter:

1. Outright sale of your screenplay

2. A development deal

3. A salaried or staff writer position on an episodic series

In this chapter, I will discuss all of those situations, the way each occurs, and the components of the deal.

SALE OF THE SCREENPLAY

Sale of the film rights to a complete screenplay is almost always based on an *option/purchase deal*. Rarely will the film rights to a screenplay be purchased by a producer outright; usually, those film rights will be optioned first.

An option in the film business is the same as an option in real estate or any other area of negotiation: it is the exclusive right to purchase property for a predetermined amount of money over a finite period of time.

Option money doesn't pay for the right to make the movie of your script; an option buys the right to *purchase* those film rights at a later date, exclusive of anybody else. What is actually being paid for is the exclusivity. This gives the person optioning your screenplay time to raise the money to produce the film, during which time no other person can offer more money and make a separate deal.

If you option your script to a producer today for $10,000, and tomorrow Martin Scorsese offers you $50,000, you have to say, "Sorry, Marty, but the rights are now controlled by another producer."

The following example will illustrate how an option/purchase deal works. The figures used are arbitrary, because everything is negotiable. I just chose these amounts because they're nice round figures and are easy to divide.

Let's say a producer makes this offer: a $10,000 option against a purchase price of $100,000 for one year, renewable for a second year for an additional $10,000. This means that if you agree to the deal, the producer will pay you $10,000 to option the film rights to your completed screenplay. This deal gives the producer one year to pay you the remaining $90,000 toward the total purchase price. (That is why it is referred to as $10,000 *against* $100,000.) If, at any time during that year, the producer pays you the remaining $90,000, then he owns the film rights to your screenplay forever. If the producer fails to raise the other $90,000 during that year, you keep the $10,000, and you can then make a new deal with someone else.

The renewal clause means that if, before the first year expires, the producer does not pay you the remaining $90,000, but instead pays you an additional $10,000, he has exclusive rights to your screenplay for an additional year. If, during that second year, he pays you the $90,000 (usually the second-year renewal fee is not deducted from the total purchase price), then he owns the rights to your screenplay forever. If the second year elapses and the producer hasn't purchased the script, then you keep the $20,000, and you can shop your screenplay elsewhere.

The producer has spent his $10,000 or $20,000 for the *exclusivity* of the deal. You can't make any other deals for this screenplay during his option period.

In addition to the option amount and the purchase amount, the other basic elements of the deal are usually negotiated at the outset as well. The following are some of the deal points that you might negotiate prior to signing an option/purchase agreement:

1. **Exclusivity.** This would guarantee that you would be the only screenwriter on the project; no other screenwriter could be brought in to rewrite your script. Only the top screenwriters in Hollywood get this clause in their contract. Unless you're up there with Nora Ephron or Nancy Meyers, you're likely to opt for the next clause as an alternative to exclusivity.

2. **Rewrites.** The more rewrites of the screenplay you can be guaranteed before another writer can be hired, the more control and input you will have on your project. This clause will set the fee you would receive for any rewrites you do, as well as the number of paid rewrites you are guaranteed, should they be needed. The producer may negotiate for a certain number of rewrites (usually one rewrite and one "polish") to which he is entitled as part of his purchase price. In other words, the producer will want as many additional rewrites as possible for no additional money.

   Obtaining a guaranteed number of rewrites, at a certain fee, doesn't necessarily mean you will do them. The producer or director may want to bring in a new writer even if you haven't written the number of rewrites you're entitled to do. But you still must be paid for that number of rewrites before another writer can be hired.

3. **Bonuses.** You might negotiate for a bonus if no other writer is *needed* to rewrite the script. Then some of the money the producer would have had to pay a second screenwriter goes to you for writing such a good script in the first place.

You may also get a bonus if and when the movie goes into production, is completed, or is released. In other words, if your
screenplay is good enough that the movie actually gets made, you
get rewarded. This clause is more likely in a development deal (see
below). In an option/purchase arrangement, the option is not usually exercised until the producer is certain that the movie is going
into production.

4. **Percentage of the profits.** Even on your first sale, it is reasonable to
   negotiate for 2 to 5 percent of the net (never gross) profits of the
   film. Of course, how net profits are actually defined is what keeps
   all those Hollywood lawyers getting all those fat fees. And dis-
   tributors seem to have a way of never going into profit with their
   films, but somehow staying in business. But it's always good to
   negotiate for net-profit participation, just in case your film turns
   into such a blockbuster that there's no way to hide the profits.

   Net-profit participation can be especially important for an
   independent, low-budget feature. Often your fee for writing such
   a film will be far less than for a studio deal, so the profit share is
   the only way you can hope to make a comparable amount of
   money. And just imagine having even a tiny piece of *Paranormal
   Activity*.

5. **Sequels, spin-offs, and remakes.** You might want to negotiate for
   the opportunity to write the screenplays for any sequels or television series that are spun off from the movie of your original script.
   This would be a "first right of refusal": you don't *have* to write the
   sequel, but you must be given the opportunity to do so, at a fair
   fee, before any other writer can be hired.

   You will certainly want a piece of the action on any of these
   sequels and spin-offs and any future remakes of your screenplay,
   for the same reason you want a percentage of the net profits of the
   original film.

6. Ancillary Rights. Ancillary rights enable you to participate financially in income generated by your movie in other arenas: video
games, record albums, toys, posters, neckties, key-chains, and
cocktail napkins. In other words, you want to share in as much of
the income that originated from your screenplay as possible. Every
time somebody buys an *Avatar* lunch box, James Cameron puts
another nickel in his pocket.

You may want to negotiate even more elements of your option/pur-
chase deal. The clearer the deal is at the outset, the less the danger of
misunderstandings, confusions, and broken promises later on.

Sometimes only the major aspects of a deal will be negotiated in the
original contract, and the rest will be left until later, so that everybody
doesn't have to pay a lot of big legal fees right off the bat. Then the phrase
"to be negotiated in good faith at a later date" is added to the contract.
The "in good faith" means that when it's time to work out the rest of the
deal, no one can stonewall the negotiations and the fees must be consistent with standard movie industry amounts at that time.

Throughout this list, I've been saying "you" negotiate this or that.
By "you" I actually mean your agent, manager, or attorney. *Never negotiate for yourself!* If a producer or financier offers you a deal, and you have
no representative, get back in touch with all the ones who wouldn't read
your screenplay before. An offer on the table can make you a much more
attractive possibility. If they're still not interested or if you still can't
find an agent or manager you like, then hire an attorney to negotiate
this deal for you.

If an offer is on the table, you can't find an agent, and you can't afford
an attorney, at least get as much information as possible before you
agree to anything. And somehow scrape up enough money to have a
lawyer check over the contract before you sign. Writing is your talent,
not negotiating.

Negotiating for yourself can also strain your relationship with a producer. After locking horns over fees and profits, friendly, creative story

conferences are harder to achieve. It's better to let your agent take all the heat and be nasty on your behalf.

The amount of money involved in any option/purchase deal varies greatly. If you are a member of the Writers Guild of America or if the financier you're dealing with is a signatory to the guild agreement, then your deal must at least meet the minimums set by the guild. (To see what the current minimums are, go to wga.org and click on Writer's Resources/Contracts and Compensation.) Most feature film deals with studios will exceed guild minimums. And if more than one studio is bidding for your screenplay, your price can climb a lot higher.

If neither you nor the financier is connected to the Writers Guild, then the monetary amounts are completely negotiable. The law of supply and demand is the rule. The hungrier the financier is for your screenplay, the more you'll be able to get.

The sum for a one-year option is often calculated at 10 percent of the purchase price. But that, too, is totally negotiable, and you might very well accept a $10 option on your screenplay—in other words, a *free option*. This might sound like a bum deal at first, but if the producer offering you ten bucks is also offering a higher purchase price on the back end, if he's the only one knocking on your door, and if you really think he has a good shot at getting your movie made, then you might want to accept the offer.

The time period for the option is also negotiable, and can range from six weeks to three years. If the producer wanting a free option requests a year, you might negotiate for only a six-month option, so your screenplay won't be tied up for such a long period of time without any remuneration. The renewal clause can then include a significant payment, so the producer will have to come up with some good-faith money within six months to prove his sincerity and abilities.

You might also reject the free option offer, but give the producer *permission to shop* your script wherever he is strongest. If you turn down the free option and the producer responds, "But I'm a close personal friend of Johnny Depp, and this is just what he's looking for!" then you might tell the producer to take it *only* to Johnny Depp. If the producer can make a deal with the star, then the producer is locked into the project. But he can't take it to any other element or financier without again getting your approval.

THE DEVELOPMENT DEAL

Now that you understand how the option/purchase deal works, I should mention that it almost never happens. Most of what you see on the big screen and almost everything on television is *developed*.

Before I got involved in the film business, I used to assume that movies and TV shows got made in the following way: a writer would slave away until he had created a complete screenplay for a movie, which would then be purchased by a studio. The studio would hire actors, director, and the like, and the screenplay would be turned into what we saw on the screen.

This process is obviously too simple, straightforward, and logical for Hollywood. Thus was born the development deal.

Developing a screenplay simply means paying a screenwriter up front to put a film story on paper. The screenwriter is a hired gun, and the script belongs entirely to the producer, studio, or network that is paying for it. The principle is much the same as for an inventor who creates some new gizmo as an employee of Apple Computer. He may get salary, royalties, and a bonus, but Apple owns the invention.

The great news about development deals is that they create a lot more work than is evident. At least ten to twenty feature-length screenplays get developed in Hollywood for every one that ends up getting produced.

The path to a development deal might go something like this:

You've been pursuing the four categories of people in power in the manner outlined in chapter 8. Then one day a producer calls you and says, "I read your screenplay, and I loved it. But I don't want to make that movie, because it's too expensive/familiar/out of my arena/hard to sell/ hard to cast/arty/soft/all of the above. But I would love to work on something else with you. Have you got any other ideas?"

In other words, now that the producer (or story editor or executive or investor) has seen your talent, he is willing to consider putting another project in the works for you to write. This is why having a completed screenplay is imperative. No one is going to risk paying you to develop a screenplay until you have proven your ability as a screenwriter.

Once you have proven yourself to a producer, you can present him with other stories for possible development. Then, and only then, is when treatments and pitches come into the picture.

Treatments

A treatment is a prose version of a film story, usually five to twenty pages long. Shorter treatments are sometimes called outlines. As with a complete screenplay, your primary goal is to elicit emotion in the reader.

A treatment looks like a short story, because it's written in paragraph form, uses quotation marks for dialogue, and omits the format devices of a screenplay. However, a treatment is always written in present tense and abides by the principle that nothing goes on the page that doesn't go on the screen. Thus a treatment, just like a screenplay, can have no interior thoughts of the characters, author's asides, or editorial prose. Treatments consist entirely of action, description, and dialogue.

A treatment follows all the basic principles of concept, character, and structure: a hero with whom we identify; motivation and conflict; other primary characters; three distinct acts based on the hero's outer motivation (although the acts are never labeled); and the use of as many of the structural principles and devices from chapter 5 as possible.

With a treatment, you outline only the broad strokes of the story; minor scenes, secondary characters, and most dialogue is omitted. Comedy treatments will require a bit more dialogue to convey any verbal humor and to illustrate your ability to write hilarious lines in the eventual screenplay.

The shorter your treatment the better; five to ten pages is ideal. A thirty-page treatment is so detailed and takes so long to read that it might as well be written in screenplay form. The best treatments seduce the reader immediately, clearly outline an emotionally involving story, and leave the reader wanting more.

A sample treatment is included in Appendix B.

Pitches

A pitch, as I discussed in the previous chapter, is a verbal presentation of your proposed film story. It is, as the name implies, a sales pitch.

Pitches fall into two categories. What I term a sixty-second pitch (which is sometimes referred to as a telephone pitch or an elevator pitch) is a very brief presentation of your project when your primary goal is to get your completed screenplay read. A pitch *meeting* is an opportunity to meet in person with a representative, producer, or financier to give a longer, more detailed description of the story for a screenplay that has not yet been written. The objective of the sixty-second pitch is to get your work read; the objective of the pitch meeting is to get a development deal by persuading the people in the room that your proposed screenplay is worth financing.

Pitch meetings are sometimes opportunities to present your approach to writing or rewriting a project that a producer already owns. You might be one of a number of possible writers competing to get hired on a particular project.

Pitching a story should take about fifteen to thirty minutes, and again, shorter is usually better. You are simply telling your story idea in such a way that the artistic and commercial (especially commercial) potential of the movie is clear.

A pitch will usually begin with a detailed opening to grab your audience, followed by the highlights of the story. The principles of concept, character, and structure are identical to those for a complete screenplay.

In pitching a story, pull anything you can out of your bag of tricks to get the listener excited. *Be sure that you have rehearsed the pitch thoroughly before presenting it to an executive.* Note-cards taken to the meeting are okay if they enhance your ability to tell the story. Some writers perform scenes from the script, do stand-up routines for their comedies, and yell, scream, and jump up and down if necessary to get the listeners' juices flowing. You must do whatever works best for you.

But don't worry that you won't have a chance if you don't put on some dog-and-pony show. Some people are naturally gifted at mesmerizing buyers with their humor or performing talent. Others are not. Ultimately, it's the story that will sell your project. If you can clearly and passionately present your emotionally involving story, you can leave the props and magic tricks at home.

So what if a producer asks to see your ideas, but you've been working on your next screenplay and have no treatments? What do you do?

You go to the little notebook or recorder you bought way back in the chapter on story concept and look over all of the ideas you have been recording on a daily basis since you began this whole process. You brainstorm, combine ideas, and select the one or two or three concepts that you believe would appeal most to the potential producer.

You then put the best of these ideas in treatment or pitch form, depending on the producer's desires. And you present it, or them, to the producer in the hope of securing a development deal to write the screenplay.

Do not write treatments until they are requested. Until you have proved yourself to an executive who is asking to see your ideas, treatments will be of no value. And after presenting your treatment or pitch to a person in power, go back to writing complete screenplays until another executive asks to see your material or until you are offered a development deal.

I am referring here only to treatments written for submission. If you find it helpful to outline your own story ideas before converting them to complete screenplays, of course you should do so. You might also want to work with a consultant on the treatment of your story idea to be sure the concept, characters, and structure are outstanding before you tackle the complete screenplay. But don't stop when the treatment is done in the hope that it alone will attract a producer. *The way to become a screenwriter is to write screenplays.*

Some established screenwriters never write treatments, because they want that first draft to be theirs alone. Treatments give others a hand in your creation before you've had the opportunity to do it your own way. Dealing only in completed screenplays at least allows you to realize your own vision on paper before everybody else starts to change it.

Development deals do not always grow out of your own concepts. If a producer or financier is really enamored of your work, or if you are already an established screenwriter, you may be given the opportunity to write (or rewrite) a concept or novel or true story or screenplay for which the producer already owns the rights. Then you simply decide whether you wish to pursue the project, and negotiate the deal.

Elements of the Deal

The money you are paid for a development deal is your fee for writing the screenplay, not a purchase price. Otherwise, a development deal includes the same basic elements that an option/purchase agreement contains: a percentage of the net profits; a cutoff point, prior to which no other writer can be hired; sequel, spin-off, and remake participation; ancillary rights; and so on.

You will usually be paid less for a development deal than for the sale of a completed screenplay, particularly in the feature film arena. With an option/purchase arrangement, the producer is getting a known quantity and is only gambling on the outcome of the finished film. With a development deal, there is the added risk that when you complete the script, the producer still won't be able to acquire financing to produce the film. But you must be paid your fee for writing the screenplay no matter how good or bad it turns out to be.

However, if the script you were paid to write ends up getting produced, you'll probably receive a bonus that will make your deal the equivalent of an outright purchase.

A development deal can include an option on the story itself, which works the same way as an option on a complete screenplay. The producer options your story for an X amount of dollars over a Y period of time. During that period, you can't set up a deal for your story anywhere else; again, the producer is paying for exclusivity. During that period, the producer will try to raise the money to pay you to write the screenplay. If he does, you get paid to write the script; if he doesn't, you keep the option money, and you can option your story elsewhere.

Development deals will often be "step deals." Your story is optioned, then you are paid to write a treatment based on the producer's input, then you are paid more to write a screenplay, then the producer is entitled to a negotiable number of rewrites, and then you are paid more for additional rewrites.

The point in this process where you can be cut off is negotiable. In other words, the producer may have the right, if that's the deal you've agreed to, to pay just for your treatment and then hire another writer to write the screenplay. You obviously hope to get a cutoff point that is later in the process. The more established you are and the more somebody wants your idea, the better your chances of getting it.

Usually your payment schedule in a development deal will be one-third to begin the screenplay, one-third upon completion of the first draft, and one-third upon completion of the rewrite. When your obligations are completed and the financier has paid you the full amount, the financier owns the film rights to the screenplay forever.

There is an escape clause to this issue of "forever." If, within a certain period of time, the producer has failed to go into production on the screenplay you wrote, it enters what is known as *turnaround*. In turnaround, you have the right to pursue a deal for the screenplay with other producers and financiers. If you locate another producer who wants to acquire the rights to the screenplay, the producer who initially purchased or developed it must sell them. However, that initial producer is entitled to all of the development money spent on the project—your fee, as well as legal fees, office expenses, salaries, and anything else that can be legitimately attributed to the development of your script.

Sometimes this figure is negotiated down. The initial producer is often pleased to recoup even some of the costs of a project that is dead in the water. But he is only *required* to turn over the rights if the total verified expenses are met.

THE STAFF WRITER

The third method of making money as a screenwriter is as a staff writer for a television series. These jobs carry several different titles and levels of responsibility, and are the only salaried positions available to a screenwriter of prime-time television or feature films.

In times past, studios had screenwriters on staff to churn out movie scripts, but those days have gone the way of the double feature and the contract player. Established screenwriters may sign exclusive or "first-refusal" deals with production companies, but those are simply variations on the option/purchase deal or the development deal. The mainstream screenwriter drawing a weekly paycheck will almost always be a series staff writer.

Staff writing positions can be obtained after you've proved your talents by writing series episodes as a freelancer. When you have shown the producers of a particular series that you can deliver the goods, then you might be hired as a staff writer.

A staff writer reports to work every day, just like in a real job, to brainstorm with the other writers on the show, contribute ideas, write or rewrite scripts for individual episodes, and rewrite them again when the directors and stars of the series have given their input.

Creators (or cocreators) of series get the same kinds of salaries and fees for their ongoing positions with the series, but in addition receive royalties and residuals for every single episode aired.

A producer on an episodic series receives even more money from each of these sources (salary, script fees, royalties). Unlike in the feature film arena, producers on television series are almost always screenwriters who have been promoted up from staff writer positions.

The highest level of producer is the show runner—the head writer who oversees the entire series. The total annual income for the executive producer of an ongoing series (who might also be the creator and the show runner) can exceed a million dollars a year.

Let me give you a specific example of how this career path can unfold:

Once upon a time, about the same time I came to Hollywood to break into the movies, a writer arrived from back East, where he had done reviews for a small film magazine. Under his arm were five completed screenplays he had written in his spare time. He began beating the pavement, suffering many rejections from agents, until he met an agent who was impressed that the writer was committed enough to complete five screenplays. So she agreed to represent him.

He told his new agent that he eventually wanted to direct features but that, in the meantime, he would be willing to write anything she advised, television included. She had him do spec scripts for episodes of two different cop shows on the air at that time, and she submitted them to many of the active series in production.

One of the story editors for one of those series (but not one for which the writer had written a sample script) recognized the writer's talent, so our hero was asked to go in and pitch a half-dozen possible episode ideas for that story editor's series. The story editor liked one, so the screenwriter was given a development deal for that episode. It never got made.

But the staff writers on the series still liked the writer's work, so another development deal followed. This second script was used as an episode, and the writer started getting noticed by the television industry.

This led to a staff writer position on a different series. The writer then was hired as a story editor for another series the following year, followed two years later by a producer credit on a third series.

Eventually, the screenwriter wrote the pilot for a new series, for which he became cocreator and co–executive producer, with a seven-figure income.

Now before you throw away your feature script and start analyzing every past episode of *The Big Bang Theory*, understand that not all episodic writers reach the level of financial success that the writer described above has. But there are currently about seventy prime-time series on the five major networks at any given time, plus more on cable and premium cable channels such as TNT, FX, Bravo, HBO, and Showtime. Each of these series has at least six staff writers, usually a lot more. Are they all happy? Probably not. But they're all making a lot of money.

Once again, the question to ask yourself repeatedly is this: "Is writing screenplays bringing me joy?" If the answer is no, then forget the issue of money and find a more fulfilling pursuit. If the answer is yes, then go for it.

SUMMARY

1. A screenwriter can earn money in three ways:

- ► Sale of the screenplay
- ► A development deal
- ► A salaried staff writer position

2. Sale of the screenplay is based on an option/purchase deal. An *option* is the exclusive right to purchase property for a predetermined amount of money over a finite period of time

3. The negotiable elements of an option/purchase deal include:

- ► Option price
- ► Purchase price
- ► Option period
- ► Renewal clause
- ► Exclusivity
- ► Guaranteed rewrites
- ► Bonuses
- ► Percentage of net profits
- ► Participation in sequels, spin-offs, and remakes
- ► Ancillary rights
- ► A turnaround clause

4. In a development deal, the screenwriter is hired by a producer or financier to write a screenplay based on the writer's own idea, or on a story concept controlled by the producer

5. A *treatment* is a five- to twenty-page prose version of a proposed film story, which adheres to the basic principles of effective screenwriting

6. A *pitch* is a verbal presentation of a film story

➤ A telephone or elevator pitch is a sixty-second pitch designed to persuade someone to read your work

➤ A pitch meeting is a face-to-face opportunity to present your story in ten to thirty minutes or more, usually to persuade a buyer to option it

7. With a development deal, a writer is hired to write a screenplay to the buyer's specifications, based on the writer's own concept, the buyer's idea, or on an existing story or screenplay to be adapted or rewritten

8. A *step deal* is a development deal outlining each stage in the process—treatment, screenplay, rewrites—plus the fee paid at each stage and the amount you are guaranteed before the project can be discontinued or another writer hired

9. Staff writers, story editors, and producers for episodic television series can receive both guaranteed salaries and negotiated fees for the episodes they write, plus royalties for rebroadcasts.

PART FOUR

THE COMMITMENT TO
SCREENWRITING

ELEVEN

THE LIFE OF A SCREENWRITER

Did you hear about the woman who was so dumb she tried to break into the film business by sleeping with a screenwriter?

—SOCRATES

IF YOU PURCHASED THIS BOOK TO HELP YOU DECIDE WHETHER OR NOT to pursue screenwriting, I would add these comments to everything else I've said. To me, there are two big advantages to being a screenwriter:

1. **You get to work in the movies.** I love the movies, and I think the opportunity to reach people by becoming a storyteller, a creator, and a writer in the most powerful medium in the world is wonderful. Regardless of the frustrations and the discouragement and the money and the hype and the greed and the rumors and the personalities and the rejection and all the other pros and cons and success stories and horror stories, when you feel the lights go down in the theater and the rush before a new movie begins and you know that you're a part of that, that is an unequaled high.

2. **Word for word, and dollar for dollar, you can make more money in screenwriting than in any other form of writing.** This doesn't mean that Dan Brown and J. K. Rowling haven't made a whole lot more than most screenwriters. And a starving screenwriter is just as unhappy as a starving poet. But once you're established and are getting paid regularly for your work, the financial rewards of screenwriting can be immense.

There are also, in my opinion, three big disadvantages to screenwriting, compared with other forms of writing:

1. **You don't have the opportunity to weave magic with words.** If the reason you wish to pursue a writing career is to revel in the beauty, glory, and depth of the English language, then screenwriting is probably not for you. If you want to make full use of everything that Noah Webster has to offer, then poetry or short stories or novels would probably be better objectives.

    Screenwriters are storytellers, and screenplays consist only of action, description, and dialogue, written at a high school reading level. Your goal is to create a story that can be told and transferred to the big or small screen, not to dazzle the reader with the power of your prose.

2. **A screenwriter is a surrogate mother.** After what is probably about a nine-month gestation period, you give birth to a creation that represents your love, your passion, your sweat, your devotion, and your pain. Then you must hand over this piece of your soul to someone else, who will stomp on it with logging boots.

    Occasionally your writing is treated with great respect, but you must be emotionally prepared to see your creation changed and possibly destroyed. Your only consolations are your Mercedes, your swimming pool, and your therapist. And the fact is that once you are sufficiently established, you can negotiate for greater control over your material through directing, producing, or securing a sole screenwriter position on your later projects.

3. **Screenwriters do not rank particularly high in the Hollywood hierarchy.**
Even though logic and evidence would support the maxim "If it ain't on the page, it ain't on the stage," the screenwriter is usually given short shrift with regard to status and power. You're not necessarily the low man on the totem pole, but you are rarely the top dog either.

If, given all these pros and cons, you choose to commit to pursuing screenwriting as a career, this is what you must do:

I. **Establish a writing regimen.** Very early in this book, I said that longtime screenwriter Art Arthur, who was my mentor and, I'll now reveal, my father-in-law, had revealed two secrets to being a good screenwriter. The first was, *Don't get it right, get it written.* At last you get to learn his other secret to success: *The seat of the pants to the seat of the chair.*

Lots of us would like to *have written* a screenplay. But if you want to be a screenwriter, you have to write. Every day. No distractions. No excuses. Because it's the *regularity* of your writing regimen that will sharpen your craft and enable you to complete a salable screenplay.

If you don't already have such a writing regimen, start with a half hour a day. Don't try to bite off a three-hour-per-day writing commitment. It will end up just like exercise commitments: you'll stick to it devotedly for three days, get burned out, and give up. Instead, start slowly, so you can feel you've kept your commitment each day. Then, when a half hour is comfortable, stretch it to an hour, and keep increasing your regimen only when you're comfortable with the plateau you're on.

You'll be amazed at the amount of work you can generate in only a half hour a day, as long as, during that time, you do *nothing* but sit at the computer or legal pad and work on your script.

2. **See movies.** Two a week. A hundred a year. And see the good ones twice or more. If you want to write for television, see *lots* of TV episodes.

3. **Read screenplays.** One a week. Fifty a year. And read the good ones twice or more.

   As I said at the beginning of this book, these two items are essential steps to improving your artistic abilities as a screenwriter. By watching and analyzing Hollywood movies and reading successful screenplays, you'll learn as much about style and craft as any single book or seminar can teach you.

4. **Stay informed about the movie business.** In addition to seeing a lot of movies, you must also be aware of what's going on within the film industry. In other words, you've got to start reading about the movie business.

   You must know which movies are doing well at the box office; which stars, producers, and directors are hot; what they're looking for; who the new and/or powerful literary agents are; what movies are scheduled for release in the future; and which categories of film are currently in or out of favor with the powers that be.

   And you must know the same things for television.

   I reveal a number of print and online resources in chapter 9 that can keep you up to date about the business of Hollywood. All this information will greatly improve the chances of your screenplay getting sold and produced. Remember, *knowledge is power.*

5. **Make contacts.** Attend film seminars and lectures. Go to screenings. Volunteer to work on someone's film. Volunteer to assist at a film festival. Get invited to parties. Hang out in theater lobbies.

   And everywhere you go, tell people you're a screenwriter.

6. **Join a writers' group.** Writers' groups can be excellent sources of contacts, information, feedback on your work, and moral support.

It can be a cold, lonely world out there for writers, and meeting others on the same rugged path can help immensely.

A word of caution about this item, though: pick your writers' group carefully. Over the years I've worked with many writers who have either had their writing dreams crushed by overly critical members of their group, or who are shocked to learn their screenplay is miles away from professional caliber because no one in their group had been courageous enough, or insightful enough, to tell them that.

Join or create a writers' group made up of committed, supportive members who only want you to succeed along with them, and who are knowledgeable enough about Hollywood movies and screenplays that they will tell you when and how your work needs improvement.

7. **Pursue other markets for your work.** This book is about mainstream movies and TV, because that's what I know about. But 90 percent of the professional film and video shot in this country is used outside of those arenas. If you can sharpen your talent and pay your bills writing industrial films, educational films, promotional films, training films, religious films, animated films, adult films, commercials, or audiovisual presentations, then do it. The goal of each is to elicit emotion in an audience, and these other markets can only sharpen your craft.

8. **Consider moving to Los Angeles.** If you live more than fifty miles from the Universal Studios Tour, here's my best advice about moving to L.A.: *Don't do it yet.*

If you're a working screenwriter, there is a decided advantage to living in Los Angeles: you're available for meetings; you're more attractive to potential agents; and you have more direct access to what's going on in the film business.

But if you haven't yet broken into the film industry, right now your main concern must be to take the principles of this book and use them to perfect your craft and to pursue the people in power. And you will do a better job of writing if you remain where you already have financial and emotional support. Rather than picking up stakes and moving to some empty apartment in Encino, stay put.

The time to consider migrating to L.A. is when someone is offering you the likely possibility of income if you do. If an agent convinces you that he can get you work if you move to southern California or if someone offers you hard cash to do so, then you have a decision to make. But until then, continue writing and pursuing the people in power from wherever you now live. (Unless you want to learn how to surf, too. In that case, come on out.)

Even with the promise of money, you may choose to stay where you are. There are working screenwriters living all over the world. It isn't as easy, but if you're determined to succeed as a screenwriter without leaving your roots, then it can be done. And as films continue to become more and more regional, with independent financing, location shooting, and local production facilities, moving to Hollywood becomes less important.

And finally . . .

9. **Evaluate your goals.** Every six months or so, ask yourself if being a screenwriter is bringing you joy and fulfillment. Is the writing itself satisfying and fulfilling? If the answer is yes, then keep at it.

SUMMARY

1. There are two big advantages to screenwriting:

   ➤ You get to tell stories for the movies

   ➤ You can make a lot of money

2. There are three major disadvantages to screenwriting:

   ➤ You don't get to weave magic with words

➤ You have no control over what is done to your screenplay after it's sold

➤ Screenwriters don't rank very high in the film industry

3. If you choose to pursue screenwriting, you should:

➤ Establish a writing regimen

➤ See movies and TV episodes

➤ Read screenplays

➤ Be informed about the film industry

➤ Make contacts

➤ Join a writers' group

➤ Pursue other markets for your work

➤ Consider moving to Los Angeles

➤ Periodically evaluate your goals

TWELVE

THE POWER OF SCREENWRITING

FROM ALMOST THE FIRST PAGE OF THIS BOOK, I HAVE BEEN TALKING about the need to create emotion in a reader and an audience. For you as a screenwriter, and for all filmmakers, that is the primary goal.

There are two direct paths to eliciting that emotional response in an audience. One is through the head. The other is through the glands.

The first path gets people thinking, gets their wheels turning

The second path gets their blood racing, gets their juices flowing.

Both paths are fine. There is nothing inherently good or bad about either method. But each, if used exclusively, becomes esoteric. That is, each, when used alone, limits your potential audience.

If you go strictly with the glandular approach—trying just to get people frightened or turned on—you can end up with splatter movies and pornography. And there is a limited audience for those.

If you attempt only to get people thinking, the result can be a provocative intellectual exercise that is seen by six people in a college basement. Because there is a limited audience for those films as well.

The tragedy of the first situation is the abundance of films devoid of any apparent thought or any contribution to the human condition. The even greater tragedy of the second situation is that filmmakers with important ideas to offer humanity are unable to find an audience or even to get their movies made.

The solution to these situations is combining the two approaches. If you can see the effectiveness of getting people excited, frightened, laughing, and crying and then can use that ability to touch them deeply and really get them thinking, then you have tapped into the immense power you can wield as an artist, a screenwriter, and a filmmaker.

That is what I call reaching people through the *heart*.

That is also what I wish for all of you reading this book.

Now be joyful, get in touch with your own power, and start writing.

FREQUENTLY ASKED QUESTIONS

WHEN I WROTE THE FIRST EDITION OF THIS BOOK WAY BACK WHEN, I began this appendix by saying, "I have now taught more than seven thousand writers throughout the United States, Canada, and England, and these are the questions that consistently arise." Since then, I've now lectured to more than forty thousand writers, filmmakers, psychologists, attorneys, and businesspeople around the world. I've heard and read a *lot* more questions. I've left the ones that are still pertinent, and added more that have arisen in the years since. I still hope the answers will help clarify the principles discussed throughout the book and will provide added assistance with individual situations you may encounter.

Where are the restrooms?

I don't know, I've never been here before, either.

You've laid out all of these rules for writing screenplays, but aren't the rules broken in *No Country for Old Men*? *Pulp Fiction*? *Eternal Sunshine of the Spotless Mind*? *The Station Agent*? *Memento*? *Zelig*? *Blow-Up*? *El Topo*? *Citizen Kane*? *Lunch Hour at the Lumière Factory*?

Yes, they are.

The point is this: your objective is (I assume) to break into writing mainstream movies and television. That's why you picked up this book.

You can probably find exceptions to almost every principle in this book. But how does spotting the exceptions help you in your own career pursuit?

If you examine the films that break the rules, you will find that almost without exception (1) the scripts were low-budget, independently financed films made outside the Hollywood system; or (2) they were written by screenwriters or writer-directors who were well enough established to get an out-of-the-ordinary project off the ground; (3) even with that established background, it took the filmmakers years to get the movie made; and (4) even with the one or two rules that are broken, the majority of principles contained in this book are met by the film.

Those screenwriters who *effectively* break the mold with their screenplays are the ones who already know, consciously or instinctively, what the basic rules of good screenwriting are and have chosen to break a particular rule to heighten the emotion. If that is honestly your situation, you can do that in your own script.

What I hope to prevent with this book is your breaking the rules because you don't know them, or because you're so caught up in the exceptions to the rules that you've gotten confused, or because you've chosen to ignore them so you won't be confined to a formula.

Screenwriting is formula writing. Screenplays probably have more restrictions to length, style, subject matter, vocabulary, and commerciality than any form of writing this side of haiku poetry. If you just can't stomach these parameters, then pursue some other form of writing.

If you are trying to launch a career, it will be much more helpful to find examples that *conform* to these rules and formulas for screenwriting, in order to increase your understanding of the principles and strengthen your own ability to employ them. That is what will get you work. Then, when you are established, you can start breaking the rules effectively, and the financiers will trust your judgment because of your track record.

Why do you say *X* but this other author (or teacher) says *Y*?

Because we've each come up with a different method for creating emotion in a reader and an audience. The underlying principles of the teachers and books I respect don't differ that greatly. Syd Field's plot points and Chris Volger's mythical take on the hero's journey and Eric Edson's Hero Goal Sequences® and John Truby's take on structure and Linda Seger's analyses of character and Bob McKee's approach to story and my emphasis on outer motivation aren't really contradictory; each is a possible method of developing your plot and characters to create an effective, salable screenplay. You ultimately have to draw from all the approaches you encounter and develop the method of writing that is true for you.

There is a danger in reading too many books and taking too many classes, however. Lots of people out there have become professional screenwriting students rather than professional screenwriters. At some point, you've got to trust that you've got enough information and just *do it*.

I recommend that when you finish this book, you write a screenplay. Then read someone else's book or take someone else's seminar and then write another screenplay. This will ensure that you haven't gotten class-happy and that the new information you glean from each successive book or teacher will mean that much more because of your added experience.

I think in very visual terms, and that is why I would like to write movies. Shouldn't I include camera directions in the screenplay to convey exactly how I see it?

No.

Why can't I write a pilot for a new television series?

You can, but if you're a new writer trying to break in, your chances of getting work from it are so slim that I strongly advise against it. The writers who are hired to write pilots and miniseries are those who have already established themselves strongly in television. Pilots are commissioned to those who have experience as staff writers on current series. You'll have much better luck launching an episodic TV career with strong sample episodes for at least two existing series.

I am finding that when I sit down each day to continue my writing, I read the entire script again to get back into the flow of my story. When I do this, I have the tendency to hate something I loved a few days ago, so I want to go back and change it—which makes the whole process very slow, and sometimes discouraging. The obvious answer is stop rereading my previous work every day. But since I am new at this, I wondered what the experts do to avoid it. Is it just me, or is this a common problem?

This is, indeed, a common problem for many writers in all disciplines. The solution is to keep trying different approaches until you find the process that works best for you. There's nothing wrong with rereading what you've done already each day—and even editing and rewriting the stuff you can improve—*provided* you're still making progress. Even if you add only one new scene a day, in the long run your first draft will be more like a second draft, because you've already rewritten most of it by the time you get to the end of the story.

However, it's possible that you "hate" what you liked before because you're subconsciously avoiding moving forward and finishing the draft. Those voices that keep telling you that your writing is shit are simply trying to block you from some deeper fear—of judgment, of change, of failure, of success, or of facing a new rewrite.

If this is the case, you must take a different approach: reread what you've written if you want, just to get in the flow each day, but don't rewrite anything until the draft is done. This means your draft will be finished more quickly, you'll have overcome a big hurdle, and from now on whatever you do will be rewriting—no more facing the blank page.

Like all questions about the writing process (as opposed to principles of structure and character), there is no one right answer. You've got to play around until you find the combination that is right for you. The only criteria for defining your own process are: (1) is your screenplay moving forward? and (2) are you having fun writing? When the answer is yes to both, you're doing fine.

Writers are often told that plot comes secondary to character development. Is that statement true or false, and why?

False. Audiences go to movies to see what happens, not just to ob-serve characters for two hours. The action must grow out of the charac-ters' motivations and conflicts, but without some goal to pursue, and some conflict standing in the way, you don't have a movie.

Plot points and paradigms and index cards and outlines often confuse writers and can also make stories flat, predictable, and boring. What do you think of the rigid three-act structure and how closely do writers need to plan their story?

I disagree with the whole premise of this question. When movies as varied as *Titanic*, *The School of Rock*, *American Beauty*, *Finding Nemo*, *Being John Malkovich*, *Gladiator*, *There's Something About Mary*, *The Ring*, and even a biography like *A Beautiful Mind* all not only adhere to the three-act structure but also contain the essential turning points within each act—all occurring at precisely the same points in the film—it's pretty hard to argue that paradigms lead to cookie-cutter screenplays. It's not the three-act structure that makes stories flat, predictable, and boring, it's that the writer hasn't added anything original or clever to that structure.

How do you "show" backstory when telling seems so necessary?

In spite of the age-old admonition to "show, don't tell," I am actually a big believer in *telling* a character's backstory.

In a screenplay, that means that instead of putting an event from the past on the screen in a prologue (as in *Batman Begins* or *Seabiscuit*) or a flashback (as in *Seven Pounds* or many episodes of *Mad Men*), you re-veal a critical moment from the character's past through the use of a *monologue*: the character actually tells a story about the key, painful ex-perience from their past that is now (unconsciously) defining their per-sonality.

So the murders of Exley's father and Bud White's mother in *L.A. Confidential*, or the hero having awakened with no memory and only a movie ticket stub in *Hancock*, are emotionally powerful because we don't actually see these things occur. We are involved in these stories because they are *told* to us, in the same way we are drawn in whenever we hear the words, *"Once upon a time . . ."*

How do I have my hero leave one woman for his true love without making him look like a schmuck?

You never want to end a love story or romantic comedy in a way that will lose sympathy for your hero, or create ambivalence about the outcome. So when your hero dumps one lover for another, you have four ways to create a satisfying ending for your story:

1. Make the other woman (or other man, if the hero is a woman, or gay) a jerk that deserves to be jilted (*Wedding Crashers*).

2. Let the rival realize the hero isn't the right person for him, and that he'll be happier without her (*Sleepless in Seattle*).

3. Give "Ms. Wrong" someone better to be with, who makes her happier than the hero can (*What's Up, Doc?*).

4. Let the hero realize that the person she was pursuing was not really her destiny after all, and her romance character belongs to someone more deserving (*My Best Friend's Wedding*, *Mrs. Doubtfire*, and, of course, the greatest of all the "I'll-leave-my-true-love-for-a-higher-calling" movies: *Casablanca*).

What do you mean by "antecedents" and why do you believe they're so important?

An antecedent is a successful movie or television series in the same genre as your screenplay, which would be marketed in the same way to the same group of people. *The Hangover* is a huge hit, but it isn't a totally unique story. Its genre, tone, and targeted demographic are the same as *40-Year-Old Virgin* and *Wedding Crashers*. They all are R-rated comedies involving immature men who don't want to grow up emotionally, and who get themselves into hilarious situations as a result.

This means if you're pitching your own Judd Apatow–type comedy, and you can say your movie is in the same arena as *Knocked Up* or *The Hangover*, the people you're pitching to immediately know what kind of story it is. And since your antecedents were commercially successful, it means they'll immediately start thinking that your script might be as well.

I often ask clients or seminar participants to name a couple of movies they can point to and say, "Because that story made money, mine will make money." When they can't think of a single successful antecedent for the screenplay they're writing, then how successful are they likely to be at selling it?

Writers often balk at the question, saying, "I don't want my story to be like any others . . . I want it to be original!" But Hollywood doesn't produce movies that are completely unique and original. They make movies that fill a slot and a mentality that's been successful in the past. So if you're pitching a genre film—a romantic comedy, a broad comedy, a suspense thriller, a big action movie, a family film, or a horror film—they will be more receptive to your idea than they will to a unique drama that defies categorization.

What is a "MacGuffin"?

Though I don't believe he invented it, the term MacGuffin is most closely associated with Alfred Hitchcock. He defined it as the thing that the characters care a lot about, and the audience doesn't care anything about. His usual examples were the chemical process revealed by "Mr. Memory" in *The 39 Steps*, the microfilm hidden in the art figure in *North by Northwest*, or the uranium dust in the wine bottle in *Notorious*.

This question highlights a much more important principle: you can come up with the most clever situation or mystery imaginable, but if we don't care about your characters, or if your clever plot line doesn't generate suspense, fear, humor, passion, and conflict, your readers won't give a damn. As I've said countless times, it's the emotion elicited by your screenplay that will determine its success. Hitchcock was the Master of Suspense, not the Master of MacGuffins.

I'm having a ridiculous amount of trouble even getting an agent to review my script. I have sent about 125 query letters with no luck. Any suggestions on agents/agencies that might be looking for some new talent with a good romantic comedy?

If your query letters, faxes, or e-mails aren't persuading people to read your screenplay, it's because they're not written in a way to compel the recipient to say yes. In other words:

1. Your writing style isn't clear, powerful, succinct, and professional. You're claiming to be a professional writer, but this is the only evidence they have of that. If you can't compose a single compelling page (their subconscious is telling them), how good could your entire script be?

2. Your description of the screenplay doesn't make it seem commercial. It can't just sound interesting; it must be a story they think a studio or financier will want to buy, or at least that a major star will want to commit to.

3. You're writing the wrong person in the first place. You must target the specific producers and agents who are most appropriate to approach by researching those who have sold or produced romantic comedies recently.

4. You're not personalizing the letter by telling the recipient why you're contacting them in particular. Nobody wants to get a form letter, and they can tell immediately if you're simply mass-mailing your request to everyone in the *Hollywood Creative Directory*. Refer to the specific credit, referral, or information (see #3 above) that led you directly to them.

5. You're not following up with a phone call. Many consultants and agents disagree with me on this, but I believe in being tenacious—phone the people you've targeted after you've approached them

with the letter. If you can't get through to the agents or producers you wrote to, ask their assistants if they'll read your screenplay.

What about services that offer to represent scripts for an up-front fee?
Avoid them.

Entertainment attorneys will sometimes charge a fee to *submit* your screenplay to a buyer who has told you they won't accept material unless it's from an agent, manager, or attorney. This is an acceptable practice, since you're paying them for their time for a very specific service.

But I don't know any legitimate agent or manager in Hollywood who charges a fee for considering a screenplay for representation. And among all my past students and clients, I have never heard a single person say that he was glad he paid someone in advance to represent him, or that the fee he paid ever led to a deal.

What if I have a great idea but I don't care if I write it or not and I would be willing to give it to an established writer for a share of the profits?
It is possible to be paid just for a story idea. There are people in Hollywood who are great at coming up with high concepts and make a living just by selling their ideas to producers, who then hire other screenwriters to come in and do all the work. Sounds great, doesn't it?

But before you decide that this is the niche for you, you'd better ask yourself if this pursuit is worth the effort.

Ideas in Hollywood are worth quite a bit less than a dime a dozen. *Everybody*'s got ideas. It's the execution of the concept that determines whether the concept has value. So the chances of finding an established screenwriter who wants to pay you for your idea or wants to team with you on a project are slim, since they've all got drawers full of their *own* ideas that they haven't gotten made.

You might interest a *producer* in your idea and make some money that way. But the amount of money you would receive is rarely very significant—maybe a couple thousand dollars for your concept. Now I know that a couple thousand dollars probably doesn't sound bad just for selling something you came up with while you were folding your laundry. But to get that two grand, you've got to get in touch with dozens of producers, find those who are willing to hear bare ideas from unestablished nonwriters, and get them to like it enough to pay even that much for it.

If you want to be a screenwriter, trust your own abilities and use your good ideas yourself. Maybe your first script won't do justice to this great concept, but a producer might want to option your script just to use the idea, so you'd still end up as well off as if you had sold the idea outright in the first place. Only now you have more experience and another writing sample. And you'll always be able to come up with more ideas.

If you really don't want to write screenplays but you like developing ideas and want to work in film or television, consider producing. If that is your career goal, you can take your ideas to an established producer with the understanding that if the producer wants to develop one of them, you will also be involved in the project, perhaps as an associate producer or coproducer. If the project goes forward, you are then launched on a whole new career path.

Can I produce or direct or star in my own screenplay?

Sure.

But every extra demand you make when negotiating for sale of your screenplay encumbers it a bit more. And the more it's encumbered, the more difficult it is to get a deal. It's hard enough just to sell your script. Until you're established, going after a *Rocky*-type deal puts your chances in the one-in-a-million category.

Don't I have any control at all over what is done to my screenplay once I sell it?

No.

Is it a good idea to work with a writing partner?

This is like asking if it's a good idea to get married. Collaboration has the same kinds of advantages and disadvantages that any other committed relationship does.

On the plus side, a writing partner is a good source of brainstorming, because you can tap into each other's creativity and feed on each other's ideas. Two heads are usually *more* than twice as creative as one, in this regard.

A writing partner can be especially helpful writing comedy, because you can try to make each other laugh as a test of your funny ideas.

A writing team can often combat block more easily as well. When one partner is getting lazy or scared, the other can insist that the team stick to the writing commitment.

And writing, like sex, is sometimes more fun if it's shared.

The downside of collaboration is the sacrifice of one's ego. The only way a partnership will work is if each member has the right to say, "I just can't accept this idea (or line of dialogue or character description or whatever)." And the partner has to agree to go along, giving up that particular idea, even though it would have changed the course of filmmaking as we know it.

Collaboration can be more cumbersome, because your writing regimen has to conform to two schedules. You also have to split the money. And if you break up, anyone reading your past scripts will assume it was your partner that had all the talent. So you'll often have to write an additional spec script on your own.

Only you can decide if those pluses outweigh those minuses. You pays your money and you takes your choice.

Is it worth it to go to film school?

Maybe.

If you want to be a lawyer, you've got to get a degree in law. But if you want to be a screenwriter, a degree is next to meaningless. Nobody in Hollywood really cares if you've got a certificate on your wall or what your grade point average was. All anyone cares about is your script. Having a film degree might persuade more people to look at your writing sample, but beyond that, I've never seen any evidence that the diploma made any difference to a screenwriter's success.

But this doesn't mean that film schools aren't of value. The education you get in pursuing that degree can offer you four valuable commodities:

1. **Information.** If you get exposed to good teachers in film school, you can develop your talent as a screenwriter to the point where you can write a salable script. The guidance and feedback of a good instructor is invaluable in learning your craft.

2. **Contacts.** Film school can be a great source of lasting friendships and associations that will pay off as you all pursue Hollywood together. The classic example is the gang that came out of USC in the 1960s (George Lucas, Francis Ford Coppola, John Milius, Terrence Malick, and others), who came into their glory in the 1970s, and continued to help and support each other as their careers grew. Both fellow students and professors can provide the information and introductions you need when you try to launch your career.

3. **A Screenplay.** Getting that degree should include writing at least one screenplay, which can then serve as your sample script when you begin pursuing your career. *River's Edge*, for example, was screenwriter Neal Jimenez's master's thesis at UCLA. And if you want to pursue directing, film school gives you access to equipment and a finished piece of film to show.

4. **A Liberal Arts Education.** Don't pooh-pooh this one. The more you know about life in general, the breadth of man's history and knowledge, and the history and forms of artistic expression (including film history), the better a writer, and possibly human being, you will be.

These four rewards of film school, or at least the first three, are essential to becoming a working screenwriter. You must have information, contacts, and a finished screenplay if you hope to achieve your career goal. However, film school is a very expensive way to acquire that necessary information, those contacts, and a finished screenplay. Tuition, books, equipment, and living expenses can add up to a six-figure investment. Even without that kind of money to spend, there are other ways to pursue screenwriting.

Since the degree itself is of little importance, you can get the information you need from seminars, conferences, books, CDs, DVDs, and online.

You can make contacts through all of the methods outlined in the chapter on marketing yourself or by volunteering to work as an unpaid intern for someone in the film business.

You can write your sample screenplay in any living or working situation.

I'm not trying to discourage you from film school, only to get you to look at it as one of several choices in pursuing your career. You may decide that the intensity and quality of education and the number of contacts and opportunities it provides make film school the best alternative for you.

In choosing a particular school, do the kind of research you would do in pursuing a job. Consider at least a half dozen possible schools. Get all their available literature and then visit the campuses you're seriously considering. Talk to the staff and members of the faculty in the media department, talk to current students, and then ask for the names of recent graduates of the program. When you talk to those former graduates, ask them for the names of some of their fellow students who may *not* have gotten film positions after graduating. And finally, call some executives and agents in the industry and ask them whether a degree from the school you're considering would increase your chances as a potential screenwriter.

How do I obtain rights to a book, play, short story, or true story?

If a work of fiction is no longer under copyright, the work is in the public domain. That means it can be adapted to the screen without securing any rights.

The same holds true for a true story if all of those depicted in the film are deceased or if the characters are only portrayed when acting as public figures. Rights pertaining to privacy and defamation basically die when the person portrayed does. So rights are not a consideration when writing a screenplay about Millard Fillmore. However, if Millard Fillmore's mistress is still alive and she is portrayed in your screenplay, her permission will have to be obtained or she must be omitted from your film.

If a person's actions are a matter of public record, these can be portrayed without danger—*but only those actions by the person as a public figure*. Once you leave the actions revealed in newspaper articles or court transcripts and move into a person's private life, rights must be obtained.

This entire matter of rights and permissions, defamation, and invasion of privacy is a very gray area. Lawyers make big bucks preventing or participating in litigation about these issues. So when in doubt, secure the rights.

If you wish to obtain the rights to adapt a work of fiction that is still under copyright, you must first find out who holds those rights and whether they are currently under option for a film adaptation. If you phone the publisher of the novel (or play, or short story, or song, or whatever) and ask for the film rights department, they should be able to tell you who controls the movie rights.

Usually the author of the original work will retain these rights. But occasionally the publisher will acquire them as part of the original deal with the author. If the author holds the rights, it is best you contact him or her directly.

Doing a little online detective work can sometimes lead you straight to an author. Or you can write to an author in care of the publisher and hope you eventually get a response. Reaching the author directly is usually best, because the author will respond more positively to your ideas and enthusiasm than would the publisher or author's representative. The author may be more concerned about your passion and respect for the original work and less about the money you are offering up front.

If you can't reach the author, you will have to deal with the author's representative. The publisher, unless they control the rights, will give you the name of the author's agent or attorney. This will usually be the New York literary agency that represents the author for publishing.

They will often pass you on to a Hollywood literary agent who represents the film rights to the author's work.

After tracking all of these people down, you may learn that the book is already under option for film. If this is the case, try to find out who has the film rights or at least when the option expires. When that expiration date is near, call again to see if it is likely to be renewed or if the film has gone into production. Books and plays often get optioned when first released, and then the producers involved can't get a deal, and the option expires.

If the film rights to the work are available, your ability to acquire them will depend entirely on what you have to offer in the way of money, experience, enthusiasm, and the likelihood you can get the movie made.

Even if you have no money to offer up front, you still might get the rights to a work of fiction if those involved think you've got a good shot at getting the movie made. Your chances will improve if your ideas about the novel's adaptation are consistent with the author's goals for the original creation, and if no one else is knocking on the author's door.

If there are all of these rules for screenwriting, why are so many movies so bad?

Because those filmmakers *still* haven't read this book.

And also because the process of making a film involves so many people, so much money, so much talent, so many egos, so many physical obstacles, and so many things that can go wrong that it's a near miracle every time a movie even gets made, let alone is any good.

I certainly believe that Hollywood's greatest weaknesses are obvious and extensive: a lack of respect for the screenplay and the screenwriter; censorship, through a lowest-common-denominator, don't-offend-anyone attitude on television or the MPAA's boneheaded rating system for features; an unwillingness to pursue a modest profit from a modest investment; undue allegiance to stars and ideas only because they've made money in the past; too many fingers in the creative pie; and a general administrative philosophy of "cover your ass."

But I also think that the film industry takes the rap a bit too often for what is wrong with the world. Any time you try to unite art and commerce, it's an arranged marriage at best, certainly not one made in heaven. I don't think the people in Hollywood have any more to answer for than those on Wall Street or in Detroit or Washington, D.C., or Battle Creek, Michigan. Creativity in the pursuit of money and power is a tricky undertaking.

And I certainly believe that any enterprise that results in *The West Wing*; *The Wire*; *Psycho*; *Play It Again, Sam*; *Friends*; *Perry Mason*; *From Russia with Love*; *Chinatown*; *Rain Man*; *The Truman Show*; *thirtysomething*; *Ben Casey*; *Body Heat*; *The Big Chill*; *Modern Family*; *All the President's Men*; *Sleepless in Seattle*; *Hitch*; *The Office*; *Shrek*; *Jaws*; *Tootsie*; *A Few Good Men*; *When Harry Met Sally*; *Working Girl*; *The Twilight Zone*; *The Graduate*; *L.A. Confidential*; *Mad Men*; *Little Miss Sunshine*; *Lars and the Real Girl*; and *The Shawshank Redemption* has to be given a nod of gratitude for a lot of wonderful moments in the dark.

Is there sexism in Hollywood?

Yes.

Also racism, ageism, plagiarism, nepotism, censorship, homophobia, dishonesty, and brain-dead executives.

So what?

Faced with the realities of the film business, you can do one of two things.

You can say, "I don't want any part of this." And then you can choose some other path and goal that will probably involve those same hurdles and obstacles or others just like them.

Or you can say, "Screenwriting is what brings me fulfillment and a sense of worth. So I'm going to pursue it, in spite of the difficult, negative, unfair people and practices I will have to face as part of choosing that particular game. I won't be naive about it, but I won't use those obstacles, or any of the 623 others out there in Hollywood as excuses to feed my fear and keep me from pursuing my dream. I'll accept the consequences of my choice as long as being on the path of screenwriting brings me joy."

And then you go for it.

APPENDIX B

A SAMPLE TREATMENT

THE FOLLOWING IS A SAMPLE TREATMENT FOR A PROJECT I WAS INVOLVED with some time ago. The true story is based on the book *The Sylmar Tunnel Disaster* by Janette Zavattero, a journalist and author who was the sister of the story's hero. I wrote the story in treatment form as a selling tool for packaging and possible development.

If you reach the stage in your writing career where you are asked to provide treatments, this offers an example of the proper layout. Remember that treatments are written in present tense, dialogue is minimal (with a bit more in most comedy treatments), only the major scenes and characters are included, and that all of the principles of concept, character, and structure apply. And the shorter the better; always leave the reader wanting more.

SYLMAR

a treatment by

MICHAEL HAUGE

from the book

The Sylmar Tunnel Disaster

by Janette Zavattero

It is another world; a place of total silence, and
total darkness. The strings of bare electric lights
which extend for the full three-mile length of the
tunnel give it the feeling of outer space, rather than
a huge, man-made cavern seventeen stories under the
earth.

As the small cage carrying the men to their jobs
descends into the earth, the miners laugh and talk
about the bonuses they will get from Lockheed if the
irrigation tunnel is finished ahead of schedule. The
men are highballers, working stiffs who have spent
half their lives under the ground, in mines and
tunnels like this. And always in their voices is the
slight trace of unspoken fear at what can happen in so
foreign a place.

***

June 24, 1971. Wally Zavattero picks up the ringing
phone. His wife Mercedes watches anxiously as Wally
listens to the phone and climbs out of bed.

"That was Loren," he tells her. "It's the Sylmar tunnel. There's been a flash fire."

"Was anyone ...?" She doesn't let herself finish the question.

"I don't know, Mercy," he replies. "Loren said they've got it under control. But they've said that before."

***

It is near dawn when Zavattero confronts the tunnel management team in the trailer that serves as headquarters for the Sylmar tunnel. "I'm yellow-tagging the tunnel," Zavattero tells them. His penetrating eyes tell them that this won't be debated. "There's no trace of gas in the tunnel now, but if the meter registers even a molecule, you shut down."

Late that evening, just as the graveyard shift is set to come on, the meter records traces of gas at the tunnel face. Wally's friend Loren Savage, the project manager, goes inside the trailer to phone Lockheed, the company running the operation. The door closes behind him. Several minutes later he emerges from the trailer. "We're going ahead," he tells the crew boss. "It's only surface gas, and the readings are clear now."

There are eighteen men in the mine at 2:30 a.m. when the face of the tunnel explodes into an inferno of fire and flying rock. The blast will be felt as far as fifty miles from Sylmar. Above the tunnel, Loren Savage can feel the rumble of the earth. "My God," he says.

Inside the tunnel, those closest to its face have been obliterated by the explosion. As the flames and gas spread up the length of the tunnel, men try hopelessly to flee the fire. Their screaming echoes through the tunnel....

When Zavattero arrives on the scene, it is a madhouse of miners, firemen, reporters, and spectators. He is just in time to see Loren Savage, his face blank and white with horror, being driven away from the confusion by his wife. Zavattero finds Bob Ree, the project engineer, who screams at him that the fire department is keeping the miners from going in to rescue their coworkers. "They're getting out their *hoses*, for God's sake!" shouts Ree. "You can't fight a gas fire with hoses!"

Zavattero sees that the confrontation between firemen and miners will turn into a fight at any moment. He marches up to the fire chief.

"This tunnel is sealed off," announces the chief.

"No it's not," replies Zavattero firmly, pushing a blunt finger against the chief's chest. "Your men don't know the first thing about tunnels, and the miners are going after anyone who might be alive down there, whether your firemen are in the way or not." The fire chief merely nods in the face of Zavattero's rage, and the firemen back away from the tunnel entrance.

The miners are outfitted with breathing apparatus, which gives each of them only forty minutes in the smoke-filled tunnel. Soon the first of them emerges from the tunnel entrance carrying the body of one of the men. As others continue the search in the tunnel, they find other bodies, or sometimes only parts of bodies, belonging to their friends.

The entire operation of retrieving the bodies takes more than forty-eight straight hours. When Zavattero is finally driven home, he is numb. "They're going to pay this time," he tells his wife. "This time Lockheed's going to pay."

***

Over the next two weeks, Zavattero waits with increasing frustration for an investigation into the explosion to be announced. His written request for prosecution is ignored, and there is no mention in the papers of the $250 million loan guarantee that Lockheed Construction is trying to secure from the government—a loan that will be seriously jeopardized by any bad publicity. When he finally hears that a public hearing on the explosion has been canceled, he storms into the office of Jack Hatton, the head of the California Division of Industrial Safety. Jack Hatton is also a former executive for Lockheed Construction Company.

"These things must follow their normal course, Wally," says Hatton. "Besides," he adds, "even if there was negligence, it's only a misdemeanor."

With this comment, Zavattero explodes. "A MISDEMEANOR?! What happened at Sylmar wasn't even manslaughter. It was murder." That afternoon he phones the *L.A. Times*.

The next day's headline, LOCKHEED VIOLATES SAFETY ORDERS IN DEATH OF 17 MINERS, begins what will ultimately be a two-year ordeal for Zavattero and his family.

Zavattero's first obstacles come from his own department, when Jack Hatton refuses to let him off his other

duties in order to concentrate on the Sylmar
investigation. Then, when Wally attempts to retrieve
the gas meter from the Sylmar tunnel, which will
prove that gas was present in the tunnel prior
to the explosion, he discovers that Lockheed has
substituted a different meter in an attempt to cover
up their own negligence. Shortly after confronting a
Lockheed attorney with this accusation, he receives an
anonymous phone call threatening his life.

When the California Senate finally begins hearings
into the Sylmar explosion, Wally is totally unprepared
at the grilling he gets from the committee chairman
when he takes the stand. Jack Fenton, a Democratic
senator, wants to show that Governor Reagan's
budget cuts and appointments have made the Bureau
of Safety ineffectual. But the result is that
Zavattero is accused of near murder and negligence in
allowing the miners back into the tunnel prior to the
explosion.

After Wally reveals to the hearing that his life has
been threatened, the tension that has been building
at the Zavattero home finally explodes. "Your obsession
with bringing down Lockheed, or appeasing your own
guilt, or whatever you're trying to do, has blinded
you to your own family," Mercy cries at him. "One of
your daughters is getting badgered by the kids at
school because her father was practically accused of
murder, and the other is out every night 'til all
hours, and I can't even talk to her. You're already
exhausted, you've got an ulcer, and you're starting to
drink too much. And now I find out that your life's in
danger."

As Mercy breaks down in his arms, Wally doesn't answer her, just holds her quietly for a long time. Later that evening, he tells her, Gina, and Paula, their older daughter, "I know you've been going through hell, and I haven't been much of a father lately, and I'm sorry. I promise I'll be there for you from now on. But I can't stop what I'm doing. I'm the only hope for those seventeen miners' families right now, and I've got to fight for them. I've got to try to see that this won't happen again."

When the Lockheed trial finally begins, the courtroom is a three-ring circus of attorneys, witnesses, spectators, and press. As Wally begins to testify, and the evidence emerges, the history of negligence, inaction, and cover-up is revealed: dozens of requests for prosecution against Lockheed and other contractors that Jack Hatton and the Bureau of Safety have ignored ... numerous injuries and deaths that went unpunished ... Lockheed's attempt to switch the gas meter at Sylmar ... the threat to Wally's life.

When Jack Hatton finally comes to testify, he enters the court a broken man, reads a prepared statement to the jury, and announces his resignation.

Then Ralph Brisette, the only miner to survive the Sylmar explosion, takes the stand, and for the first time the courtroom is silent. In a soft, shaken voice, Brisette quietly breaks down as he recalls the screams of the miners trapped inside the tunnel, and the agony of hearing his friends die while he wondered if he would be rescued. There is no cross-examination when he finishes his testimony, only silence. Ralph Brisette shakily gets up from the stand and slowly, quietly walks out of the courtroom.

After months of testimony, arguments, appeals, and legal maneuvers, the trial finally ends and the jury is sent to render its verdict. Walking out of the courtroom for the last time, Wally sees Loren Savage sitting alone. "Well, it's finally over," Wally says quietly.

"Thank God," his friend replies.

"I guess some good will come of it all," Wally says. "Maybe next time companies like Lockheed will be a little more cautious. Still I wonder if somewhere along the line, with all the politics and legalities and money, those seventeen men weren't forgotten."

The two men sit quietly for a moment, each with his own thoughts, and then they say good-bye. It is the last time the two friends will ever see each other.

Word of the verdict reaches Zavattero as he drives past a newsstand and spots the headline: LOCKHEED GUILTY! Lockheed has been found guilty of a wrongful death misdemeanor, and has been fined the maximum in real and punitive damages. In addition, the families of the seventeen miners have received the largest civil award in California history: a total of 9.5 million dollars.

In a sidebar of the newspaper, a separate article reveals that Senator Jack Fenton has spearheaded passage of a bill increasing the possible penalties for wrongful death employer negligence. From now on, incidents like the one at Sylmar will be felonies, not misdemeanors.

The fight is over.

Wally pulls away from the curb and snaps on the car radio just as the station is playing "John Henry." Zavattero smiles and begins to whistle the tune softly to himself as he heads home to his family.

INDEX

ABOUT THE AUTHOR

MICHAEL HAUGE is a story consultant, author, and lecturer who works with writers and filmmakers on their screenplays, novels, movies, and television projects. He is currently on retainer with Will Smith's company, Overbrook Entertainment, and has consulted on projects for every major Hollywood studio, including films starring Will Smith, Julia Roberts, Jennifer Lopez, Kirsten Dunst, Robert Downey Jr., and Morgan Freeman.

As a top corporate keynote speaker and consultant, Michael works with attorneys, psychologists, individuals, and companies on employing story principles in their projects, their presentations, and their work with clients and patients.

Besides *Writing Screenplays That Sell*, Michael is the best-selling author of *Selling Your Story in 60 Seconds: The Guaranteed Way to Get Your Screenplay or Novel Read*. A number of Michael's seminars, including *The Hero's 2 Journeys* with Christopher Vogler, are available on DVD and CD at bookstores nationwide, and through his Web site below.

Michael has presented seminars and lectures to more than forty thousand participants throughout the world. He is on the board of directors of the American Screenwriters Association and the Advisory Board for *Scriptwriter Magazine* in London.

He can be reached through his Web site at storymastery.com.